Entrepreneur
MAGAZINE'S

ULTIMATE

GUIDE TO

PERSONA

FINANCE

FOR ENTREPRENEURS

PETER SANDER with J. JEFFREY LAMBERT

EP
Entrepreneur Press

Editorial Director: Jere Calmes
Cover Design: Beth Hansen-Winter
Production: CWL Publishing Enterprises, Inc., Madison, Wisconsin, www.cwlpub.com

© 2007 by Entrepreneur Media, Inc.

This publication is designed to provide accurate and authoritative information in regard to the subject matter covered. It is sold with the understanding that the publisher is not engaged in rendering legal, accounting, or other professional services. If legal advice or other expert assistance is required, the services of a competent professional person should be sought.

            –From a Declaration of Principles jointly adopted by a
               Committee of the American Bar Association and
                a Committee of Publishers and Associations

ISBN 13: 978-1-59-918032-8

Library of Congress Cataloging-in-Publication Data

Sander, Peter J.
  Ultimate guide to personal finance for entrepreneurs / by Peter Sander.
    p. cm.
  Includes bibliographical references and index.
  ISBN 13: 978-1-59-918032-8
  ISBN 10: 1-59918-032-4 (alk. paper)
  1. Businesspeople–Finance, Personal. I. Title.
  HG179.S2358 2007
  332.0240088'33804--dc22

                                   2006031840

Printed in Canada

Contents

Introduction

THE NEW BOAT JUST APPEARED IN THE DRIVE-way. You know a few facts. The owner, relatively new to the neighborhood, owns a small machine shop specializing in sheet metal fabrication. It's not a business you understand that well, but you hear that it has been doing OK, despite overseas competition. You know your neighbor and his family just got back from a week in Hawaii. His oldest daughter is about to start college. Yet, a new boat? And he has a comfortable, contented look as he saunters down his driveway in the morning, past his new watercraft, to pick up The Wall Street Journal. Regardless of the ups and downs of the business, you know he must be doing something right.

Your other next-door neighbor just refinanced his house—again. He owns a nearby flower shop that needed a new delivery van. Neighborhood gossip indicates that he and his wife cancelled summer camp for their kids because of money. In fact, they haven't been on a family vacation in years. A new car almost got repossessed a few years ago. It seems that something always comes up in the business that gets in the way. But by the looks of things, the business seems to be doing OK: plenty of customers, attractive store, good merchandise, positive word-of-mouth from everyone in the community. In fact, the local Chamber of Commerce bestowed its "best local business" award on it last year. From all appearances, the business seems as healthy as the flowers it sells—and it is. But while the business is vibrant and full of color, the family's finances constantly seem to wilt and die. What's wrong?

You made the decision a few years ago to stick your toe into the waters of entrepreneurship. As a professional photographer working for a studio, you've longed for years to hang out your shingle—to work for yourself, to be your own boss, to make the most of your professional credentials, abilities, and clients. The time seems right to make a full go of it. You've written your business plan, arranged financing, talked to your clients, networked with others in the business. You've done your homework.

But as you look at your entrepreneur neighbors, you get nervous. Something holds you back. It's held you back before. That something is a nagging notion that successful entrepreneurship is about more than business plans, knowledge, employees, skills, tireless work, and boundless energy. The experience of your neighbors says something about the need to manage money. It says that your personal success really depends on how well you manage what goes into the business and what comes out of it. That's a whole new can of worms.

Rich You, Poor You

Sure, you've read books on personal finance. Make it, keep it, grow it. Figure out what you need, budget, save, invest, and … oh, by the way, don't forget about those pressing needs of college education, retirement, insurance, and planning your final exit—estate planning. And, in essence, all of those books seem to be basically tax guides, since most of what you read about, beyond self-discipline, concerns how you get the most after taxes. And it's all important, too—in an age of do-it-yourself personal finance brought on by the absence of guaranteed pensions and benefits, changing government entitlements, a growth in personal investing, and, most pervasively, the Internet.

But what does all you read have to do with your business? The answer: these books talk about you. About your family. About your goals, short term and long term. About making the most of your income, once it's yours. About making the most of your assets and net worth. These books don't care how you get your money. You'd be hard-pressed to find the word "entrepreneur" or "small business" or "business ownership" or "business plan" anywhere in a personal finance book.

FURTHER DOWN THE BOOKSHELF

Where do you find the words and phrases of entrepreneurship? In the books you've carefully read about starting and running a small business. And there are lots and lots of these books too—probably as many as line the bookshelves on the topic of personal finance.

But do these small business books talk about your personal finances? About how to earn, save, and grow your own personal funds? About how to save the most on taxes? In a word, no. There might be a section on how to organize the business and how some of the choices—proprietorship, partnership, corporation, or LLC—might create a different tax situation for you. You might find a short section on life insurance coverage or benefits. But while a few pages might be devoted to such topics, most small business books stay well clear of providing knowledge and expertise to help you run your personal finances.

OUR APPROACH

Ultimate Guide to Personal Finance for Entrepreneurs is designed to fill this rather obvious gap. We cover personal finance, and we cover it from the viewpoint of active entrepreneurs, considering their needs and their life context.

Ultimate Guide to Personal Finance for Entrepreneurs is divided into three parts. Towards the goal of having you understand personal finance basics and how they apply to you as the entrepreneur, Part I explores those basics and how your personal and business situation are tied together. Part II gets into strategies and the nuts and bolts of starting the business and managing its—and your—day to day finances. Part III shifts focus towards how to get the most out of your business—how to build and preserve wealth, and finally, how to create an advantageous exit strategy.

Part I includes:

- Chapter 1, The Golden Triangle of Entrepreneurial Personal Finance, explores in some depth how your finances are tied to the finances and the operations of your business. As in chemistry or physics, every action gets a reaction; what you do at one "point" of the triangle will affect an outcome at the others.
- Chapter 2, Personal Finance Basics, covers basic "textbook" principles of personal finance, first by defining what is meant by the term, then explaining some of the key principles and tools involved.

- Chapter 3, It's (Mostly) About Taxes (A Short Tax Course for Entrepreneurs) digs into the truth you already expected: making the most from your business means learning how to play the tax system to keep your fair share while governmental authorities get theirs.

Part II includes:

- Chapter 4, Organizing Your Business is a fairly detailed discussion highlighting advantages and disadvantages and basic tax treatment of different forms of organization – proprietorships, partnerships, corporations, and LLCs.
- Chapter 5, Budget It: The Art and Science of Budgeting for Entrepreneurs switches gears from business structure to how to plan—and execute—a budget, both in your business and personal life, and how these budgets and the behaviors around them tie together.
- Chapter 6, Finance It: Cash, Credit and Capital covers another area of strong ties between business and personal finances: the strategic use of debt and credit.

Part III includes:

- Chapter 7, Keep It: Turning More of What You Earn Into Wealth. Now we get into the down and dirty of how to use the tax rules to your advantage, particularly in terms of using tax deductions and credits to maximize what you take from the business.
- Chapter 8, Protect It: How to Protect Your Business and Yourself from the Unexpected covers the topic of risk, how to manage risk, and how to use insurance products to manage risks that aren't practical to manage otherwise.
- Chapter 9, Grow It: Investing for Entrepreneurs lays out the premise of building a nest egg and using it ultimately to replace your business income and/or to meet other financial goals.
- Chapter 10, Avoiding Future Shock: College and Retirement Planning covers two "big ticket" items most need to plan for with their personal finances
- Chapter 11, Transition It: What To Do When It's Time to Move On lays out the various forms of exit from your business, by sale or succession, and the personal financial aspects of each choice.

Finally, our appendices offer handy tables, tips, tricks, forms, and lists of other resources designed to help you navigate special situations and make the best of the "normal" ones.

We realize this book doesn't explain everything. It isn't a manual, and if it were, you'd get so quickly bogged down in detail that you'd miss many important concepts. As much as we'd like you to become an expert, we'd rather have you know what opportunities lie out there and what questions to ask. You probably don't have time to the nuts and bolts anyway, nor to keep up with all the rules and changes in the financial and tax world. That is for specialists—your CPA, your tax attorney, your financial planner. But if you know how the pieces fit together, and if you're able to understand what needs to be done, and whether it has been done properly and to your greatest advantage, we've achieved our objective.

ACCOMPANYING CD

This book also includes a CD-ROM with detailed tax charts and sample startup budgets.

ABOUT THE AUTHORS

Peter Sander is a professional author, researcher, and consultant in the fields of personal finance, business, and location reference. His 15 book titles include *Cities Ranked & Rated, The 250 Personal Finance Questions Everyone Should Ask, Everything Personal Finance, Niche and Get Rich,* and *Value Investing For Dummies.* He also produces material for TheStreet.com and TheMillionaireZone.com and does occasional consulting work for financial planning firms and other small businesses. His formal education includes an MBA in logistics management from Indiana University and a B.A. in urban affairs and administration from Miami University of Ohio, and he has completed professional training and examination as a Certified Financial Planner (CFP®). His career includes 20 years as a marketing and logistics specialist for a major high tech firm. He has appeared on *NBC Today, CNBC, CNNfn,* and *Fox News* and has been a frequent radio guest and commentator about personal finance and relocation across the U.S and Canada. Originally from Cincinnati, Ohio, he now lives with his family in Granite Bay, California.

Jeff Lambert served as contributing consultant to this book and is a nationally acclaimed Certified Financial Planner® practitioner and partner of Lighthouse Financial Planning in Sacramento, California, a fee-only comprehensive financial planning firm. He is a founding board member of the Financial Planning Association and was instrumental in the early work of FPA's community, pro bono and career development initiatives.

He has directed the Personal Financial Planning Certificate program at University of California Davis, Extension since 1996 and is founder of the Sacramento Financial Education Center.

Jeff has received many awards including Certified Financial Planner® of the year and has been named one of *Mutual Funds Magazine*'s "100 Great Financial Planners" in 2001 and 2002. *The Wealth Factor* by Sydney LeBlanc and Lyn Fisher devotes a chapter to the story of Jeff and his practice partner, Jim Johnson, CFP® calling their firm, Lighthouse Financial Planning, "A Beacon for World Class Financial Planning."

The Personal Finance of Entrepreneurship

CHAPTER 1

The Golden Triangle of Entrepreneurial Finance

W**E HAVE ALL MET PEOPLE SUCCESSFUL IN** business and personal life. Without going into all of the reasons for their success, suffice it to say we all aspire to be more like them. Likewise, we all know of people who are "good with money" but fail in business, and similarly, we know of others who are "good in business" but never seem to get things quite right with their personal finances.

The ultimate goal of any entrepreneur going into business or already in business is to make money—not just for the business, but for *themselves*. Those business books just described are all aimed at one thing—to help you as an entrepreneur make more money in the business. Hiring and managing employees, funding the business, creating good contracts, managing cash flow: all of those activities benefit one thing—the bottom line of the *business*.

But how much of this bottom-line performance makes its way to you, the owner of the business? Isn't that the true meaning of success? It is all too common for a business to be successful in the marketplace without creating profits for the owner. Stated differently, it's all too common for a business owner or entrepreneur to *put more into* the business than he or she *gets out*

of it. Is that because the business performs poorly? Sometimes yes—clearly any one of a number of issues can cause a business to perform under its potential. This is a given, and we'll let all the other small business books analyze the issues and take care of the causes. But all too often a successful business fails to create a financially successful owner, and the reasons are many.

WHY SMALL BUSINESSES FAIL

Most small business experts are quick to flash the common wisdom that half of all businesses "fail" in the first year and that 95 percent "fail" in the first five years. "Fail" turns out to be a relative term, for many close voluntarily or are absorbed into larger businesses; only a small fraction actually end up in bankruptcy. (Refer to the federal Small Business Administration Web site, *www.sba.gov*, for more details on this topic.) The business literature is ripe with analyses of why businesses fail; the reasons group fairly well into market-driven, operationally driven, and financially driven reasons.

- **Market-driven:** competition, poor location, product or service not needed, underpricing, bad luck/bad timing, poor understanding of market

- **Operationally driven:** poor inventory management, excessive fixed costs, internal theft, poor hiring decisions, too many or too few employees, poor quality product
- Financially driven: inadequate capital, poor credit arrangements, poor accounting controls

Any one of these factors or, more likely, any combination of these factors will cause a business to underperform or even fail. But that's not what this book is about. As the title states, we're more concerned about *personal* finances.

WHY PERSONAL FINANCES FAIL

Even more has been written about why people fail with their individual personal finances. We hear about the "D" word—debt—clearly the "canary in the coal mine" of personal financial problems. A great number of personal finance books and financial consultants focus their readers and clients on debt and how to get out of it or reduce the cost of it (the *symptom*) without properly addressing the *causes*. Truth is, most individual personal financial failures result from poor financial *awareness, commitment,* and *control.* (We'll discuss these three in Chapter 2.) These three factors result in overspending, failing to correctly foresee income or expenses, and not maintaining sufficient reserves to meet them. These difficulties are compounded by failure to properly plan major life events or transitions, such as college education, retirement, and children.

So what do these failures have to do with the entrepreneur? Did we once mention "business" in any of the above?

It is especially common for entrepreneurs to spend so much time focused on the operations and finances of their businesses that they sort of forget to keep their own houses in order. They have limited time and, after all, the business is the source of their pride and income. The day-to-day attention required by the business soon supersedes the need to attend to personal and family financial matters. Whether by deliberate decision or default, these entrepreneurs soon drift into a paradigm of thinking that if they take care of the business, personal finances will take care of themselves.

Nothing could be further from the truth.

The American landscape is littered with households having a high income and little net worth to show for it. Why? Because they spend too much, save too little, and rely on entitlements (public Social Security and Medicare, private pensions, and insurance) to take care of the financial "bad stuff." As an entrepreneur, you've already decided to give up some of your entitlements—the pension, the health insurance, the matched 401k—so you're well aware that you're more responsible for your financial future than the average working Joe or Joni. But somehow, with many entrepreneurs, that notion fails to turn into focus on personal finances.

Beyond simple neglect, many entrepreneurs, especially those more talented in marketing and operations than in finances, don't make the best financial decisions, especially when it comes to their own finances. They don't take the time. They fail to see the true costs, short term or long term, for a purchase or other financial decision. They fail to fully understand the tax consequences. They overextend themselves in their business and personal lives. There may be too much overhead in the business—and there may be excessive "overhead" at home.

CHIPS ON THE TABLE

As we'll see, tax code provisions create many nuances in the relationship between business and personal finances. Many entrepreneurs simply "don't know what they don't know." Further, entrepreneurs are—well—entrepreneurial. Many want to do things themselves, but underestimate the complexities of personal finance and the complex relationship between business and individual finances. They fail to get the proper help when necessary.

Such an omission may not lead to business failure directly but it leads to a failure to realize potential income. In other words, money is left on the table.

Leaving money on the table means that the business doesn't produce for its owners what it could. If the business is highly profitable, perhaps the owner doesn't feel the effects. But in the more typical case, business incomes are modest, so wringing every possible dollar out of the business becomes undeniably important. Why? First, to finance its growth and future operational needs. Second, and almost as important, to pay the owners, not only for their hard work and "sweat equity," but also for a decent return on their own capital dollars deployed. We see many cases, even when entrepreneurs know the ropes and/or get the proper help, where they just don't think through business operational and financial decisions carefully enough to get the most from the business.

Of course it gets worse that that—a bad business funding or capitalization strategy can lead to outright failure and bankruptcy for the business and the entrepreneur. Lack of capital and inadequate protection from a variety of business and financial risks can transcend the business and attack personal finances, particularly where no corporate protections are in force.

WHAT THIS BOOK IS ABOUT

If you haven't already figured this out through your business planning and/or experience, you know that most likely you and your business are one. Your business and personal finances are firmly joined. Depending on what kind of business you're in, that bond may be total—that is, you *are* your business—while in other cases, it might be a little less—that is, the business is shared with other owners, so what happens to the business has something less than a one-for-one effect on you personally. But regardless, if you're in business, you realize that somehow you need to simultaneously manage business finances,

personal finances, and the connection between the two. Otherwise, you will inevitably leave something on the table—or worse, come apart. Managing your finances—and particularly the connection between your finances and the finances of the business—is what this book is about.

WHO THIS BOOK IS FOR AND WHY

This *Ultimate Guide to Personal Finance for Entrepreneurs* is *not* a business book. If you bought this expecting to find the secrets to the successful financing, marketing, and operation of your business, you bought the wrong book. *Personal Finance for Entrepreneurs* is not about what business to start or how to start it; in fact, it isn't really about the business at all, *except* where it touches personal finances. The "pure" business topics are left to the broad range of material already available on the topic. (Consider, for example, such books from Entrepreneur Press as *Ultimate Small Business Advisor, Managing a Small Business Made Easy,* and *Accounting and Finance for Small Business Made Easy.*)

This book is also not, strictly speaking, a personal finance book. It covers the major topics of personal finance, but from the perspective of the entrepreneur. It is personal finance *for entrepreneurs.* It covers personal finance topics as the entrepreneur needs to address them.

What this really means (and you probably saw this coming) is that this book aims squarely not at the business itself or exclusively at personal finances, but at the *linkages* between the two. Do you need a new vehicle for the business? Considering tax laws on depreciation and the many ways to finance that vehicle, some or all involving your own personal capital, what's the best way to do it? What's the best way to set up your retirement plan to save the most on business and personal taxes and to meet your personal retirement goals? When does it make sense to buy property for the business? Should you buy it through the business or should you own it yourself and lease it to the business? If you have employees, does this affect your retirement or benefit options? How? These are the sorts of questions addressed in this book.

Finding the right answers to these questions often means the difference for a small business between success and just keeping up—or failing. Getting your entrepreneurial finances right means getting the most *out* of the business, often with putting the least *into* the business, and oh, by the way, with the least amount of risk.

With these statements we get to the stated objective of this book:

> **Objective:** Lay out a framework to help entrepreneurs take care of personal financial needs while taking care of the business. The framework helps entrepreneurs get the most out of the business, short and long term, while minimizing the risk of failure.

THE TIES THAT BIND

In that *Personal Finance for Entrepreneurs* takes aim at the linkages between business and personal finances, we think this book and its approach are fairly unique. Let's now elaborate on those linkages.

Figure 1.1 shows what we call the "Golden Triangle" of personal finance as it relates to entrepreneurs. As the figure illustrates, business operations, business finances, and personal finances are inexorably linked. Decisions and actions at one point in the triangle will most likely—in at least some way—affect a decision made in another. Some of these influences are obvious; others are more subtle. But like a balance equation in chemistry or physics, there will always be an effect. The question is, how large an effect?

For example, the effect of an operational decision to hire employees has an obvious effect on business finances—wages or salaries paid, benefits paid, insurance covered, facilities required. But does this decision affect your personal finances as an entre-

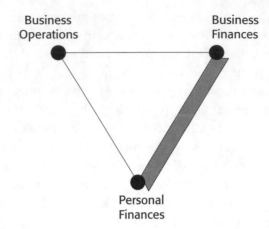

FIGURE 1.1. The Golden Triangle of Entrepreneurial Personal Finance

preneur? Obviously it might affect the cash flow you take from the business, but hopefully not much, as the return on investment of these new employees should be positive. But more subtly, the number and kind of employees you have can affect the choice of retirement plans and employment benefits and, in many cases, open up options and alternatives for your own personal retirement plan. The employees may also help you qualify for group insurance plans or for better plans than you have already. That's the kind of effect we're considering in this book.

For the sake of clarity, it's worth taking a moment to explain the points of the triangle as a stage in explaining how the pieces fit together.

Business Operations

As an entrepreneur you will make hundreds—thousands—of operational decisions in setting up an infrastructure and producing your product or service. All decisions that involve money involve the finances of the business, of course, and many, like employment and facility decisions, will affect your personal finances as an owner. And these decisions are never finished: they will adjust and evolve as your business evolves—and so will your business and personal finances. Business operational decisions include the following:

- **Employment and employees.** Whether to have employees, how many, and what kind of compensation to provide are decisions that affect business finances in obvious ways. Decisions about employee benefits and retirement plans will affect you, for whatever you decide to do for them may have consequences for you: you can participate in benefit and retirement plans, often to your advantage. Also, your decision on how to use yourself and your spouse and/or family members as employees can impact your finances.

- **Facilities and location.** Early on, you'll have to decide what kind of location and building your business needs. That decision will likely have to be modified as the business grows and evolves. Naturally, like employee costs, facility costs are a major factor in the finances of most businesses. But key decisions on building ownership—buy vs. lease, owner buys and leases to business—are important to personal finances. Depending on the business, many entrepreneurs look to buy their facilities to build the asset base as part of a retirement or other exit strategy for the business. In addition, the use of a home or other personal space in a business has important personal finance consequences.

- **Growth strategy and plans.** Every viable business has a strategy and a plan to grow and evolve. Decisions on how to evolve and how fast must be made in the context of both business and personal finances. Many good businesses fail because they grow beyond the asset base and working capital required to support them.

- **Organization.** Every entrepreneur must decide how to organize his or her business. Not only are we talking about organizing facilities and human resources, but also the basic legal structure of the business. The decision of whether or not to incorporate is important. If the decision is not to incorporate, important decisions must be made between or among partners, if there are partners, and contingency plans must be in place in case things change. Like most operational decisions, the organization decision is never finished.

- **Risk.** Every business has risk, and there are several kinds of risk. Operational risks—the risk of accident, mistake, or omission—produce potential liability for the business and can produce liability for the owners, depending on how the business is structured. Continuation risks concern the ability of the business to function in the case of unexpected catastrophe or unavailability of a key employee or owner. *Financial risks* concern the capital structure and the availability of capital and are covered below. Many of these risks are assumed and covered at the business level, but the owner must consider the risks at the personal level as well.

Business Finances

The term "business finances" refers to the assets, liabilities, capital, revenue, and expenses of the business. For you, "expenses" may or may not literally include taxes, but however you want to slice it, taxes and tax considerations obviously have a big impact on how businesses are organized and run. These financial components are tightly intertwined with each other and with the operational decisions made by the business.

- **Capital purchases and assets.** Almost all businesses need to acquire and use fixed assets. That acquisition, of course, can be through purchasing or through renting or leasing. Purchase and lease decisions in turn require return-on-investment (ROI) analysis and financing decisions. Then, once an asset is acquired, it must be *recovered*, or expensed, over time to reflect its depreciation and plan for its replacement. The financing and cash flow decisions involved in acquiring assets will affect both business operations and owner finances, especially in proprietorships, partnerships, and closely held corporations.

- **Capital structure.** "Capital structure" refers to how much of the business financing is through owner equity and how much is through debt or other liabilities, and how it is done, that is, the mix of financial instruments and ownership vehicles. Business capital requirements and owner decisions influence the capital structure, which in turn influences the owner's personal finances. Entrepreneurs must decide how much of their own capital to invest in the business, how they will be "paid" for that capital (in profits, wages, interest, or other ways), and how procuring capital through loans will affect their own financial well-being.

- **Working capital.** This is a tough concept for many entrepreneurs to grasp. It is capital used to finance the flow-through, what goes into the business and what goes out of the business—not the fixed or tangible assets of the business. It is used to pay for inventory and to provide cash for other items necessary to the day-to-day running of the business. Any business that must pay a supplier or an employee before providing a product or a service to its customers or must provide a product or a service to customers before receiving payment needs working capital to make this happen. Working capital is *part* of the total capital required to run a business—and the most dynamic part. Insufficient working capital can choke business operations—insufficient inventory, inability to offer satisfactory customer purchase terms, inability to pay employees or suppliers. It is very common for a business and its entrepreneurs to underestimate its need for working capital. The usual result is that the owner must kick in more cap-

ital from personal finances—or accumulate more debt. Working capital mismanagement is a common cause of personal financial failure for entrepreneurs.

- **Cash flow.** This is the bigger picture for working capital. Does the business have enough cash to meet its ongoing business needs? Does it generate enough cash through operations to replace assets, pay its owners, and fund its growth? Poor cash flow leads to inadequate business resources. It can cause an assortment of financial problems, from decreases in owner returns to severe shortages of capital that must be met eventually by the owners. Cash flow becomes especially critical when the owners must replace key assets or as they're implementing important growth and competitive strategies. Many a business has declined or failed because of inadequate cash flow to replace assets or to execute key competitive strategies—and these problems almost always come back to the doorstep of the entrepreneur.

- **Risk management.** We mentioned risk under Business Operations, but needless to say, any business faces various financial risks. Customers don't always pay, interest rates don't always stay the same, tax rules change, sources of funds don't always come through as expected, owners or investors can leave, and the list goes on—all with obvious personal financial consequences.

Personal Finances

Chapter 2 and the rest of the book bring a deeper discussion of what we mean by personal finances. For now it's sufficient to say that personal finances include the income and expenses and the assets and liabilities of the individual entrepreneur and his or her household. Within those parameters, individual personal finance includes managing cash and money, setting short- and long-term goals, and putting plans in place to achieve those goals. Here are some important pieces to the personal financial puzzle and how they relate to the operations and especially the finances of the business:

- **Cash and money management.** Just as in the business, the key to a financially healthy and secure household lies in managing day-to-day money flows—income and expenses. Here we talk about the use of personal budgets and banking and credit to manage family finances and lay bricks in place to achieve longer-term goals.

- **Income from business.** Every entrepreneur has to decide when, how, and how much to be paid from the business. This key decision obviously impacts personal finances, but it is also important to the financial health of the business. The amount and timing of such payments should be right for both the entrepreneur and the business. Also, it should generally—but not always—be done in a way to minimize tax impact. The amount and regularity of income from the business must, of course, be accounted for in the personal financial budget. "Payment" may be in forms besides cash—benefits, retirement savings, or use of assets. However entrepreneurial compensation is structured, it must be thought through carefully.

- **Management and growth of personal wealth.** We mentioned income, but income most surely doesn't translate directly to wealth. Just ask the thousands (millions?) of entrepreneurs and other individuals with substantial incomes but little to show for them. The slogan is "*make it, keep it, grow it*"—but many never get past "make it." Why? Poor money management—lack of awareness, commitment, and control—gets in the way of keeping it, and poor or inattentive use of investing and savings vehicles gets in the way of growing it. Now, we know that most entrepreneurs are too busy to be very active investors, but we will offer some invest-

ing basics to help savvy entrepreneurs figure out where to stash their cash.

- **Risk management.** Just as in business, your personal life involves risks, including loss of income, health problems, liability, and loss of property. Risk management isn't *just* about insurance, although insurance is an important tool used to manage risk. Entrepreneurs and their families incur the same risks as other people, but business owners may face some additional risks—and may also have some other alternatives to help manage them.

- **Benefits.** If you're a corporate or public service employee, your fringe benefits—insurance coverage, retirement, bonuses, discounts, use of facilities, etc.—are usually fairly well defined upfront or at least defined as a set of choices. When you're an entrepreneur, the sky's the limit, at least within the law. The business can provide your benefits; if it is large enough, it can take advantage of group plans and rates. Good entrepreneurial personal finance means choosing the right combination of benefits to get you the most personally, while not compromising the business and while minimizing total taxes.

- **Retirement planning.** "Retirement planning" means figuring out how much you need for retirement and how you will achieve that "number" or goal; "retirement plans" refer to the specific savings vehicles you use to move toward achieving that goal. The first is a matter of pure planning and number crunching; for the entrepreneur, it must include an exit strategy, a way out of the business. The second is really part of the "benefits" package—choosing the right retirement savings package to maximize savings and tax advantages for both you and your business. There are many choices, complex choices that depend on both the finances and the operations (specifically, number and type of employees) of the business.

■ **Transition and distribution planning.** Sooner or later, for financial or other personal reasons, every entrepreneur needs to figure out an exit strategy from the business. Needless to say also, sooner or later, we all die. In personal finance, estate planning concerns the preparation to transfer assets and decision-making authority to others. When a business is involved, the process is first more complex and second should usually start earlier. If something happens to you, what happens to the business? If something happens to one of your partners or key employees, what happens to the business? And what happens to your personal finances as a result of these events? Should you sell your business? When and why? How do you maximize your personal wealth as you close the doors? Again, many, many choices—all begging for careful planning.

The above bullet points cover many of the basics of personal finance and touch on how those basics relate to the finances of a business and to business ownership in general. The rest of the book digs further into personal finances and these relationships.

OUR "MODEL" ENTREPRENEUR

There are many, many types of entrepreneurs. By now, you're probably wondering what kinds of entrepreneurs we are addressing this book to—or, more specifically, whether or not it's for you.

Of course the term "entrepreneur" applies to a range of small business owners and partners—people who own a side business/hobby, a local espresso cart, a franchise, a $100-million-a-year cement contractor, or any of so many possibilities. The location of the business can be anything from a corner of a garage to a multinational expanse of factories and offices. It would be disingenuous to target this book to one specific type of entrepreneur. However, the issues and needs of the man making bird feeders in the corner of his garage differ from the issues and needs of the man or woman owning the $100-million corporation.

FOR THOSE WHO PREFER DIAMONDS

You may have felt that the triangle model presented Figure 1.1 and illustrating the connections among business operations, business finances, and personal finances was incomplete. What about marketing costs? Especially for start-up businesses or businesses requiring substantial marketing resources, where does this fit in? For those curious, Figure 1.2 shows a more complete picture.

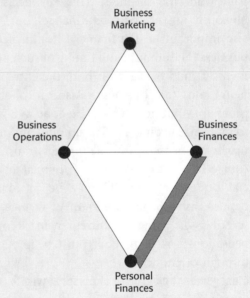

FIGURE 1.2. The Golden Diamond of Entrepreneurial Personal Finance

In this more complete model, marketing costs and decisions affect business operations and finances—and vice versa. There is no direct impact on personal finances. Remove the "Personal Finances" portion of the picture and you have the standard business triumvirate studied in any business school.

When looking at the broad spectrum of entrepreneurs, we see several factors that will impact personal finance needs and the relationship between business and personal finances:

- **Size of business.** Obviously, the coffee cart business and the $100-million corporation have different personal financial ramifications. The coffee cart entrepreneur is most likely a proprietor; he or she and that business are largely one and the same. Life becomes a matter of managing cash flow and acquiring a few assets. What the business earns is what the owner earns; it's a one-for-one relationship. The large corporate entrepreneur, on the other hand, faces key decisions on how to get paid, how to maximize benefits, and how to tailor ownership to best suit his or her personal needs.

- **Number of employees.** Adding employees increases financial complexity—and opportunity, especially in the area of benefits.

- **Type of business.** Different businesses have different asset and cash flow requirements and they suggest different forms of organization and structure. A business handling radioactive waste has a different risk profile than one serving espressos.

- **Degree of involvement.** Some entrepreneurs *are* their business; others are minority owners or not actively involved in managing the business.

- **Life stage of business.** It makes a big difference where you are in the lifetime of the business. Start-up entrepreneurs have different needs from mid-career or late-stage entrepreneurs. Start-up entrepreneurs face important decisions on how to organize the business and how to capitalize or fund it—what to put into the business. As a business approaches the middle stages of life, decisions shift to how to protect the business and get the most cash flow out of it. Finally, in the latter stages of

> ## WHO THIS BOOK IS *NOT* FOR ...
>
> We will say here at the outset that our aim is to help "active" entrepreneurs, as the IRS defines them—that is, those managing an active business—as opposed to "passive" entrepreneurs—those managing real estate or other passive investments. These entrepreneurs may be fully or only partially involved, but they are active and the business is active. The tax rules for passive entrepreneurs are quite different; also, most of the discussion about benefits and income-planning tools is of no practical interest. Our span of coverage includes entrepreneurs with home-based businesses, but mainly such businesses that are operated for profit, not so-called "hobby" businesses.

ownership, focus shifts even further into how to get the most out of it, but then it's about wealth, not just cash flow.

If you consider each of the five factors listed above as a continuum, you as an entrepreneur are at a certain point on each of these five continua—this mix of five points makes your entrepreneurial profile unique. There is no single "model" entrepreneur. You may be a new entrepreneur with a coffee cart, no employees, simple structure, producing one income from the business. Or you may be a late-stage owner of a corporation with 100 employees; you remain on the board of directors but you've delegated most day-to-day responsibilities to others and your chief source of income is an annual dividend. Or you could be anywhere in between.

In a book like this, we can't write an exact personal finance formula for such a diverse universe of unique sets of needs. All we can hope to do is to is stick to the most universal principles and philosophies of entrepreneurial personal finance. In so doing, our approach is more to teach you how to fish than to give you fish. We can't prescribe the best specific financial approach for your situation. We can only illuminate the various alternatives and issues you'll need to consider and to provide enough information about those alternatives to motivate you to get more advice and to feel more competent in doing so.

THREE "MODEL" BUSINESSES

The best way to teach is by example. Therefore, throughout the book, we will use examples where it makes sense. We have identified three model businesses, each with different characteristics and circumstances. These businesses are fictitious but based on real businesses we know about and have worked with. Our hope is that you can identify with at least one of these models. You may have to use your imagination a little. Where it makes sense, we will look at principles and thought processes from the perspectives of these entrepreneurs.

Here are the three businesses.

DG Commercial Photo

Three years ago, Dave Green was a staff photographer and ran the professional photography studio for a large photographic firm in a big Midwestern city. He didn't always agree with the owner, who was more interested in running the photo-finishing operations than anything else. Dave saw a more clearly defined and underserved set of niches in commercial photography—more specifically, product, architectural, and aerial photography. Dave also saw the writing on the wall about digital photography and the future of photo-finishing. Over time he became increasingly lured by the notion that he could make it on his own.

So he read the books on starting a business, talked to suppliers, costed out $50,000 in start-up gear, and talked with friends and bankers about financing.

Ready, aim, ready, aim …. Finally, he decided "go" and went to tell his boss. He expected a curt rebuff and a vow to compete to the death. The response was 180 degrees from what he expected: "Dave, you want to go into the business? How would you like to buy my studio? I'll finance it for you."

So, that's what happened: Dave bought the studio, accepted the owner financing, and paid it off five years after starting. He runs the studio as a sole proprietorship from a small home he purchased next door to his residence. He has no employees. He has maintained the business at an average of about $150,000 in annual revenues. But the client base is shrinking and the ubiquity of digital imaging has made his once-predictable client base less predictable; the boom-and-bust cycles have become sharper. He wonders how best to manage these cycles, whether or not he needs to grow or add something to the business. Although only 35 years old, he wants to start building a retirement and recognizes that the business won't bring much as an asset, for he faces the same issue as many other professionals: without him, there's really no business.

Wheeler Dealer

Some ten years before Dave Green was venturing into the photography business, Henry Wheeler was making a life change. He was part of the San Francisco Bay Area daily grind: his job paid modestly and he was finding it hard to keep up, especially now with two toddlers in the family. The future was somewhere else, Henry decided, so he quit his job, sold the house, and used the proceeds to move the family, to start a new life in a small city in the Pacific Northwest—the same city where a cousin was living after making a similar move. He and his wife had no jobs, but he aspired to do something, to start some kind of business. He did not know what.

Soon, Henry heard about a bike shop that had come available; the owner was retiring. But he didn't have enough cash to buy the business *and* support the family. So he and his wife had dinner with the cousin, who, as it turns out, had worked in a bike shop and had extensive experience. They decided to become partners. They bought the shop and renamed it Wheeler Dealer.

Fast-forward about 15 years. His cousin decided to move on. Henry bought him out and now runs a $400,000-a-year shop, the biggest and best in town. Recently a building more suitable for his business came up for sale; after a grinding decision-making process filled with pros and cons, he bought it. His children are now approaching college age. As the business has become a stable source of income, Henry wonders how to best meet his family's growing financial needs and how to fund his future retirement.

MicroMetal Precision Machining

MicroMetal Precision Machining does custom work with sheet metal. Its specialty is custom job-lot manufacture of designed parts from sheet steel and aluminum for a range of customers. The business, founded in 1990 by northern California entrepreneur Tim Cutter, started as a small single-owner traditional machine shop with traditional equipment, traditional customers, and two employees.

Five years ago, new laser machine tools became available and offered an opportunity for MicroMetal to carve out a niche in manufacturing higher-precision parts. With complete computer control and easier setup, the new flatbed laser machine tools allow greater precision and shorter lead times. This would allow MicroMetal to make more high-end parts and position it better in the just-in-time manufacturing environment. Machine shops are everywhere and Taiwan and China are getting a growing share of the business. But Taiwan and China can't compete with MicroMetal on the lead times or, for most jobs, the precision of the products. So there's clearly a niche. The only problem is that the laser machines cost about $2 million

each, and, to offer a complete solution, MicroMetal needed two of them.

So, for this and other reasons, Cutter decided to incorporate and find an angel investor for capital. He succeeded and now, in five years the closely-held company has grown further by acquiring other small machine shops in northern California. The $5 million company is considering future expansion plans, including moving into the lucrative Los Angeles market. Cutter, now 55, is quite satisfied with the business he has created. After living lean for years, he now wants to expand his take from the business and wants to start developing a plan to sell or transition it to others.

THE REST OF THE STORY

From here, we move into Chapter 2 to explore basic principles of and tools of personal finance. In Chapter 3 we take on taxes. Upfront, we mentioned the profound influence of taxes on business and personal finances; Chapter 3 gives a short course on what these effects are and how you should manage them.

Part II gets more practical about how best to start up and grow a business within the context of your personal finances. Chapter 4 outlines the usual forms of business organization and their pros and cons. Chapter 5 gets into the nuts and bolts of budgeting and managing business and personal cash flows. Chapter 6 examines the use of debt and credit and the acquisition of business assets. Chapter 7 digs deeper into the tax system and getting the most out of your business after taxes.

Part II is about what you put into the business; Part III, "Building Long-Term Wealth," shifts focus to what you get *out* of the business. Chapter 8, "Protecting Yourself," examines risk management and the role of personal and business insurance and other financial buffers in managing risk. Chapter 9 covers the management and growth of personal assets through investing. Chapter 10 covers college and retirement savings strategies and the many choices of savings vehicles. Chapter 11 concerns the exit strategy for your business, whether it is passed on or sold.

Finally, the vast array of entrepreneurial situations begs for special treatment of certain topics likely to be of interest to certain entrepreneurs. So we offer short reference tips for family businesses, home-based businesses, and franchise businesses and more tips about how to hire accountants and financial planners and, finally, other resources for working out the business finance–personal finance equation for your unique situation.

CHAPTER 2

Personal Finance Basics

WHAT *IS* PERSONAL FINANCE? IN MUCH the same way as 20th-century author Ayn Rand led us into the depths of defining her objectivist philosophy in *Atlas Shrugged*, we now start the journey toward defining what we really mean by "personal finance" and what you should know about it. This chapter gives a big-picture overview of personal finance and adapts it to the entrepreneurial experience and lifestyle where it makes sense.

DEFINING *PERSONAL* FINANCE

It's never *too* basic to start with a working definition:

> Personal finance is the management of individual or family financial resources to create enough wealth to achieve the basic needs, chosen lifestyle, and aspirations of that individual or family.

Breaking the term down into its components, personal and finance, clarifies its meaning a little more.

Personal means that it's about you and your family. It is not about the business and its revenues, costs, and profits. It is about what comes into your household, what goes out of your household, and what stays in your household,

saved. The goals are personal, as are the means and tools to achieve them. True, you may watch your investments from your desk and your health insurance may actually come as a business health plan. But these factors influence your *personal* well-being, not your *business*.

Finance means, of course, that it's about your individual or family monetary wealth. This wealth, however temporary or permanent, is earned, used, and saved as a means to meet personal and family wants and needs, to achieve personal and family life goals. The term "finance" refers to both monetary flows *and* contingency plans to deal with unexpected events that might affect those flows. Your unexpected death, disability, loss of job, or unforeseen expenses are examples of unexpected events.

THE PUZZLE AND ITS MANY PIECES

As we presented the "Golden Triangle" of entrepreneurial personal finance in Chapter 1, we introduced some of the major components of personal finance. Simply put, the phrase "make it, keep it, and grow it" is really what it's all about. Personal finance tools—budgeting, banking and credit, investing, tax planning, college planning, retirement planning, risk management, and estate planning—are the big pieces of the big picture.

Just as a technical understanding of accounting or marketing doesn't necessarily make for a good business leader, good personal finance doesn't just mean understanding the individual pieces separately. Good finance is about how they fit together. It is about the underlying principles, practices, and habits that *make them* fit together *best*. In entrepreneurial personal finance, it isn't just how they fit together in the personal finance "space," but also how they connect with your business.

In this chapter we develop the underlying context, principles, and *thought process* of personal finance. We talk about how to fit the puzzle pieces together. The rest of the book develops each puzzle piece in more detail, all within the context of the big picture.

BASIC PRINCIPLES

People often associate personal finance with endless number crunching, detailed line-by-line spending plans, dry and dull bank and brokerage statements, counting this, counting that. Well, personal finance does involve those things, but good personal finance requires sound judgment and a good set of personal financial habits to go with the numbers. Just as in business, really. You can make a number, but if you fail to satisfy a customer, develop an employee, introduce a new product, or work towards some goal, then the thrill of making that number soon disappears.

Growing Imperative

Personal finance is taking on a rapidly growing importance and role. People everywhere—not just entrepreneurs—are taking more individual responsibility for their financial destiny. Financial needs, especially for the long term, are growing. We live longer. Health-care costs are rising. Big-ticket items, like housing, have become considerably more expensive relative to incomes. Jobs—and the companies that provide them—have become less stable, work stints are shorter, and transitions are more fre-

quent. It now takes a college education to get a high-paying job. Income tax laws, reflecting the effects of almost a century of tinkering, have become more complex than ever. We want to retire early and do more in retirement. Government entitlements—Social Security, Medicare—are not keeping up and will never be able to keep up.

It takes good, solid personal financial decisions and planning to deal with these issues. No longer can we work 40 years for the same company with a $10-copay employer-provided health care plan now and a guaranteed pension and health benefits for our retirement. And you know the rest of the story—as an entrepreneur you have no such long-term financial security.

Financial Planning

As a result, personal finance has become less about *managing finances* from day to day (although this is still a vital part) and more about *financial planning*. Financial planning helps individuals and families set goals and then develop means to achieve them. Financial planning starts with where you are now, plots where you want to go, and then supplies the means—and the choices—to get there. Much as a business or marketing plan provides a strategic framework for operating a business, financial planning provides a strategic framework for making day-to-day tactical financial decisions.

Good financial planning is systematic—that is, it considers individual or family personal finances as an integrated system of inflows, outflows, needs, wants, assets, and liabilities and finds the best balance of savings, investments, insurance, and other planning tools. It doesn't merely focus on insurance as an end in itself but it tries to fit insurance into the larger financial equation that includes income and income needs, investments, retirement, and so forth.

Integrated financial planning is thus, to the specific concepts and tools of personal finance, what an MBA (master of business administration) is to a person engaged in business. MBA students learn about individual business components—like marketing, accounting, production and operations, human resources, and so on. But most of all, they learn how to work with all those components together to develop and maintain a good business. Such it is with the financial plan: it takes the elements of personal finance and blends them to best accumulate wealth and achieve goals.

You as CFO

You may be the chief financial officer of your business or you may have hired one. Either way, someone is ultimately in charge. The CFO's function and importance in business are fairly clear, and most entrepreneurs understand them. Someone must monitor the financial pulse of the business, maintain integrity, and adapt to changes that affect finances, no? Someone must control the budget and cut the checks, right? Absolutely.

Well, someone needs to pay the same attention to your *personal* finances as the CFO pays to business finances and to perform much the same role. Just as in your business, the CFO responsibilities are yours—unless you choose to farm out some or all of them to a spouse or a significant other. The point is that *someone* is CFO of your personal finances and should behave that way—because personal finances are important enough to merit CFO treatment. Furthermore, just as being a business CFO is an acquired skill, so it is with the personal financial CFO. Like any job, it works out better if you *learn* to do it. You've made that commitment by reading this book. It also works better over time as you become more experienced.

Money, Income, and Wealth Are Not the Same

People mix up these terms and concepts. Just because you have a lot of money doesn't mean you have a lot of wealth or income. (You may have bor-

rowed it.) Having a lot of income doesn't always mean you have wealth. (You may be spending it all.) Having a lot of wealth doesn't always mean you have money. (It may be tied up in expensive business assets, real estate, etc.) Effective personal financiers realize that money, income, and wealth are all important at times, but that wealth—real wealth as measured by net worth—is the real goal.

Business Profits Do Not Equal Personal Wealth

For the entrepreneur, it is also important to realize that business *profits* and personal wealth aren't the same, A business may be highly profitable, but consume its resources in growth, acquisitions, or investor payments like interest. Further, if those profits are retained in the business, they could disappear in the next downturn. Unless there is a plan to transition business profits into owner wealth, the owner may come up short.

Business Value Does Not Equal Personal Wealth

Likewise, business *value* and personal wealth are not the same. Just because a business has a high stated value (which may be as much an accounting illusion as reality) doesn't mean that the owner is wealthy. Again, there could be a downturn. Also, it may be difficult for the owner as an individual to make much use of an obsolete $2-million laser machining bed. Bringing business wealth into the personal space may trigger a large tax bill, especially if the business is a corporation and is sitting on a large capital gain.

That brings us to a point we'll discuss throughout the book. There needs to be an "invisible wall" between owner and business finances: they must be managed as separate entities or "spaces." There also needs to be a well-defined set of doors to allow the owner to move resources back and forth between the two financial spaces—and assets and wealth need to move between the spaces at the right moment.

This may be a bit confusing, since, as we'll discuss later, in sole proprietorships and partnerships, business and personal incomes are considered one *for tax purposes*. But taxes aren't everything. Beyond taxes, for the purposes of managing cash flow, asset ownership, insurance, and general financial planning, business assets and incomes and their management should be separated from personal assets and income. Separated physically—separate checking accounts, checkbooks, and most physical assets— and separated in the mind of the entrepreneur.

Personal Finance Isn't Just Tools—It's Behavior

Woe unto the individual—entrepreneur or not— who simply thinks that he or she can sit down with a set of statements once a month and do personal finances with a calculator! Sure, calculators and a bunch of other planning tools come into play. Sure, there are many choices of investments, credit cards, savings plans, insurance policies, and trusts used for estate planning. But while personal finance uses these tools and platforms, it goes beyond. It is *behavior*—how you use the tools, how you manage your finances on a daily basis—that really counts. When you play golf or tennis, you use clubs or rackets as tools, but it is really behavior—stance and swing and club selection and so on in golf, position and stroke and placement and so forth in tennis—that makes a player successful. The best tools—just like the best clubs or rackets—won't make you successful alone. Further, tools won't work if you aren't in charge.

Successful personal financial behavior breaks down into three character traits: *awareness, control,* and *commitment*. We find that no individual or family can achieve financial success without these traits—unless through luck. Not surprisingly, these are traits you'd expect in a CFO in a business.

Awareness. Success in personal finance means becoming aware—and *staying* aware—of where you

are financially. Just as you should know where you are on the golf course or a tennis court, it is important to know where you are financially. It's important to maintain a good notion of your net worth, debts, and where you are with this month's expenses, credit card balances, and recent income. Whether this is kept "back of mind" or researched and tabulated daily, it doesn't matter. What's important is that you know enough about where you are to make ends meet and handle contingencies.

The tricky part for most entrepreneurs, again, is separating the business space from the personal space. It seems like most entrepreneurs can tell you a lot more about their business finances than about their personal finances. They live the business day in and day out, but they tend to their personal finances once or twice a month when bills are due and then again at tax time. Good personal finance requires staying more on top of things, especially when there are family members in the household.

Control. In the business, "control" refers to making sure funds are used correctly and that all assets are accounted for. It also means clearly outlining who has authority to spend what and putting processes in place to ensure compliance. In the personal space, "control" is much the same concept, although different means will be used to achieve it. Much of personal financial control is *self*-control. It relates not only to physically controlling the flow of money, which is important too, but also to making prudent financial decisions "on the fly." Control in personal finance is the ability to resist tempting buys and bargains and to restrict spending to a predefined limit. It is making and meeting budgets and making savings deposits according to plans. If you realize that control can't happen without awareness, you're getting the point.

Commitment. Commitment is a combination of effort and persistence required to get in control and stay there. It doesn't do any good to be aware only part of the time and in control only part of the time, in either the business or the personal space. Just as in business you need the commitment of your employees and suppliers to help you achieve a goal, so it is in personal finances. Particularly where family members are involved, you need a clearly defined plan and modus operandi to keep things working on a daily basis. Every member of your personal space must buy into it. Each must share in the rewards when it works and each must share in the fix when it doesn't work. Just like in the business.

Lifetime Endeavor

Personal finance isn't something you do once in a while, yet many deal with it this way. They write the checks, balance the checkbook, and check a bank balance or a credit rating only when they get ready to buy something. College for the kids? "That's 10 years off—and we'll just borrow the funds." Retirement? "That's 25 years away—and there's always Social Security and we're sure to inherit some money someday."

Could a business operate this way? Could you write checks, cash and deposit checks, execute payroll, and just run out and buy another machine or store fixture when you think you need it? Hardly. As a business owner, you need to think short and long term. You need to plan for the long-term things and stay on top of the short-term things. Most entrepreneurs are pretty good at this: they keep their finger on the pulse of the business, they know how and where its lifeblood is flowing, and they seek help and think through their decisions. For the most part, anyway. But somehow the personal finances don't get this kind of attention.

Personal finance is filled with short- and long-term considerations. Individuals and families must plan for the future, for the expected (college, retirement, large purchases) and the unexpected (income disruptions, unanticipated expenses, unplanned events, changing needs). More importantly, needs and the *priority* of those needs change over your

lifetime. In your earlier years, your priorities may consist of acquiring a home, building savings, and caring for the needs of your children. As you get older, those children go to college and health care becomes more important. You settle into a way of life based on your income, so you need to protect that income. As you approach retirement, health care becomes even more important, and now you must decide what lifestyle you want in retirement. As we'll see, by this latter stage it is too late to start thinking about saving for retirement; you need to start sooner. So some personal financial decisions must be made far in advance and others as you pass through the various stages of life.

THE PERSONAL FINANCIAL LIFE CYCLE

So now we arrive at one of the most important concepts of personal finance, especially as it relates to the entrepreneur: the *personal financial life cycle*.

Any entrepreneur or business professional understands that businesses don't stay the same from conception to termination, that they change over the course of their existence. The needs and issues of a start-up business are far different from one that's well established or one that's nearing the end of its useful life. What's going on, strategically and operationally, at Google or Genentech is radically different from what's happening or being discussed in the conference rooms at General Motors or Western Union. What we're talking about here is the *business life cycle*. We'll see in a minute that the business life cycle ties in closely with the *personal finance life cycle* and in many ways drives it. Many decisions you make, both day-to-day and strategic, in both business and personal finance, are influenced by understanding where you are in the respective life cycles. The connection *between* the business and personal financial life cycles is also important and is one of the key lessons in entrepreneurial personal finance.

The Business Life Cycle

Anybody who has studied business at the college level and most people who have read up on the art and science of business have encountered the business life cycle concept in some form. In brief, the business life cycle describes the phases of a business from start-up to dissolution. The goals, needs, challenges, and style of management evolve radically as the business evolves.

At start-up, the business needs to establish market position and learn to build and deliver its product; to do so requires a lot of capital and cash. As the business matures, the focus shifts from more rapid but erratic growth to a more stable and moderate growth. The imperative shifts from establishing market position to becoming profitable. As this mature phase continues, growth opportunities start to diminish and the focus shifts to becoming more efficient and thus more profitable. Finally, as the business shifts toward its final stages, in many cases the strategy shifts to defense; that is, preserving market position and profits. For many entrepreneur-owners, the trick is to foresee this phase and work on a dissolution or sale plan while the business still has maximum value. For some entrepreneurs, the sale or dissolution is driven by personal or family needs as the entrepreneur gets older, rather than by a decline in market or business viability.

Figure 2.1 shows a typical business life cycle.

Clearly a lot more could be said about the strategies and tactics congruent with these stages. Again, this is not intended to be a business book. As the business life cycle progresses, some very important themes become apparent. You'll soon see why they're important as we develop the personal finance life cycle:

1. **Risks decrease.** The initial stages of any business entail taking a lot of risk. Many operational and financial decisions are all-or-nothing; one of many unforeseen events could sack the business. As the business matures, the risks become more

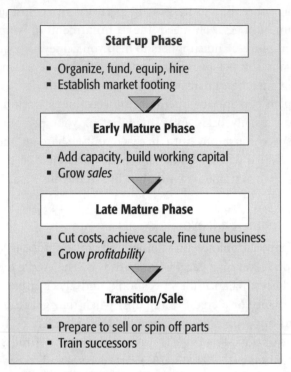

FIGURE 2.1. Typical Business Life Cycle

calculated, more certain of generating a measurable return. As it gets older and more stable, the risks become smaller.

2. **Profitability becomes the point.** The early stages emphasize establishing product and market and growing sales, often at a loss. At some point—and this point varies among businesses—the business crosses the line to become profitable. Then, the push becomes to become more profitable and to generate more *free cash flow*; that is, cash unencumbered by the investment needs of the business. As the business matures, focus shifts toward becoming more efficient with the current products or services and markets to deliver stronger products or services and gain a larger share of those markets.

3. **Growth "push" decreases.** Achieving rapid growth requires taking more risks and consumes resources that impact profitability.

4. **Direct entrepreneurial involvement decreases.** This

depends to a great extent on the business involved, but as the business matures, the entrepreneur does less and less of the day-to-day work. Others are hired to take on responsibilities and bring more vitality into the business.

The Personal Finance Life Cycle

Now let's move over to the personal financial space. Although the issues are not the same as in the business life cycle, we find that the personal life cycle has many parallels. Such parallels include declining risk, improved cash flow, reduced debt, and, more generally, wealth accumulation and then preservation. In many cases, as the individual grows older, there is more to manage and thus greater involvement in personal finances.

Financial planners define three major phases: the *accumulation phase*, the *preservation phase*, and the *distribution phase*. These terms are somewhat self-explanatory; Figure 2.2 will help.

Most of the personal finance bookshelf is concerned with the accumulation phase—how to invest, how to buy real estate, how to save for retirement, how to become a millionaire, and so forth. Only in recent years—as more people age and approach retirement—have books started to appear about preservation and distribution of wealth. *You're Fifty—Now What?* by Charles Schwab is a good example.

Figure 2.2 shows the personal finance life cycle.

Personal Financial Life Cycle Phases

Most entrepreneurs and business professionals understand the business life cycle. However, the phases of the personal financial life cycle merit more detail.

Accumulation phase. Typically, this is the startup phase experienced by younger people, newlyweds, and new families starting out in new careers. It is characterized by low net worth or a high ratio

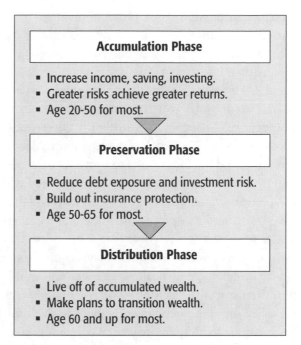

FIGURE 2.2. Personal Finance Life Cycle

of debt to net worth. In this phase, individuals and families borrow to buy homes and establish households, budgeting tightly and saving where and when they can. When starting out, savings are low and it is common not to start saving for retirement at all. Insurance needs are relatively modest, unless a large fixed commitment has been made to a home or other expenses. As time passes, incomes increase while the largest expenses, especially housing, remain fixed. Cash flow begins to run positive, the household starts to save, assets appreciate, and the nest egg starts to build, in both retirement and other assets. The household begins to invest these assets and may do so fairly aggressively (that is, in higher-risk investments) because there are relatively few risks to the income stream and there is plenty of time to recoup any losses.

As we'll see in a minute, entrepreneurs may have a "pre-accumulation" phase where net worth decreases and debts are incurred to get the business off the ground: we will call this the *investment* phase.

Preservation phase. In this phase, individuals have started to accumulate some wealth, usually in the form of their homes, some retirement savings, and some other investment assets. They have enough *liquid assets* (cash or equivalents) in reserve, usually at least six months' worth of income, to get by in case of a major income disruption or large unexpected expenses. Net worth is stable to rising, debt is declining, and the focus shifts to protecting the nest egg. Investment risk is gradually reduced. People in this phase become more aware of life's risks and they have more assets to protect, so they increase their insurance protection to cover disability and similar income disruptions, and they may acquire more casualty, liability, and health coverage. The transition between the accumulation phase and the preservation phase happens gradually. Many families continue to accumulate while taking more steps to preserve what they have; in fact, the accumulation might accelerate as they learn to live on less—or as their businesses produce increased profits.

Distribution phase. This phase begins when individual or families start to feel they've accumulated enough to achieve their goals or to spend on things they want without jeopardizing some future need or goal. Like the transition from the accumulation to preservation phase, this transition can be subtle. Focus may shift from generating income and wealth to using that wealth to help others, i.e., charitable giving. If there's a business involved, at this point the owner has likely turned over the reins to someone else. Thoughts start to move toward gifting and transitioning assets to family members and to downsizing life style towards Sun City-style simplicity.

It's important to note, as we have already, that there are no clear boundaries of age or behavior separating the phases. People tend to think and act as though they were in two phases or even all three simultaneously. And people can be moved backwards through the cycle by events, such as an investment downturn—or even starting a business. Backwards isn't always bad—it may be part of a conscious decision.

SIDE BY SIDE

Now, you can probably see where this is going. Entrepreneurs have a business space and a personal finance space. Each space has its life cycle phases and clearly the two life cycles and their phases influence each other. A business in start-up mode will place different demands on the personal financial side than a business throwing off thousands in excess cash. Likewise, a personal situation driven by a special need, like a college education, will place special demands on the business and may influence, for example, decisions about how much short-term risk to take.

For most entrepreneurs, these two life cycles run side by side. But the life cycles do not always line up in "textbook" model fashion, particularly when age is considered. It is becoming increasingly common for people during midlife to leave careers as employees to start businesses. Those people may be late in the accumulation phase or even in the preservation phase, but only starting out in the business life cycle. As mentioned earlier, the age boundaries we suggested don't always apply. A person could be 60 or older and still be in a start-up business phase. At 60, he or she could have some preservation needs and maybe even some distribution planning needs, but be starting a business, presumably with the intent of accumulating some wealth from it!

Figure 2.3 shows how the two life cycles run side by side for a "typical" entrepreneur. First, and most important, you'll notice that we've added a phase on the personal finance side.

Entrepreneurs experience a phase not experienced by other people, one we call the *investment phase*. In this phase, entrepreneurs are doing everything necessary to start their businesses. Their needs clearly do not fit into the three phases of accumulation, preservation, and distribution.

It's important to understand the dynamics connecting the business and personal financial life cycle phases. We've added them in the center of the graphic in summary form. These dynamics indicate what should be happening in each phase and also

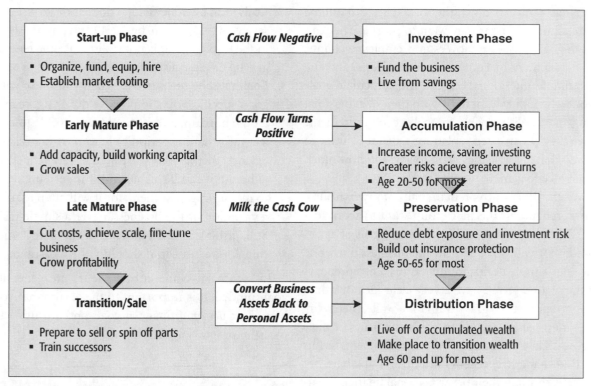

FIGURE 2.3. Personal Finance Life Style for Entrepreneurs

define the transition from one phase to another. For instance, as cash flow turns positive, it makes sense to surmise that the entrepreneur is moving from the start-up phase to the early mature phase on the business side and from the investment phase to the accumulation phase in his or her personal financial space.

This model shows general tendencies. It is quite common for an individual to have characteristics of the accumulation phase or the preservation phase mixed with characteristics of the investment phase. If you quit a job in your 50s with solid retirement savings and home equity, but set aside a couple of hundred thousand or take on some debt to start a business, you may operate largely in the preservation phase, but have some needs and characteristics of the investment phase.

What's important is to understand the life cycle model in terms of general tendencies and to understand the ramifications of each phase and the transition from one phase to another. The model provides a great backdrop for discussing personal finance tools and best practices. As the adage goes, if you don't know where you are, it's hard to know where you're going.

GOALS AND GOAL SETTING

Many basic personal finance books and classes start with a lengthy treatise on setting goals. The notion is that you need to plot a direction or you are not likely to achieve what you want to achieve financially. We agree with this notion, but we will not spend a lot of time on setting goals. As an entrepreneur, you doubtless had some pretty clear goals in mind when you decided to start your business.

We are not minimizing the importance of having clear personal financial goals. From our observations, entrepreneurs are commonly clearer about their business goals than their personal ones. They know where they want to be with the business this year, next, five, ten years down the road. They can outline in detail new markets they want to pursue. They can quote goals about employees and employee counts, new machinery or equipment acquisitions, and site or building intentions. But can they articulate goals about where they want to be with their own personal net worth? With saving for college or retirement? Have they constructed a plan for when they want to retire, what life style they want to live, and how much it will take to achieve that life style?

We find that entrepreneurs fall into two groups. Entrepreneurs in the first group want to work forever. They have no specific retirement goals or age in mind; they will work to grow the business until, one day, they simply decide to call it quits. Entrepreneurs in the second group have a very clear idea of riding the entrepreneurial gravy train for a while, then retiring, often before age 65, to enjoy the fruits of their success. They have very clear retirement goals. But we find that entrepreneurs in both groups have *not* thought through their other personal financial goals in great detail.

Whether or not you have retirement goals, there are a few important characteristics of good goal setting. This is probably familiar territory for all but the most "seat of the pants" entrepreneurs:

1. **Goals must be focused.** If there are too many goals, the strategies and tactics to achieve them become diffuse; we've all experienced trying to do too many things at once and doing none of them well. Similarly, if there are too few goals, something is probably being left out. Just as the ideal presentation slide covers three to seven points, the ideal goal matrix probably contains three to seven goals.
2. **Goals must be specific.** You must state your goals in terms specific enough to measurably achieve. A goal of "get rich" won't work; "Achieve a net worth of $1 million by age 45" is better. "Pay for college" is OK, but it's better to specify a sum, developed in context of likely college choices and inflation rates with a specific time horizon.
3. **Goals must be achievable.** It doesn't make sense to set a goal (e.g., "Retire by age 40 and buy an island in the tropics") if it is not realistic. People tend to give up on unrealistic goals.
4. **Goals must be measurable.** When you make your goals specific, you should set a dollar figure and a time horizon, and it should be possible to collect information periodically to measure results against them. Net worth goals are effective, although it can be a challenge for entrepreneurs to measure against them, for it will often require a valuation of the business, never a simple task. Still, just because it's difficult to measure something doesn't mean it shouldn't be measured.

In summary, while entrepreneurs are generally goal-minded, it is important to make sure that you have clear *personal* financial goals and a routine to measure progress against them.

TOOL TIME

Now we switch gears just a bit. Before going further, it is important to touch on a few mathematical tools and principles vital to understanding and executing a good personal financial plan.

Most entrepreneurs are familiar with the concept of time value of money: a dollar today is worth more than a dollar in the future. We want to expand that concept to cover the power of compounding, a vitally important principle in the financial planning process. Building on the compounding principle, we explain the concept of *distribution* and *accumulation annuities* and offer tools, in the form of simple tables, to help with the financial planning process.

Time Value of Money

A dollar in hand now is worth more than a dollar in the future. Any entrepreneur will tell you so. The reasons are more obvious to the entrepreneur than to most people. Running a business requires cash; cash that isn't on hand today the owner must borrow and then pay interest or some other form of return on the cash—that is, capital. Business professionals and financiers speak of *present value* and *future value.*

Present and Future Value

Present value is today's equivalent value for a dollar received at some specific time in the future, *discounted* according to the current cost—the applicable interest rate. That rate, incidentally, corresponds most closely to the market rate of return that someone else, presumably the lender, could have earned on the funds during the discount period.

Personal financial math can be explained by words, formulas, tables, or pictures. We've found that words, by themselves, don't do justice to explaining present value, future value, or annuities. So in the next few pages, we use pictures and tables. Figure 2.4 illustrates the concept of time value of money and, in so doing, present and future value.

A sum is deposited today and accumulates *compound* interest (that is, interest is paid on the principal *plus* the interest received to date). The amount deposited today is the present value; the accumulated sum is the future value. If you deposit $100 today, ten years down the road you'll receive a future value determined by the interest rate or rate of return paid. If, on the other hand, you expect to receive $100 ten years from now, $100 is the future value and the present value is a discounted amount taking into consideration the implied rate of return and the ten-year period.

We can now add to the explanation using tables, with actual figures to make it easier to understand and to give you a tool to use in the future to manage your finances. We'll start with future value (Figure 2.5), since that is a bit easier to grasp intuitively.

The figure has a lot of numbers, but they will soon make sense if they don't already. If you have $100 today and want to know the future value in ten years, just assume a rate of return (an interest rate or some other investment rate of return) and find the corresponding factor on the table.

Suppose you plan to invest that $100 in your business for ten years and earn 10 percent on it. The table factor is 2.59; multiply that factor by $100 and you'll get $259, the future value of your $100 ten years from now at 10 percent.

Now we move along to present value. The table in Figure 2.6 shows the factors used to *discount* a sum in the future back to the present value.

From the table, you can see that $100 received ten years from now, assuming an 8-percent rate of return, is worth only $46 today ($100 x 0.46). So in both your business and personal finances, it's helpful to know that that barroom offer to buy your business from you for a million bucks 20 years from now isn't worth quite that much.

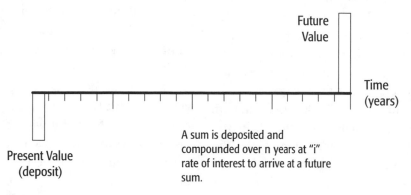

FIGURE 2.4. Time Value of Money

Future Value of $1 Present Sum								
Number of years	**1**	**2**	**5**	**10**	**15**	**20**	**30**	**40**
4.0%	$1.04	$1.08	$1.22	$1.48	$1.80	$2.19	$3.24	$4.80
5.0%	1.05	1.10	1.28	1.63	2.08	2.65	4.32	7.04
6.0%	1.06	1.12	1.34	1.79	2.40	3.21	5.74	10.29
7.0%	1.07	1.14	1.40	1.97	2.76	3.87	7.61	14.97
8.0%	1.08	1.17	1.47	2.16	3.17	4.66	10.06	21.72
9.0%	1.09	1.19	1.54	2.37	3.64	5.60	13.27	31.41
10.0%	1.10	1.21	1.61	2.59	4.18	6.73	17.45	45.26
12.0%	1.12	1.25	1.76	3.11	5.47	9.66	29.96	93.05
15.0%	1.15	1.32	2.01	4.05	8.14	16.37	66.21	267.86
20.0%	1.20	1.44	2.49	6.19	15.41	38.34	237.38	1,469.77
25.0%	1.25	1.56	3.05	9.31	28.42	86.74	807.79	7,523.16

Rate of Return (%) (row label)

FIGURE 2.5. Future Value Factor Table

Present Value of $1 Future Sum								
Number of years	**1**	**2**	**5**	**10**	**15**	**20**	**30**	**40**
4.0%	$0.96	$0.92	$0.82	$0.68	$0.56	$0.46	$0.31	$0.21
5.0%	0.95	0.91	0.78	0.61	0.48	0.38	0.23	0.14
6.0%	0.94	0.89	0.75	0.56	0.42	0.31	0.17	0.10
7.0%	0.93	0.87	0.71	0.51	0.36	0.26	0.13	0.07
8.0%	0.93	0.86	0.68	0.46	0.32	0.21	0.10	0.05
9.0%	0.92	0.84	0.65	0.42	0.27	0.18	0.08	0.03
10.0%	0.91	0.83	0.62	0.39	0.24	0.15	0.06	0.02
12.0%	0.89	0.80	0.57	0.32	0.18	0.10	0.03	0.01
15.0%	0.87	0.76	0.50	0.25	0.12	0.08	0.02	0.00
20.0%	0.83	0.69	0.40	0.16	0.06	0.03	0.00	0.00
25.0%	0.80	0.64	0.33	0.11	0.04	0.01	0.00	0.00

Rate of Return (%) (row label)

FIGURE 2.6. Present Value Factor Table

The Power of Compounding

OK, it's good to know about present and future values and to be able to calculate these values simply. But other than estimating the future value of my savings or comparing immediate and deferred cash offers for my business, what's the point?

Present value and future value are useful in both business and personal finance, for they help you gauge the relative worth of funds now and later. But the most important personal finance lesson is really the power of sums of money, when left alone, to accumulate additional sums of money. Wealth builds wealth, as the adage goes. Good personal financiers understand it as the *power of compounding*.

Again, the best way to illustrate is to use the future value factor table (Figure 2.5). Set $100 aside for five years and earn today's historically moderate interest rates on it—let's say, 4 percent—and you'll wind up with $122 (five years at 4 percent gives a factor of 1.22). Nice. But what if you set that $100 aside for 20 years and earn a handsome return of 15 percent, as you might in your business? The factor for 20 years at 15 percent is 16.37—you'll end up with $1,637, 16 times your investment. (Yes, the

Rule of 72 works too: 72 divided by 15 percent is roughly five, so your sum doubles every five years for 20 years; that is, it doubles four times. $100 becomes $200 in five years, $400 in ten years, $800 in 15 years, and finally $1,600 in 20 years.)

The sum of $1,637 isn't bad. But what if you leave that sum invested for another ten years? The factor jumps to 66.21—you'll wind up with $6,621. If you bump the return to 20 percent over 30 years, the factor explodes to 237.38—that is, you'll wind up with $23,738 on your $100 investment.

Little wonder that we hear so much in the media about starting your retirement savings early. Little wonder also that Albert Einstein was just as fascinated with the power of compounding—some say more so—as he was with the physics of space-time and relativity. It shouldn't be hard to see how the principle of compounding is important to your own financial planning.

Annuities, Financially Speaking

You probably have heard of financial products known as *annuities*, usually bought in many shapes and forms from insurance companies as investments to provide a stream of income some years down the road. These products have a place, and we'll get to them briefly when discussing retirement savings vehicles.

For personal finance and financial planning, what is important here is to understand the underlying mathematics of annuities. If you deposit a sum of money today, say $100 at 5 percent for 20 years, we've already seen how it can grow. But what if you deposit *another* $100 each year for the next 20 years? Your first $100 compounds to $265 (from the future value factor table, Figure 2.5) and each subsequent investment of $100 earns a return for the amount of time held. $100 for 20 years becomes $265, $100 for 19 years becomes $254, $100 for 18 years becomes $241, and so on to the $100 for the final year, which becomes $105. The happy result: more money

invested, more interest earned, more interest on the interest, and so forth.

There are two types of annuities important in personal financial planning: *accumulation annuities* and *distribution annuities*. *Accumulation* annuities represent the scenario just described: that is, a fixed amount is added to the savings kitty every period and it builds with compounding to achieve a future sum. A *distribution* annuity, on the other hand, reverses the process. Instead of building to a future sum, you want to receive a stream of fixed payments from the kitty for the next *n* number of years, such as during retirement. What is the sum of money you must have, at present, to fund this annual stream, as the balance continues to earn a rate of return? Again, some pictures and tables will make these concepts less abstract and more useful.

Accumulation Annuities

With an accumulation annuity, a fixed amount is added each period. (In our model we'll use a yearly, end-of-year contribution, but the concept works for other time periods.) Figure 2.7 shows this process.

At the end of the time period, individual payments and their compounded interest add up to a fixed sum. Often that is a target savings amount determined by college or retirement needs, but it can be anything—including the amount required to buy the latest flatbed laser machining bed for your business.

To calculate the future accumulated sum, simply find the factor corresponding to the number of years and the expected rate of return. Deposit $100 each year for 20 years at an expected 7-percent rate of return, and what do you get? In the accumulation annuity factor table (Figure 2.8), we find the factor for 20 years at 7 percent is 41.00. Multiply by $100 to get the tidy sum of $4,100 at the end of 20 years. Contrast this with the $387 you end up with if the $100 is deposited in Year One only, without any subsequent deposits (Figure 2.5, 20 years at 7.0 percent).

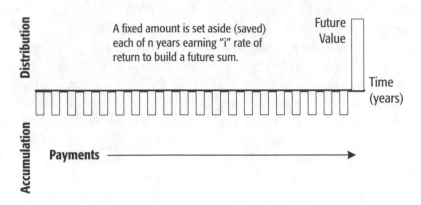

FIGURE 2.7. Accumulation Annuity

TWO BUGABOOS: TAXES AND INFLATION

Put away $735.64 a month and you'll be a millionaire in 30 years. Indeed that sounds attractive; but taxes and inflation darken the story just a bit. Unless you invest tax-free, the interest or other returns earned will be taxable; if you pay the tax from the proceeds, it puts a dent in the compounding power. So the model works only if you (1) pay taxes from other funds or (2) let the assets ride (you don't sell and incur capital gains), and (3) use tax-deferred or tax-free retirement savings vehicles, like IRAs, 401(k)s, or other qualified plans to manage your savings. And about inflation: just remember that the million bucks you save probably won't be worth as much in 30 years. You can calculate more accurately, if you want, by lowering the effective rate of return by the tax rate. If you want to go further, you can deduct an inflation rate, too.

You can see how this kind of calculation helps for retirement and other kinds of savings planning. It works even better when used backwards. Suppose your goal is to accumulate $1 million in 30 years. You think you can earn an 8-percent rate of return between your investments and your business cash flow returns and keep those funds invested. The factor for 30 years at 8 percent is $113.28. So divide that into your million bucks: $8,827.68 is what you must invest every year (or $735.64 every month). Simple—stop sending your kids to private school and you too can be a millionaire!

There may be no more useful set of numbers offered up in this book. It's fun—and quite enlightening—to figure out what you have to do to reach a goal or, alternatively, where you will end up with what you're setting aside today.

Distribution Annuities

Distribution annuities essentially reverse the process outlined for the accumulation annuity. A sum is deposited with the goal of receiving a fixed payment "n" number of years in the future. The rate of return is important here, for the funds that remain will continue to earn interest, which will continue to feed the fund. Figure 2.9 illustrates.

Retirement is where most distribution annuity computations come into play. You decide you need or want $30,000 per year in retirement income (in addition to Social Security and other entitlements). What do you need to have on hand today in order to

Sum accumulated with $1 deposited end of each year for n years								
Number of years	1	2	5	10	15	20	30	40
4.0%	$1.00	$2.04	$5.42	$12.01	$20.02	$29.78	$56.08	$95.03
5.0%	1.00	2.05	5.53	12.58	21.58	33.07	66.44	120.80
6.0%	1.00	2.06	5.64	13.18	23.28	36.79	79.06	154.76
7.0%	1.00	2.07	5.75	13.82	25.13	41.00	94.46	199.64
8.0%	1.00	2.08	5.87	14.49	27.15	45.76	113.28	259.06
10.0%	1.00	2.10	6.11	15.94	31.77	57.27	164.49	442.59
12.0%	1.00	2.12	6.35	17.55	37.28	72.05	241.33	767.09
15.0%	1.00	2.15	6.74	20.30	47.58	102.44	434.75	1,177.09
20.0%	1.00	2.20	7.44	25.96	72.04	186.69	1,181.88	7,343.86

Rate of Return (%)

FIGURE 2.8. Accumulation Annuity Factor Table

ensure receiving that $30,000 for 30 years? The answer is found using a table of distribution annuity factors (Figure 2.10).

Assuming a conservative 5-percent return in retirement (from, say, U.S. Treasury securities and similar), the 30-year factor is $15.37. That means you'll need 15.37 times your annual dollar payout requirement as an initial, present-value lump sum, or 15.37 x $30,000 or $461,100. That figure is your retirement savings goal, the number you need to hit in order to achieve your downstream income objectives. If you can achieve a return rate a few percentage points higher, you can clearly see how your retirement savings goal decreases—but you may end up taking on more risk to achieve this return.

Note: as in the accumulation annuity example above, these calculations do not include the effects of taxes, which will reduce the $30,000 you will receive. Also note that there are no raises or cost-of-living adjustments, so the $30,000 you receive 25 years from now will simply have to suffice, regardless of inflation. Additionally, this calculation assumes you plan to consume the original nest egg, leaving nothing to your heirs—and nothing if you live beyond 100 years. There are other calculations available, beyond our scope here, to build a plan that preserves some assets for your heirs.

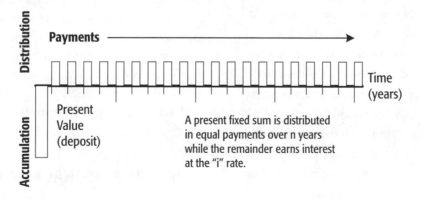

FIGURE 2.9. Distribution Annuity

Sum required to receive $1 paid out each year for n years								
Number of years	**1**	**2**	**5**	**10**	**15**	**20**	**30**	**40**
4.0%	$0.96	$1.89	$4.45	$8.11	$11.12	$13.59	$17.29	$19.79
5.0%	0.95	1.86	4.33	7.72	10.36	12.46	15.37	17.16
6.0%	0.94	1.83	4.21	7.36	9.71	11.47	13.76	15.05
7.0%	0.93	1.81	4.10	7.02	9.11	10.59	12.41	13.33
8.0%	0.93	1.78	3.99	6.71	8.56	9.82	11.26	11.92
10.0%	0.91	1.74	3.79	6.14	7.61	8.51	9.43	9.78
12.0%	0.89	1.69	3.60	5.65	6.81	7.47	8.06	8.24
15.0%	0.87	1.63	3.35	5.02	5.85	6.26	6.57	6.64
20.0%	0.83	1.53	2.99	4.19	4.68	4.87	4.98	5.00

(Rate of Return (%))

FIGURE 2.10. Distribution Annuity Factor Table

Putting Two and Two Together

Put the accumulation and distribution annuity concepts and calculations together back to back and you'll get an idea of what quantitative financial planning is all about.

Suppose you want $50,000 per year in retirement, which you assume starts at age 65 and goes for 20 years. You want to feel financially safe during this retirement, so you expect a modest 4-percent return on your investments during that period. You're 50 years old today. How much will you need to have on Retirement Day and how much will you need to save to achieve that goal?

First, calculate your goal. A 20-year distribution annuity at 4 percent gives a factor of 13.59 (Figure 2.10), so you'll need that number times your $50,000 annual stipend upfront. Your goal—the number to hit by Retirement Day—is $679,500.

Now, to get to that number, how much will you have to save each year for the next 15 years? You're willing to invest a bit more aggressively and hopefully your business investment is generating a nice return, so let's say 8 percent is the right rate of return. From the accumulation annuity factor table (Figure 2.10), we get a factor of 27.15. Divide that into $679,500 to get your annual savings set-aside, which is $25,027.62.

Maybe you're not convinced yet that starting early is a good idea. Suppose you are 35, not 50—you have 30 years, not 15, to achieve your goal. The factor becomes 113.28, and the annual savings required drops to $5,998.41. Quite a difference—and yet another great illustration of the power of compounding.

STRATEGIC PERSONAL FINANCE

These tools and concepts help us move into strategies for managing your personal finances for greater

> ### ▼ BUT I SAVE MONTHLY …
>
> The accumulation and distribution annuity tables used in this chapter assume an annual savings contribution or payout at the end of each year. Monthly savings and withdrawals are probably a more realistic scenario and, of course, compounding would produce slightly higher returns if done monthly instead of annually. So the factors rise somewhat if a monthly assumption is used—and more for longer time periods. The 113.25 accumulation annuity factor used for 30 years at 8 percent is 124.90 when calculated monthly, that is, across 360 months..

power. This chapter offers a few building blocks; the following chapters do likewise. The ultimate goal is to figure out how to use these building blocks to set and achieve goals. Hopefully we've done some of that successfully in this chapter. But there are more building blocks and puzzle pieces yet to come. The next chapter brings taxes into the mix—not really a tool but a heavy influence on any and all personal finance decisions—especially where businesses are involved.

CHAPTER 3

It's (Mostly) About Taxes: A Short Tax Course for Entrepreneurs

SOME SAY THAT PERSONAL FINANCE IS REALLY pretty simple. It boils down to two things: *cash flow* and *protecting* that cash flow. Manage your cash flow so that you get the most and keep the most. Put proper protections in place for that unexpected emergency. Make sure your nest egg isn't gobbled up by an accident or a medical crisis. Keep on top of everything—make it, keep it, grow it.

Such a simple model serves well. Indeed, set a few goals, manage your cash, and keep the bogeyman away and you'll live happily ever after. However, managing that cash flow to consistently get the best outcome can be pretty tricky. There are countless factors that can get in the way of perfection. One of the biggest factors determining how much you *get* and how much you get to *keep* is—you guessed it—taxes.

Taxes influence just about every corner of personal financial life and, as we'll see, they become more complex—and more influential—if you have a business. To understand all taxes and tax rules is virtually impossible: any attempt to do so would be a huge drain on an entrepreneur's time and energy. But it's important to have a basic understanding of taxes and their effects on major (and many minor) business decisions. You need to know the basic principles and you need to know what you don't know so that you can work with professionals to figure out your best course. The tax consequences, both business and personal, of a poor business decision can be in many cases expensive and in some cases disastrous.

That's why we put this chapter toward the beginning of the *Ultimate Guide to Personal Finance for Entrepreneurs*. While most personal finance books address the topic of taxes—mainly income taxes—somewhere along the way, we feel that understanding taxes and the tax system is important enough to merit an early overview chapter and then greater details in later chapters. This chapter is about breadth, those that follow give the depth, and taxes will be a recurring and pervasive theme throughout this book. Some of details described in this chapter may be familiar if you are already in an entrepreneurial situation, but a basic review of underlying principles is nonetheless important.

THE IMPORTANCE OF TAXES

If in doubt about the importance of learning about taxes, realize that the self-employed typically face not only federal and state income taxes but also the full burden of *self-employment* taxes collected to provide for eventual Social Security and Medicare coverage. Add fees, licenses, local taxes, etc, for a typical entrepreneur in a typical income range, and the total can amount to almost 50 percent of business income diverted into government coffers. The tax hit on cash flow is huge. While we will touch on other taxes in this chapter, federal income and self-employment taxes will be the center of our discussion here and throughout. Federal estate and gift taxes will come later, in Chapter 11, as we move toward transitioning the business to others.

Entrepreneurs at the Helm

You might want to stop here, resigned to the idea that taxes are taxes and, like death and a few other things, you can't do much about them. That's the impression that many of us, once employees, take away. Sure, you can massage your finances a little by tinkering with retirement plan contributions, pretax set-asides for child care and medical expenses, and various and assorted line-item deductions for interest and taxes. You can influence capital gains by effectively timing investment sales to qualify for lower long-term capital gains tax rates. But there aren't too many knobs and levers to grab and twist; it's hard to change your tax situation very much.

But when you own a business, you take on far more control of your taxes. Your personal income is determined by your business income, and you have much more control over the timing of revenues and especially expenses. First of all, you're in control of those expenses. Aside from direct costs of producing your product or service, you can decide how much to spend for that computer or printer and when. You can decide what kind of vehicle you need and how to recover its cost on your books through depreciation. You can hire your kids or other family members to help and write off fair wages paid to them. You can decide what kind of tax-deferred retirement savings plan you want to use and, believe it, there are many more choices available to entrepreneurs. You can decide how traditional employee benefits like health coverage and life insurance will be paid for; owning a business opens up more options.

Tax Philosophy

Philosophy? In the nitty-gritty world of taxes and taxation? Yes: it's worth stepping back to look at the big picture. Why taxes?

This may seem obvious, but taxes are collected to support a greater good, to fund government and reallocate resources to areas of greater need or public preference. Good, but this isn't a social science book, right? The point is that taxes, tax policy, and the specific tax laws that arise from tax policy reflect the intent of Congress. The members of Congress make tax law—and the thousands of changes to tax law that all become part of the nearly 8,000-page *Tax Code* or more formally, *Internal Revenue Code*—to raise revenue in a way that, at least in their eyes, does the most social and economic good overall. How well they do that job is not the point here. Clearly the tax code, as it has evolved, is enormously complex and contains some pretty strange stuff. The point is to recognize that the tax code, enforced by the Internal Revenue Service (IRS), is a creation of Congress, a true "camel designed by a committee" that has been in session and has answered to a large number of interests for a long time.

The IRS Isn't "Out to Get You"

Congress creates and modifies the *Tax Code;* the job of the IRS is to enforce it. Put simply, the IRS employees do the best they can with what they have to work with.

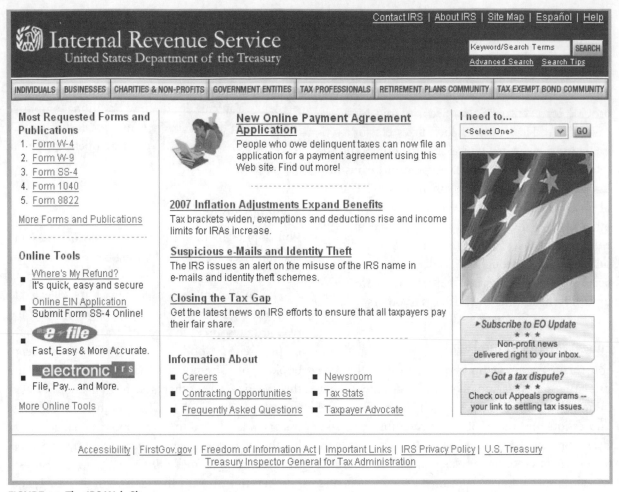

FIGURE 1.1. The IRS Web Site

If you take away nothing else from this discussion, it is important to know that the intent of the IRS is to enforce the law. The agents are not out to get what they can from you; they are out to get what you owe.

From your side of the table, that means that tax *avoidance*—that is, reducing your tax liability within the law—is perfectly OK. It is tax *evasion*—the willful and knowing dodge of tax law or fudging or obfuscating records—that bothers them. If you manage your business and your taxes within the law and have sound basis and rationale for what you do, backed up with good records, avoiding taxes to the fullest extent of the law will do nothing but save you money.

In fact, the IRS will even help you, with helpful Web tools and in person by phone. The IRS Web site (*www.irs.gov,* Figure 3.1) is remarkably well organized and easy to use and there are answers to most questions in plain English. If you have an issue you're not sure about, it's usually easy to find an answer in one of many IRS publications if not online.

The Importance of Tax Planning

Why are we making these last few points about tax avoidance, evasion, and the role of the IRS? Because you, as an entrepreneur, should learn to approach taxes with a positive, affirmative attitude. We've

▼ DON'T WAIT UNTIL TAX TIME

The IRS has taken a decidedly more helpful and consumer-friendly approach in the past 10 to 15 years. Gone are the days of mysterious behind-closed-doors dealings with no interaction until you were called on to face the IRS in a full audit. Today, the agency reaches out with toll-free numbers and ample, easily accessible publications and the Web site. But remember that the agents get busy during the late winter and spring months leading up to the April 15 filing deadline.

seen, over and over again, entrepreneurs and especially *new* entrepreneurs refuse to "take risks" with taxes; as a result, they leave a lot of potential net income (after taxes) on the table. We're not saying that entrepreneurs shouldn't have a healthy respect for the IRS and the tax code behind it. Instead, we're saying that the tax code is there to define your tax liability as was intended by Congress.

▼ LET THE ADVISEE BEWARE

The tax code is so complex that even the IRS doesn't always get it right. Through its telephone advisory services, it has occasionally made misleading recommendations, and unfortunately the IRS does not always stand behind its advice. The agency claims to having fielded 33 million taxpayer calls and to have "... achieved an all-time high for the accuracy of [its] answers." Still, despite what an IRS advisor may tell you, you are responsible for the accuracy and legality of your taxes. For tricky issues, it's a good idea to write down what the agents say—and to get a second opinion from a tax professional. especially for complex issues..

Now, once again many people would walk away from this statement with the idea that Congress is just "out to get what it can." Yes, taxes can take a lot: as much as 50 percent. But Congress knows about the 50 million-plus entrepreneurs in this country, how much business they do, how many people they employ, and how much political clout they have. Do they want to hit small businesses with excessive taxes, especially when they're just getting off the ground? Not really.

The reality is that the tax code is packed full of benefits, small and large, for small businesses. That 50-percent tax hit applies, of course, to *net* business income—not to total business revenue or sales. As we'll see, there are many ways to deduct costs and expenses against income or to set aside funds in ways to avoid current taxation. The tax rates *are* high, but there are lots of ways to manage and optimize *taxable income*. Congress has enacted changes—some recently—to make sure that entrepreneurs get at least the benefits that their corporate-world counterparts get, like writing off 100 percent of the cost of health insurance or employment taxes or even the cost of on-site health facilities. Congress wants its fair share, but that "fair share" might be less than you think!

Enter the idea of *tax planning*. Tax planning means managing income, expenses, benefits, retirement, and other set-asides in such a way as to minimize taxes. It is legal. It is moral and ethical. It is about paying your *true* fair share. It requires knowing the rules of the game and playing by those rules. It requires hard work to figure out the best thing to do in a situation; in many cases, the game is played to the fullest with the help of professionals.

Most entrepreneurs should have a tax advisor or a CPA somewhere within reach if not directly involved in personal and business tax planning. Why? It isn't just to prepare tax returns, although this too is important for the busy entrepreneur. It is to do appropriate and effective tax planning, to figure out how to make the rules work for you, as well as to keep up on the latest rules. You're most likely too busy for this. Doing your own detailed tax planning will inevitably distract you from your business purpose. Tax advice isn't necessarily cheap, but it can be quite cost-effective in the long run.

If you're just getting started in business, it's wise to engage a tax professional early on, so you can begin with a good tax strategy. Organizing the business, that is, choosing a legal and tax structure, is one of the first tasks facing new entrepreneurs. As we'll explore in the next chapter, this choice can have important tax implications, although taxes aren't the only consideration in choosing a particular organizational form.

This chapter and much of the rest of this book are intended to make you savvier about taxes, to the point where you can work with the IRS and tax professionals. You'll be able to recognize opportunities and ask the right questions at the right time. You'll be able to incorporate tax principles in strategic and day-to-day thinking. Knowing about taxes doesn't make you a tax expert (unless *that's* your entrepreneurial field), but it will make you a better small business professional.

KINDS OF TAXES

What taxes do you face as an entrepreneur? Most of the taxes listed here are assessed at the personal level, but some, especially for corporate organizational forms, are assessed against the business as well. Many of these taxes are assessed not only by the federal government but also by the state and even many local entities, like counties or municipalities.

INCOME TAXES

Income taxes, particularly federal income taxes, come to mind immediately when someone mentions "taxes." As a percentage, they most likely consume the largest piece of your potential take-home income. Income taxes also tend to be the most man-

ageable; that is, operational and financial decisions you make will influence the taxes you pay. Not surprisingly, the structure of income taxation isn't simple, starting with the fact that there are income taxes at multiple levels—federal, state, and local. There are *personal* income taxes and *corporate* income taxes.

Personal Income Taxes

In the purest form, income taxes are levied against *earned* income. "Earned income" is defined by the IRS as "salaries, wages, tips, professional fees, and other amounts received for pay for work you actually perform." It is, thus, income earned from employment by an employer or self-employment, i.e., from your own business activities or activities in which you share a business interest.

But income taxes cover a much wider swath of income types, including investment income, capital gains, or other activities in which you were involved less directly. If you take payments from a corporation you own as dividends, those will be taxed as investment income. If you sell the business or assets in the business, gains on that sale will be taxed as capital gains. As income taxes are central to many topics examined later in this chapter and this book, we won't go into detail here.

Figure 3.2 is a tax table for federal personal income taxes on ordinary income. For the sake of simplicity, we show only "married filing jointly" tax status here and use it in most examples throughout the book. Tables for Single, Head of Household, and Married Filing Separately are easily found on the IRS Web site or in most tax publications.

The table in Figure 3.2 covers *federal* income tax rates; for those interested, we have included a summary table for *state* income tax rates in the Appendix.

Corporate Income Taxes

These taxes are levied against the net income of corporate entities. For those entrepreneurs who own all

Married, Filing Jointly, 2006				
Taxable Income		Tax		
Over	But Not Over	Tax	+%	On Amount Over
$0	$15,100	$0	10%	$0
15,100	61,300	1,510	15%	15,100
61,300	123,700	8,440	25%	61,300
123,700	188,450	24,040	28%	123,700
188,450	336,550	42,170	33%	188,450
336,550		91,043	35%	336,550

Source: IRS

FIGURE 3.2. Federal Personal Income Tax Rates

or part of a corporation, these taxes introduce *double taxation:* profits are first taxed at a corporate level and then again at the personal level on returns or dividends paid to the corporate owners. Managing this double taxation is important for the corporate entrepreneur.

In addition to standard corporate income tax rates, there are also taxes that may be levied against profits retained in the corporation. While it might be wise for an entrepreneur to accumulate modest earnings in the corporation each year, in order to pay lower tax rates on dividends and avoid double taxation on the earnings retained, an *accumulated earnings tax* of 15 percent may apply to retained

2006		
Over	But Not Over	Tax Rate
$0	$50,000	15%
50,000	75,000	25%
75,000	100,000	34%
100,000	335,000	39%
335,000	10,000,000	34%
10,000,000	15,000,000	35%
15,000,000	18,333,333	38%
18,333,333		35%

Source: IRS

FIGURE 3.3. Corporate Income Tax Rates

amounts greater than $250,000. This tax is usually not a problem for smaller businesses.

EMPLOYMENT TAXES

Employment taxes are collected by the federal government for the primary purpose of funding income security entitlements, that is, Social Security old age, survivor, and disability benefits and Medicare health care benefits for seniors. These are called *payroll taxes* in the employer-employee world and *self-employment taxes* for self-employed individuals and partners.

Payroll Taxes

Payroll taxes include FICA (Federal Insurance Contributions Act), the standard tax for Social Security and Medicare, which is split 50-50 between employer and employee. The total FICA tax rate is 15.3 percent for wages up to $90,000 (2005) but above that figure drops to 2.9 percent, the Medicare portion. All employers, small or large, must file and pay their portion of FICA quarterly using IRS Form 941. Employees pay the other half as a deduction from their gross pay, reported on a year-end W-2 form.

Employers must also pay FUTA (Federal Unemployment Tax Act) taxes up to a maximum of $56 per year to fund unemployment compensation programs administered at the state level.

Entrepreneurs need to understand these taxes and the impact on their business bottom line: typically the 50 percent of payroll taxes will cost employers approximately an additional 7.15 percent of their payroll, which can be deducted from the *business* income as a business expense. The administration of payroll taxes is fairly complex and is usually done as

GETTING A TAXPAYER IDENTIFICATION NUMBER

When you go into business, there's so much to do and so many forms to fill out. A critical form, at least for businesses with employees, is the application for an Employer Identification Number (EIN). It's fairly easy and there is no charge, but not having one causes big trouble. The IRS has almost no tolerance for payroll tax delinquencies and will pursue vigorous actions and assess large penalties against businesses that fail to pay payroll taxes. Payroll taxes are important: if a corporation closes through bankruptcy, payroll taxes can be collected from the owners, despite normal corporate liability protection. If you have more than one business, you need an EIN for each.

EMPLOYEE OR SELF-EMPLOYED: WHO'S BETTER OFF?

Most folks sitting in corporate cubicles relish the idea of entrepreneurship and self-employment—do your own thing, be in charge, work when you need to. Self-employed folks envy corporate employees—half of self-employment taxes paid, benefits paid, steady income.

What if you own a corporation? Should you hire yourself as an employee? Why or why not? A corporation pays income tax, so the wage paid to you comes directly off the bottom line and reduces that tax. But then you pay payroll taxes on your wage, half through your corporation, half through your paycheck. Maybe you could avoid payroll taxes by taking your compensation as a dividend, instead. But then there would be no deduction against the profits of your business, so these profits would be subject to the corporate income tax—which just happens to be 15 percent for the first $50,000 in income. That amount would come off the top of your dividend. Either way, you'd pay 15 percent, possibly more if you take dividends, since corporate tax rates increase quickly above $50,000 in net income. Further, you wouldn't get credit toward accumulated Social Security wages, which could affect your Social Security payout someday. Bottom line: it's complicated. You should examine the alternatives carefully; in more cases than not, it makes sense to become an employee of your corporation. This is a great example of the complex intersection between business and personal finances.

part of a larger payroll process, often handled by bookkeepers or outsourced payroll specialists.

Self-Employment Taxes. Just because you work for yourself doesn't mean you're exempt from paying your fair share of Social Security and Medicare costs. In fact, your "fair share" is the same as collected in the employer-employee scenario—except that you are liable for the entire 15.3 percent. You pay self-employment tax, filed with your annual tax return on Form 1040-SE. You can deduct one half of your self-employment tax from your personal income. There is another adjustment: total business income is multiplied by .9235 (92.35 percent) so that you don't pay tax on the tax. (Don't worry—the math detail isn't important!)

Capital Gains Taxes

Capital gains taxes are assessed against income derived from the sale of assets. They are generally not considered earned income unless you are an invest-

ment professional. In personal finance, most capital gains occur on the sale of investments—stocks,

▼ WHAT IS A TAX BRACKET?

A bracket is simply the range in which a taxpayer falls, based on total taxable income. A taxpayer married filing jointly with an income of $50,000 thus would be in the 15-percent bracket (see Figure 3.2). The bracket determines the marginal rate, that is, the rate at which the next earned dollar would be taxed. It is very important to know this rate for making short-term business decisions, so you know how much you will give up in taxes for new dollars earned—or, just as important, how much you'll save in taxes on the next dollar spent.

▼ WHAT IS A "BASIS"?

Capital gains come into play when an asset is sold for more than its *basis*. The basis is the total acquisition cost, less normal wear and tear as represented by *depreciation,* plus the value of any improvements made to that asset. Basis must be tracked not only for business assets but also for personal assets. Keeping track of basis among a number of assets is a big job for any entrepreneur.

bonds, real estate, and so forth. When a business is involved, capital gains can occur when any fixed business asset—or the business itself—is sold for a gain.

Capital gains are taxed at ordinary personal income tax rates, as shown in Figure 3.2, for assets bought and sold within a year. For longer holding periods, Congress has capped the maximum tax rate at 5 percent for individuals in the 10-percent and 15-percent ordinary income tax brackets and 15 percent for individuals in higher brackets.

Capital gains taxes may impact what you decide to sell and when, although, especially for personal investments, most financial advisors suggest basing selling decisions on factors other than taxes. Assets sold for more than their *book value* or *cost basis* may be subject to capital gains taxes at higher rates against the "recaptured" depreciation. (Remember: you got a write-off for this depreciation.) Finally, it's worth noting that corporations pay capital gains taxes too, but at the standard corporate rates. There is no cap as instituted by Congress for individuals. This places a lot of important decisions for entrepreneurs on ownership of key business assets. Often it makes sense for an entrepreneur to buy a building and lease it to his or her corporate business—to pay

lower personal capital gains tax rates on eventual appreciation.

So far, we've spoken of capital *gains.* As you might have guessed, there is a flip side—capital *losses.* No one wants to lose money on anything, but it happens occasionally. When we lose money, the government subsidizes the loss. You can deduct capital losses against other capital gains, then against your other taxable income. But there's a limit to this break for personal capital losses. You may deduct only a maximum of $3,000 per year of net capital losses (gains less losses) against ordinary income. Additional losses may be carried forward or backward: you can use the excess of a loss above that maximum to get a refund from taxes you paid in the most recent three years or to reduce taxes due in the next 15 years. it may make more sense to own certain capital assets where there is risk of loss—in the business. (We should note now that capital losses do not include losses due to ordinary wear and tear—that's depreciation. In addition, we should note that capital gains are also taxed by state and local authorities. In most cases, they are taxed at ordinary income rates and no rate caps apply.)

Death and Gift Taxes

In addition to taxing income, Congress also considers the transfer of assets from one person to another, often a descendant or other family member, as an ideal taxing opportunity. Not only does it raise revenue but it also, as a social objective, levels the playing field by redistributing wealth from those who might be considered excessively wealthy.

Estate or "death" taxes apply to assets transferred at the time of death; *gift* taxes apply to assets transferred while the transferor is still alive. The good news is that there is a large exemption, known as a *unified credit*; only amounts over $2 million are subject to the tax as of 2006, rising to $3.5 million in 2009. In 2010, federal estate taxes are scheduled to go away completely, but then revert again – unless

▼
SUNRISE, SUNSET

We mentioned that estate taxes are scheduled to go away in 2010. Let's clarify: "in 2010" means that the disappearance is currently slated for *that year only*. In 2011, estate and gift taxes are currently set to revert back to the $1 million unified credit and higher tax rates of 2002. The subject is currently under debate and likely will be for a while. In our opinion, Congress will probably reinstate the estate tax, but with the higher unified credits and hopefully a much lower rate, e.g., 20–25 percent, as it probably should have been designed in the first place.

We should also note that for many years state inheritance taxes followed federal practice, effectively allowing heirs and recipients of their gifts to pay their state taxes and eliminate an equivalent amount from the federal taxes. However, most states are not following suit with the 2010 elimination or even changes in exemption amounts. The changing landscape of gift and estate taxation is causing considerable uncertainty in today's financial planning process for asset transfer. Business owners should follow the changes in this area.

Congress decides differently—to the schedule in place during 2002. The bad news is that the tax rates are extremely high—generally 48 percent, dropping to 45 percent by 2007. Needless to say, this is a huge chunk to take out of a family estate whose wealth is tied to the value of a business; it has forced sale of many business just to pay estate taxes.

Estate and gift taxes are *unified;* that is, every individual is entitled to one exemption amount through his or her lifetime, to be used against assets given away in life or in death. Otherwise, you could just give away your business and personal assets from your deathbed—and what a scene that would create! So gifts in excess of the unified credit amount are taxed at the same rate. Fortunately, there is an annual exclusion: every individual is now entitled to give $12,000 each year per recipient with no taxes. These amounts do not count toward the lifetime uniform credit. Gifts and amounts bequeathed to charities are also exempt.

Obviously such high and complex taxes have spawned quite a cottage industry of estate planning tools and attorneys to administer them. There are a number of tricks—quite legal and legitimate—that can be used to transfer large pools of family wealth, including family businesses. We explore this topic in Chapter 11.

Sales Taxes

All but five states at the time of this writing collect some form of sales tax on goods and many services sold in those states. Specific tax laws vary by jurisdiction and are beyond our scope in this book. For the most part, collecting sales taxes is an operational and financial issue for the business and doesn't involve personal finances. It's worth mentioning, however, that sales tax receipts should not be booked as income and the sales tax payment to the taxing authority should not be booked as an expense. It is also worth noting that failing to meet sales tax obligations at the state level is almost as bad as missing federal employment tax payments. Many businesses have been shut down over sales tax issues.

Property Taxes

Government authorities, primarily state and local, can enact taxes on real and personal property. Real property is mainly real estate, including land and building improvements upon that land. Personal property can include investments and certain valuables. Generally the taxing authority for these taxes is set by the state; the tax rates and administration are handled by county or other local governments. Real property taxes may allow certain exemptions and exclusions for owner occupancy and there may be special offsets for businesses located in certain favored economic development zones. Property tax considerations can affect where you locate your business; in some cases they may affect the decision of whether to conduct business from a home.

Property taxes levied against a business are normally deductible from business income. They are deductible on a personal income tax return to the extent that the individual *itemizes,* that is, has enough deductible expenses to exceed the threshold of the *standard deduction.*

Related to property taxes are special assessments by state and local governments to fund specific improvements like water and sewer systems, schools, and so forth. While normal property taxes can generally be deducted, such special assessments are more likely to be treated as an increase in the cost basis of the property. As such, they are expensed through normal depreciation methods, covered in Chapter 7.

Other Taxes

Does this list seem long so far? We're not done yet. The typical business faces many more taxes, mostly smaller taxes that can add up to a lot and increase the administrative work for the entrepreneur. Here are a few of the many that entrepreneurs might run across:

- *Excise taxes* are federal taxes paid on specific items like fuel, tires, and firearms. Entrepreneurs selling these items will become quite familiar with these taxes.
- *Inventory* taxes are still collected in a number of states and jurisdictions; however, there has been a trend toward repealing them. Why? Because of business disruptions involved in minimizing inventory at tax time—or shipping it across a border just to ship it back after the tax date!
- *Licenses and fees* are required of almost all businesses, ranging from a general business license to a license to practice or operate a certain kind of business.

TAX CONCEPTS

With the rather ominous and lengthy listing of taxes already in the books, the next step is to highlight a few overarching income tax concepts well worth the time to understand. These concepts—and the terms surrounding them—will come up over and over as you move through the tax maze in your business and personal finances. The objective, again, is not to turn you into an accountant, but to give you wisdom to influence business and personal financial decisions and to work with any tax professionals.

Adjusted Gross Income

For individual federal taxes, we have discussed earned income, investment income, and capital gains. The IRS uses the term *Adjusted Gross Income* (AGI) to sum up all forms of income for an individual and make certain adjustments to that income, which will be described below. The resulting AGI then becomes the basis for calculating the tax. But just as important, it also provides a figure used in income thresholds in the tax code, determining eligibility for certain deductions, credits, and so forth. AGI, in the eyes of Congress and the IRS, is the true yardstick of your income.

▼ FOLLOWING ALONG IN FORM

For some it's easier to grasp tax concepts by looking at the specific tax forms involved; for others it's too much detail and, frankly, overwhelming, especially for those who don't do their own taxes. Most people fill out their taxes using Form 1040, *U.S. Individual Income Tax Return*. Total Income is the first section, ending on line 22 (2005 return). Schedule C captures income generated from sole proprietorships; that income is reported on line 12. Schedule E is used to report income from partnerships and S corporations, for which the individual's share is calculated on Form 1065, *U.S. Return of Partnership Income*. That income is added to the personal AGI on line 17. These forms are separate from those used to report income expenses and taxes of the business.the warning against forming oral partnerships!).

Total Income

The IRS, in fact, identifies 15 types of income that can roll up into your *total income*, including wages and other earned income, pensions, Social Security, unemployment compensation, dividends, interest, and alimony. Of most interest to the business owner are business income derived from a sole proprietorship, "other income" received from partnerships and S corporations, and ordinary dividends, which may include payouts from C corporations. As a business owner, you are likely to have at least one of these forms of income on your personal return, in addition to any wage, salary, dividend, interest, or other income earned as an individual. All become part of your *total income*.

Deductions *for* AGI

After all the income amounts are totaled, the IRS provides for certain adjustments, or deductions, *prior* to determining AGI. These are called *deductions for AGI* and are all-important, since many deductions and credits depend on the AGI figure. AGI is used, for example, to determine eligibility for the $1000-per-child Child Tax Credit. Some or all of this credit is disallowed for any married-filing-jointly taxpayer with an AGI exceeding $110,000. Similarly, joint filing taxpayers with AGI in excess of $160,000 cannot contribute to a Roth IRA.

There are 13 kinds of deductions for AGI. Most important for entrepreneurs are those related to retirement plans: IRAs, SEP-IRAs, and other quali-fied plans (discussed in Chapter 10), health insur-ance, health savings accounts, and self-employment taxes. Any deduction "above the line" (that is, the AGI line) is better than one below the line, because of the importance of the AGI in determining eligi-bility for other items.

The net result is AGI (Form 1040, line 37). From there, more deductions and some credits are applied to arrive at the final tax liability.

Deductions *from* AGI

Once the AGI is calculated, another series of deduc-tions is applied to get to taxable income (Form 1040, line 43).

First along are exemptions—one for you and one for each qualifying family member. Each qualifying exemption turns into a $3,200 deduction. At AGI levels above $109,475, this deduction amount may be cut back slightly.

Next are itemized deductions. On Schedule A you list deductions for medical expenses, taxes paid, mortgage and certain other kinds of interest, chari-table donations, and certain other miscellaneous expenses. The detail is beyond our scope here. Most, but not all, individuals owning a home will qualify for itemized deductions through mortgage interest and property taxes. Entrepreneurs, especially those with home offices or home-based businesses, need to decide whether to deduct certain mortgage interest or taxes here or on the business statements; it usually makes more sense to deduct against the business. Why? To reduce self-employment taxes.

The deduction taken against AGI is the total of itemized deductions or the standard deduction, whichever is larger. For a married-filing-jointly couple, the standard deduction is $10,000 (2005).

Tax and Tax Credits

Tax tables, using standard tax rates like those defined in Figure 3.2, are used to compute personal tax liability (Form 1040, line 44). That isn't the bottom line, however, as any of a series of *tax credits* may reduce that figure.

Congress uses tax credits the way auto manufacturers use rebates—to deliver substantial incentives for certain activities or behaviors, sometimes for a limited time period. Credits are usually more important than deductions for many taxpayers. That's because a deduction saves taxes only to the extent of the tax rate: a $2,000 deduction means only $200 in savings for people in the 10-percent bracket. A $2,000 credit, on the other hand, reduces tax liability "one for one": it's worth the full $2,000.

There are a number of tax credits; it isn't worth going into all of them here. Child tax credits and credits for child and dependent care are two of the more commonly used credits. Entrepreneurs need to be familiar with a series of business-related credits explained in Chapter 7 and may also find new credits for driving hybrid vehicles especially appealing.

WHAT ABOUT BUSINESS INCOME AND DEDUCTIONS?

As a reminder, this section is centered on personal income taxes—personal income, personal deductions, and personal taxes, although we touch on personal tax items of particular interest to entrepreneurs. Business income and expenses drive personal taxes (and business taxes, in the case of a C corporation). We've treated the net business income

as a *result* on personal tax forms, but obviously that result is driven by a long series of expense deductions and credits unique to the business. Chapters 6 and 7 discuss acquiring business assets and operating the business to deliver the most favorable tax and financial result to its entrepreneurial owners. Many of these deductions and credits are listed and explained there.

For example, there are a number of business tax *credits* under the heading of "general business credits" (GBCs). Examples include credits for providing child care facilities and for investing in certain economically disadvantaged places or employees. These credits are taken against individual taxes and appear on the individual Form 1040, rather inauspiciously as "other credits." Entrepreneurs should become acquainted with these credits.

"SPECIAL" FEATURES

As if this subject were not already complicated enough, there are two more tax features with which any entrepreneur should become familiar: Net Operating Losses (NOLs) and the nefarious Alternative Minimum Tax (AMT). NOLs are generally a good thing for entrepreneurs, while the AMT can cause bad things to happen for particularly successful entrepreneurs.

Net Operating Losses (NOLs)

Congress and the IRS recognize that not all business ventures are profitable and, moreover, not all business ventures are profitable *all the time*. The result is a concept known as a *net operating loss,* generally only available to business owners. NOL amounts from a given year can be written off against income derived from other sources and/or carried forward or backward to offset income generated in other years.

NOLs can be written off as other income for any pass-through taxation structure—sole proprietorships, partnerships, S corporations, and many limited liability companies (LLCs). We're getting ahead of ourselves here; these structures are covered in detail in the next chapter. The point here is to be aware of NOLs and to think about them strategically.

An example of such strategic thought might be to start a business as a sole proprietorship or a partnership and then migrate to a larger C corporate structure. Why? To write off start-up costs and initial losses against current income from a job or other sources or even income generated by a separate business.

The details of NOL write-offs and, in particular, carry-forwards and carry-backs, are probably best left to your tax professional. It's important, nonetheless, to grasp the concept.

▼ CASH AND CARRY (FORWARD AND BACK)

"Carry-forwards" and "carry-backs" sound like the IRS version of a time machine—and indeed that's what they are. NOL rules state that losses must first be used to offset the current year's income (unless you're running a farm). Beyond the current year's income, business owners may elect to *carry forward* losses to future years to smooth out anticipated rises in income and possibly to stay in lower tax brackets. Amounts carried forward are usually declared in writing or by using an IRS form, Form 3621, *Net Operating Loss Computation–Individuals, Corporations, and Estates and Trusts*. NOL carry-forwards are allowed for as much as 20 years into the future. Similarly, a business owner coming off a very good year into a bad one can choose to *carry back* the loss by refiling for the previous year. Such losses can be carried back two years. Carry-backs can be more expensive, as more work is required on the part of your tax professional, but in many cases, they still make sense.

Alternative Minimum Tax (AMT)

Many years ago, Congress decided to do something about the growing tendency for wealthy taxpayers to avoid taxes through excessive write-offs and other tax loopholes. So they created the *alternative minimum tax* as a supplemental tax to recover some of the taxes lost through these write-offs.

The alternative minimum tax process sits as an adjustment on top of the regular personal tax process described above. Taxpayers first calculate their personal income tax normally—through AGI, deductions from AGI, and normal tax rates. Then they take an AMT test. In this test, certain deductions normally taken as an individual taxpayer, like state and local taxes, certain kinds of mortgage interest, and personal exemptions are totaled and compared with a ceiling, $58,000 in 2005 for married-filing-jointly. If those deductions exceed this limit, they can trigger the AMT. Similarly, if other *tax preference* items are involved, like certain forms of stock options, tax credits, passive income, and a host of others, the AMT can be triggered.

When the AMT comes into play, it brings different and usually higher tax rates—26 percent up to AGI of $175,000 and 28 percent beyond that figure (married filing jointly)—without the normal stairstepping throughout the brackets. These adjustments can bring an AMT, which is added to the tax calculated previously, as a tax adjustment.

Does this sound complex? Actually, the description above is really a considerable oversimplification.

Entrepreneurs need to be aware of the AMT, especially if they are in higher income brackets or have a large amount in common personal deductions. Further, certain business accounting practices can enter into the AMT. Depreciation and the difference between normal and accelerated depreciation on some kinds of property can enter the calculation. Oddly, expenses for circulation of media, such as a magazine or newspaper, which can be written off as incurred for "normal" taxes, must be amortized over three years for AMT purposes. Who thought of that one?

It goes without saying that those who might be subject to the AMT are wise to get professional advice. A tax professional should give a straightforward take on when and how the AMT might affect you. The AMT has gotten a lot of media coverage lately. One reason is that, while incomes have risen due to inflation over the years, and normal tax rates and brackets have risen commensurately, the AMT amounts have stayed largely unchanged. The result is that many, many more taxpayers are being snagged by the AMT; indeed, it is no longer an adjustment for only the wealthy but also for a growing segment of the middle class. For example, families with lots of children can be caught because of the personal exemptions—hardly what Congress intended. Bottom line: if you own a successful business, beware!

Note also that there is a corporate AMT with a similar list of preference items to be tested. The corporate AMT comes into play only for C corporations and is beyond our scope here, but if you own a corporation, you should be aware of it.

TAX PRACTICES

From the conceptual we move to a handful of more tactical tax items that come into play when operating a business. These items include the choice of accounting methods, record-keeping requirements, and filing estimated taxes during the tax year.

Accounting Methods

Again, we're not trying to turn you into an accountant, and the choice of accounting methods will have little effect on your taxes *in the long term*. But entrepreneurs should be familiar with the choices and prepared to operate their business according to the method chosen. There may be short-term consequences from that method. Basically the choices are cash, accrual, and a hybrid of the two.

Cash method accounting means that all income and expenses are recorded *as paid*. If you write a book for a publisher, you record no income when you sign the contract or during the months that you are writing the book. You record the income when you receive the check from the publisher. Similarly, if you buy business insurance, you record the expense in the month when you paid it, even if the coverage applies through the year.

Accrual method accounting means that you record income and expenses as you incur them, regardless of when you pay them. A deposit received for a service to be performed won't be recorded until it is actually performed. Materials bought to complete the service may be recorded as an expense when they are received or when they are used—not when you pay for them. Businesses that buy and sell goods and thus carry *inventory* are generally required to use an accrual system. Why? Because if you bought a truckload of bicycles in December to sell over the next six months, you would record a big expense in that month and that tax year (assuming you use a January–December tax year) and then produce a lot of revenue without corresponding expense in the following year. The IRS doesn't like that; that approach would effectively defer taxes for one year. (It also may not be good for you either, as it might drive you into a higher bracket in the second tax year.)

The *hybrid method* is available to certain businesses: inventory is accounted for using the accrual method, while income and expenses are accounted for using the cash method. This is only for small businesses; if the business has gross revenue of more than $5 million, the IRS must grant permission.

Not surprisingly, accrual accounting is more complicated, but in many cases it's a more accurate way to report business activity. The two methods will allow different expenses to be recognized more quickly, producing some tax advantages. Doing it right will often require the help of a tax professional and/or good bookkeeping software. IRS Publication 538, *Accounting Periods and Methods,* is a good resource.

▼ **SMALL IS GOOD**

Cash method accounting is usually simpler and often allows faster recognition of expenses and slower recognition of revenues. The IRS generally allows businesses in one of two situations to use the cash method:

1. when they are *unincorporated* (even with inventory) and have gross annual receipts of less than $1 million

2. when they are *incorporated* with inventory and have receipts of less than $5 million.

Record-Keeping

It's essential to keep good records—both in the business and for personal finances—not only for tax preparation but as a general practice. Remember the three "habits" of good personal finance: awareness, control, and commitment. Good records are a first step to awareness.

The IRS is concerned with good business and personal finance practice, but it is even more concerned about having good records to support tax outcomes. Business owners must keep records for their business and for their personal taxation. Often these records are kept separately, for business results are flowed into personal taxes, as described earlier.

Business records should be kept for income, expenses, and assets.

Generally, income and expense records are kept as receipts, invoices, or copies of invoices. Where it's not clear and especially for expenses, the purpose or reason for the expense should be noted. Dates are also important.

Asset records must be kept in detail, to track basis and to manage depreciation. The asset should be described, with purchase date and amount. Any major modification, outside of routine maintenance of the asset, should be recorded, as well as the sales price and date if the business disposes of the asset.

How long should you keep records? You'll read and hear different answers to this question. Normally, the IRS has *three years* to audit you or your business from the date of filing. This *statute of limitations* can increase to *six years* if there is evidence that you've misreported taxes in the past and can be indefinite in cases of outright fraud. This timing applies to normal income and expense records. Asset records obviously should be kept longer to the extent that assets have a useful life longer than three years. One guideline for assets is that records should be kept for *six years after* you dispose of the asset. Also it should be noted that some *states* have longer statutes of limitations.

Bottom line: it is good practice to keep records as long as practical, both for your business and for your

▼ **PUTTING YOUR PC TO WORK**

How you actually keep and computerize your business and personal records is a matter of the size of your business, convenience, and personal preference. QuickBooks and QuickBooks Pro (Intuit, *quickbooks.intuit.com*) are the gold-standard programs for managing business transactions and keeping records for most small businesses. Smaller, simpler businesses or homebased businesses can record income and expense transactions in an Excel spreadsheet. For personal income taxes, you can use TurboTax or any of many other programs. Your tax professional probably has some advice in this area and may want you to use specific methods or software tools to conveniently feed into his or her tax and record management programs.

personal taxes. It's better to have something and not need it than to need something and not have it.

Estimated Taxes

Estimated taxes are installment tax payments usually due quarterly throughout a tax year. The IRS wants taxpayers who own businesses to pay in installments to speed the flow of cash into the Treasury and to avoid problems later on with businesses that do not have sufficient funds available to meet their tax obligations.

Estimated taxes are just that—estimates. The business owner cannot know his or her tax liability until the business year is complete. The point is to estimate what taxes will be (the previous year's taxes are a good basis for many businesses) and then pay that amount in four equal chunks using Form 1040-ES. Estimated taxes cover both personal income taxes (including but not limited to those of the business) and self-employment taxes.

The IRS can impose penalties and interest for underpayment of estimated taxes, particularly if the total paid in comes to less than 90 percent of the ultimate tax liability. Generally if your estimates fall short only once in a series of years, it isn't a problem, especially if your income is less than $150,000. Estimated tax payments aren't required if you expect to owe less than $1,000 in total federal taxes or if you have substantial withholdings from another source, like a job. Finally, most states require estimated payments too; find out about this probability.

THE TAX SYSTEM

To deal with something as complicated as the tax code and the IRS system, it helps to understand a little more about it.

The Tax Code—and Other Stuff

Income tax law is formulated in what is known as the Internal Revenue Code, "The Tax Code," or simply "The Code." It is but a small part of the United States Code, but not that small—some 7,500 pages and growing. And as if that weren't enough, there is a whole system of written *regulations, rulings,* and *procedures* to go with the code. These supplemental documents don't so much *update* the code as *interpret* it. They tell both us and the IRS how to apply the code in situations where it may not have been clear.

Regulations, more formally known as Treasury Regulations, less formally as just the "Regs," interpret large portions of the code, often with examples. The body of regulations today takes six volumes; it is also available on the IRS Web site. *IRS Revenue Rulings* are announcements, some long and some short, of how the IRS would interpret a particular set of facts. (To interpret a specific tax case, a *Letter Ruling* is issued, generally for a specific individual.) Finally *IRS Revenue Procedures* tell you and, more often, your tax preparer how to do certain things. They do not provide an interpretation of the code.

> ## ▼ TAX LAW: A GROWING INDUSTRY
>
> As measured by pages in the Commerce Clearing House (CCH) *Federal Tax Reporter*, which records the latest code changes, new tax regulations, rulings, and procedures, the tax law is growing by leaps and bounds. Originally, when the federal income tax was implemented, the CCH *Reporter* was 400 pages. By 1939 it had grown to 504 pages. In the 1950s it started to expand more rapidly, reaching 14,000 pages by 1954. Things were fairly quiet for the next 15 years: by 1969 there were "only" 16,500 pages. Then began the "boom years": 40,500 pages by 1995, 60,044 pages by 2004, and 66,498 pages by early 2006. Oh, if one could have only invested in such growth! Well, there are some happy bookshelf makers out there, anyway.

Do you need to follow all of this? Clearly not. This is what tax professionals do. Also, if there's a major change in business or personal tax practice with a wide effect, you'll probably find out about it from another source.

What You Need to Know About Audits

The mention of the word "audit" will make neck hair stand on end for most taxpayers and particularly for entrepreneurs. The IRS uses a number of techniques to decide which returns to audit—and small business owners often end up in its crosshairs.

There are three principal forms of audit—letter audits, office audits, and field audits.

Most common is the letter audit. A computer-generated letter arrives querying certain items on a tax return. You must return an explanation, supported by documentation, for what you did and why or pay the adjusted tax due, usually within a month.

Office audits are the next most common, especially for smaller businesses. The IRS asks you to come into a local field office, with your tax records, usually just for the most recent year.

Field audits are the really scary ones. An IRS representative visits you on site and goes through everything. Field and office audits are likely to be more comprehensive, examining the entire return, not just certain items.

Much has been written on how to prepare for an audit and what to do during the audit; you can check out those specialized guides, should the need arise. If you use a tax professional, he or she should handle most of your audit issues and responses.

The IRS and IRS Publications

The IRS Web site (*www.irs.gov*) and toll-free help lines—(800) 829-1040 for individuals and (800) 829-4933 for businesses—offer considerable tax information and advice and, as mentioned earlier, are fairly easy to use. The IRS has hundreds of pub-

THEY PICKED ME—WHY?

The exact algorithms and triggers used by the IRS to determine who gets audited and who doesn't are kept secret, of course. As a business owner, in general, your chances are higher. If you're a sole proprietor, your chances are highest. Mathematical algorithms look at the size and pattern of deductions in comparison with averages for similar taxpayers, among many factors. You get a differential income factor, a DIF score, which works much like a credit score; if that score is above a certain threshold, beware. If you write off 50 percent of your gross revenue as food, travel, and entertainment expenses, you're exposing yourself, especially if most owners of businesses of your kind write off only 10 percent. Businesses that deal in a lot of cash, like restaurants or transportation services, may also be more likely to be audited.

lications available on a multitude of topics; those of most interest to businesses are listed on the IRS Small Business page, *www.irs.gov/businesses/small*. A list appears in Appendix C.

GETTING PROFESSIONAL HELP

We've hinted all along that you might be best off to get professional advice, particularly if your business is at all complex. Any business that carries inventory, has employees, or is owned by more than one person probably qualifies as "complex." Not only will it save you time and enable you to focus on the business, not the taxes, but you're likely to discover a trick or two that will save money—more than you spend on the advisor. It may be the case, after a while and once the business is up and running, that the tax model is well developed, that each year's taxes look like the previous year's taxes, and so forth. At that point you might consider taking over the job yourself.

There are different kinds of tax advisors. And, predictably, their services become more expensive as you move up the food chain.

The most basic is the *tax return preparer*, whom you might find at an H&R Block or a similar company. Preparers can prepare your personal returns, but most won't know how to handle complex businesses and they won't be able to offer much advice. Most individuals with a business should steer clear.

An *enrolled agent* (EA) is licensed by the IRS; in fact, many EAs have worked for the IRS previously. Some will do your bookkeeping *and* your taxes—a nice blend.

Next up the food chain is the certified public accountant (CPA). Those with complex businesses or tax issues should find a local CPA, especially one specializing in small business.

Finally, for really tricky business or personal tax issues, including estate planning, and where legal representation for tax problems is required, a *tax attorney* is the best choice. And, of course, his or her services will be most expensive.

Finding a tax advisor is like finding any other professional help. Referrals are a good source, as may be the local Better Business Bureau. It may be helpful to find a tax advisor specializing in small business and especially with clients in your industry. For example, if you own a construction company, find an accountant or advisor with a lot of construction company owners as clients. Such specialists might be found through your local trade association or a publication in your field of work.

You'll typically pay a per-hour charge for advice and additional charges for preparing tax returns. Of course, the benefits should be weighed against the costs, but remember that your time is valuable and your best judgment is usually needed for other things—especially when the business is starting out. It's all too common, as we said at the outset of this book, to forget about personal financial matters while swirling around in your business activities.

PART II

Building Your Business

CHAPTER 4

Organizing Your Business

YOU SEE THE DISCUSSION AGAIN AND AGAIN in most small-business books, in magazines, and on Web sites. How should you organize your business? It seems like just when you think you understand the choices someone writes another article extolling yet a few more advantages for setting up an S corporation or a limited liability company (LLC).

What's the best business structure for your business and personal financial situation? What structure does the most for you given the effort invested? What structure pays the most, protects the most, is most tax-efficient, and makes it easiest to manage, invest, develop, and eventually sell your business?

The choice is important. Each structure has its advantages and disadvantages—some clear, some quite subtle. Many of the plusses and minuses depend on your type of business; many depend on your personal financial needs. This chapter takes a look at business organization choices from your personal financial perspective as entrepreneur/owner.

HOW BUSINESS ORGANIZATION AFFECTS PERSONAL FINANCES

On the surface it may appear that the choice of business structure would have more impact on the business than on personal finances. The reality is quite the opposite. Business structure is about ownership, and ownership determines how your personal finances—and those of any investors or partners—are connected to the business. The connection is narrow and specific in the context of cash flow and taxation. How you organize determines how income, expenses, start-up costs, gains, and losses flow through to your personal finances and how those flows are taxed. But the connection between your business and personal finances, through your choice of structure, is broad and far-reaching in terms of liability protection, attracting and retaining business capital, administration and paperwork, and the effort required to make it work.

As we'll see, business and especially personal taxation are a big factor in making the choice. Income tax laws have, over the years, created quite a maze of rules, forms, and processes to distribute business income and expenses into your personal finances and the personal finances of other owners. These processes also involve start-up costs and gains from eventual sales of assets. Each organizational form has its own set of rules and accounting and tax practices. To decide which business form makes sense, entrepreneurs need to have at least some working knowledge of the income distribution and tax consequences of each organizational form. Approaching business without that knowledge can result in unintended business and tax consequences. The specific details and forms can be left to the tax professionals. The pros will deliver good advice on which form to choose and when it's best to migrate to another form, at least for tax reasons. But you, as entrepreneur and owner, need working knowledge of the consequences of your organizational decisions, now and in the future.

As we said earlier, cash flow and taxes aren't everything. A host of other factors enter the picture. Different organizational forms entail different amounts of formality, paperwork, and administration. Different forms offer different liability protection, a very important consideration for some types of businesses. Different forms can make it easier or more difficult to raise capital for the business and also affect your ability to sell it. We'll examine the factors, compare the forms, and offer a few pointers on how to migrate from one form to another as the business evolves.

FIVE MAIN CHOICES (AND A FEW OTHERS)

We'll examine the characteristics, advantages, and disadvantages of five organizational forms in some detail. So that you can begin to connect with what you've already read and heard about, here's a summary of the primary organizational forms available to individual entrepreneurs. These are high-level definitions:

- **Sole proprietorship.** In this structure, you alone own the business and it is an extension of your personal finances. There is no separate entity; revenues, costs, and profits flow directly into your personal finances.
- **Partnership.** This structure is like a sole proprietorship, except that there is more than one owner. Again, there is no separate legal entity. Revenues, costs, and profits flow into each partner's personal finances in proportion with his or her investment in the business.
- **C Corporation.** A corporation is a separate legal entity recognized under U.S. and state law. In this structure, the business and its revenues, costs, and profits as well as its legal obligations and liabilities—are separate from its owners. Owners are shareholders. The C corporation (so named because it is covered under Subchapter C of the United States Code) conducts business as a separate entity and is also *taxed* as a separate entity. The implications of this statement are tricky but important and will be covered below. The C corporate form is used by most major U.S. corporations and all corporations that trade stock publicly on stock exchanges. There are no size requirements for a C corporation. You can organize your small business as a "C corp" with you as a single owner if it makes sense, but the administrative burdens and costs of setup and annual filing are high.
- **S Corporation.** Years ago lawmakers decided that for many businesses it made sense to create a separate legal entity that would provide the liability protection and other benefits of legal separation but would not be taxed separately. This is a pass-through entity: its owners/shareholders share directly in its net profits. For S corps, there is no income tax at the corporate level, but corporate tax returns must be filed. Though the S corp is not quite as complex as the C corp, setup and administration are generally more involved than for non-corporate forms.
- **Limited Liability Company (LLC).** The LLC, defined under state statutes rather than federal, affords much of the liability protection enjoyed by traditional C or S corporate forms. The LLC provides this protection but is simpler to set up and operate. In many ways it operates like a partnership, but with protec-

YOU GUESSED IT—THERE *ARE* OTHERS

Doubtless, if you've been reading up on this topic, you know there are more than five organizational forms. It couldn't possibly be *that* simple, right? Right.

Licensed high-level professionals such as doctors, dentists, attorneys, and engineers find many economies in working together as partners but also need a degree of liability protection from the potential misdeeds, malpractice, and liabilities of other partners. Personal service corporations (PSCs) and limited liability partnerships (LLPs) have evolved to meet this need. Effectively they operate like partnerships with a veil of liability protection from other partners. LLPs offer little liability protection for the partnership as a whole but provide partners protection from each other. PSCs offer similar liability protection and certain other advantages of a corporate form but at a higher administrative cost. The tax rules differ slightly from their traditional corporate equivalents. With these forms, all partners must generally be licensed to practice in the same profession. We won't examine these forms in detail; they aren't used by traditional entrepreneurial product and service businesses. There are also a number of not-for-profit organizational forms; but again, these are not relevant to our discussion.

tion and a higher degree of flexibility. As a best-features compromise, the LLC has become very popular with today's small business owners.

FACTORS IN CHOOSING A STRUCTURE

Many factors come into play as decision criteria for choosing an organizational structure. Some are straightforward and simple in terms of effects on your business and personal finances; others are more subtle. There is no such thing as the "perfect" form for your business—oh, if only it were so simple! Your choice will be a balancing act among the various factors, advantages, and disadvantages. To a large degree, it will reflect what you are most comfortable with as well as the size and type of your business and your plans for the future.

It should be pointed out that most choices are not irrevocable. It is possible to migrate from one form to another as needs change; we will touch on that topic at the end of this chapter.

The following are some of the major characteristics and criteria we will examine for each organizational structure.

CASH FLOW AND TAXATION

Cash flow and especially tax considerations are the "600-pound gorilla" for many small businesses. Each organizational structure we will cover is taxed somewhat differently. The structure of your business can have significant personal tax consequences, depending on the nature of your business and your stage in the business life cycle.

Congress has tried over the years to mitigate some of these differences, so businesses don't choose the wrong form just for tax reasons. Congress also wanted to avoid creating loopholes. For that reason, for example, you'll discover that whether you pay self-employment taxes on all of your business income or pay half out of your corporation and half personally as FICA, you'll pay the same amount. You'll also find that if you decide to not pay yourself at all, as a corporation, you'll still pay a similar rate—15 percent—as a corporate income tax. Yes, they have you one way or the other. Trying to avoid income or self-employment taxes altogether is a fool's errand, just as it's a myth that you can avoid estate taxes altogether by setting up trusts. But there are, as we'll see, some advantages to different structures depending on your situation.

Here are a few with respect to taxation.

Tax Structure and Flexibility

The primary choice is between *flow-through* entities and a *separately taxed* entity—a corporation. In a flow-through entity, you are taxed on the net income of the business as if it occurred in your personal financial space; the business finances and your individual finances are treated as one for tax purposes. In that case you have less control over your taxes, for you cannot keep earned income out of your personal statements once it gets through the gauntlet of business expenses related to producing that income. While those business expenses do give you some levers to pull (which we'll examine more closely in Chapter 7), you'll end up paying taxes on what your business produces as accounting income, whether or not a dime of it finds its way into your personal checking account.

More flexible is the corporate form, specifically the C corporation, in which the business exists as a wholly separate legal entity. As such, it is taxed as a separate entity for all the income it generates. That income can be kept within the corporation *as retained earnings;* as such, none of it flows into your personal finances. The happy result: you pay no personal income taxes on this income.

Double Taxation

But alas, we may not stay happy for long. When you finally pass some of that business income into your personal checking account, in the form of dividends (or wage compensation, if you work for the corporation you own), that income is taxable—for the second time. This is known as *double taxation.* If it's not managed well, the C corporation can clearly

cost you more in taxes than would a flow-through business form. But if managed correctly, you can save in taxes and reinvest funds in the business that have been subjected to relatively lower tax rates.

> ### ▼ DOUBLE JEOPARDY
>
> While C corporations are subject to double taxation by the federal government, S corporations as flow-through entities are exempt, at least at the federal level. But at the state level—watch out! There are still some states that tax S corporation profits at the corporate level. Your tax professional will know.

Income Splitting

With corporate forms, you can decide how to pay yourself and others in the business. You can pay yourself and your investors in the form of wage compensation, dividends, stock, stock options, or some combination of the above. Sharp-penciled entrepreneurs and their tax professionals navigate these choices with business and personal needs in mind; they can reduce the total taxes and the timing of those taxes at least to a degree. This is known as *income splitting;* we'll see more about how that works in Chapter 7.

Treatment of Losses

We've talked so far mainly about income—positive income—and the taxation of that income. What about *negative* income—losses? We talked about the relatively inflexible taxation of income with flow-through entities. While that's a negative for income, it can have a positive flip side in the case of losses. When you're in the investment phase, and even beyond, if your business produces a net operating loss (NOL), you can write off that amount against future income or current income generated from another source (like a job). While a flow-through entity is not flexible in the sense that you can choose how much of this loss to take, it is nice to think that, in the initial stages of a business, you can organize in such a way as to capitalize on these losses, then evolve to another form later on.

Capital Gains Treatment

So far we've covered *earned* income—profits and earnings from business activity. But many businesses with fixed or investment assets also produce capital gains over time, as many have done in recent years from real estate holdings, for example. We know that personal long-term capital gains—for assets held for more than one year—are taxed at preferential rates for individuals. As such, they are taxed preferentially for flow-through entities, for the individual is the

entity. On the other hand, the corporate form does not generally recognize separate tax rates. So businesses with considerable capital gains may be set up as C corporations for other reasons but then, using one popular strategy, hold real estate assets personally or in some other entity, lease them out to he business, and pay taxes on them personally.

▼ TAKEAWAYS

From a taxation perspective, a C corporation is taxed as a separate entity. Other forms—sole proprietorship, partnership, S corporation, and LLC—are taxed as flow-through entities. C corporations thus have more taxation flexibility but they also incur the burden of double taxation. Different forms may make more sense in different stages of the business life cycle.

▼ ORGANIZATION CHOICE–OR TAX STRATEGY?

What this capital gains taxation example illustrates is not so much a reason for choosing a business organization as it is a strategy formulated on the framework of the business structure you've chosen. Entrepreneurs should weigh all the factors in choosing an organizational structure, not just taxes. Then they should use strategies to make the best of the structure they choose. Where time and clarity permit, it makes sense to think through future business events and needs and then formulate a tax strategy around them. Will you want or need to buy a building someday? Think through the tax implications and your organizational structure to figure out the best way to do it. It may include changing your organizational structure at some point, but most likely not. That's what tax planning is really all about.

LIABILITY PROTECTION

We'll return to tax considerations in a moment, but now it's time to introduce a critically important consideration—at least for most businesses: *liability protection*. Stated simply, corporate forms—and we'll include here C corporations, S corporations, and LLCs—protect their owners against most forms of liability and risk of the corporation. Stated differently, the corporation, as a wholly separate legal entity, bears all risk and responsibility for the losses, debts, and liabilities it creates. These liabilities stay within the corporation; they cannot pass through to its owners. This is known as the "corporate veil" through which creditors and their lawyers cannot penetrate.

As with almost everything, there are some exceptions. It's well established that the corporate veil can be pierced to collect unpaid payroll taxes. Also, if the owners have committed themselves personally to support loans made to the business (as many lenders require), the lenders can collect unpaid obligations from the owners. But for most issues arising in the ordinary course of business, the owners are protected.

This is a major consideration, especially for businesses operating in hazardous professions and industries. For a trucking company, a demolition firm, or even a medical practice, where there is significant risk of physical injury, tort damage, malpractice, or so-called "errors and omissions" (the "malpractice" of the non-medical professional world), a business owner must consider a corporate form. Otherwise, if one of your employees runs over someone with a bulldozer, you could lose your entire personal wealth. It should be noted that some states have personal homestead laws that may protect business owners from losing their personal residences and that federal government rules protect most qualified retirement savings. However, the basic principle is that if your non-corporate business causes injury or damage to any person or entity, even unintentionally, you could be held fully liable.

Unfortunately, in our litigious society, the risks posed by business activities for business owners have grown by leaps and bounds. If you have a homebased business and a delivery person slips and falls on your doorstep delivering something to your business, you and your business together might be held liable. For this reason, the notion of liability protection must be considered by every business, though in many cases it may make more sense to mitigate the risk with insurance than by choosing an overly complex business structure.

It's Not *Just* Accidents

Mention the word "liability" and images of injury, death, defamation of character, and so forth immediately leap to mind. But the umbrella of corporate liability protection extends further—and this may be more important for most businesses—to cover financial losses and insolvency. If your business runs

into tough times, borrows too much, or otherwise overextends, creditors can come to the business to collect. Then they can come straight to you or your business partners to collect—unless you're protected by a corporate form. If you and your business are one, you're just as liable for business debts as your company is. If you're running a financially risky business, like an oil drilling venture, you should think about incorporating.

TAKEAWAYS

Corporate ownership forms—C corporation, S corporation, and LLC—provide significant (but not total) liability protection for owners. Other forms do not: the business and its owners are one for liabilities and debts.

BENEFITS

Work as a 9-to-5 employee of a typical corporation and you enjoy an assortment of fringe benefits, like health insurance, life insurance coverage, pre-tax dependent care accounts, retirement plans, stock options, company cars—you name it. But in most cases, you don't *pay* for those benefits. The corporation pays for most of these benefits for you (though you may extend some of them, such as by buying supplemental life insurance at very low rates). Is the corporation being generous? Yes. But the corporation is able to deduct most such expenses from its taxes, saving typically 50 percent of the cost. And do you pay taxes on the benefits? With the exception of the company car, generally not, so long as they fall within federal government guidelines.

Now we change the scenario. You own a business. What about those fringe benefits now? Can you still have them? Mostly, yes. But who pays and who gets to deduct what?

The general answer is that you can pay for most benefits out of your business or you can pay for them personally with income generated from the business. Does it make a difference? Not as much as it used to. As for other tax consequences, Congress has moved in recent years to make it a wash. If you own a corporation, you can have it pay for your health insurance and get a 100-percent deduction for the premiums paid. But can you deduct 100 percent if you're a sole proprietorship or partnership? Until 2004, no. You could deduct a portion, but not 100 percent. Congress recently moved to level the playing field: now individuals in a flow-through entity can deduct 100 percent of their health insurance premiums from your AGI so long as the cost does not exceed net business income.

Likewise, for retirement plans, it doesn't make that much difference how you set up your business. The big difference is that you *have* a business; that fact opens up a whole cornucopia of more powerful retirement savings vehicles. (We'll get to that in Chapter 10.) It doesn't make much difference how you're organized from a legal point of view; however, many retirement savings vehicles have legal requirements for including employees, so it matters how you're set up from a personnel point of view.

In this more level playing field there are still two small loopholes that may influence organization choices, albeit not dramatically. While you as a sole proprietor, a partner, or an LLC member cannot deduct the cost of life insurance, a corporation can—up to the amount that provides $50,000 in coverage. So if you own a corporation, your first $50,000 of protection (which isn't much now) will be effectively subsidized by the government. There is no double taxation on the amount paid for premiums; in fact, there is no tax at all. Somewhat more appealing—especially for those with health issues—is that a corporation can pay and deduct *all* medical expenses (not just health insurance premiums) paid for its employees. If you're an owner/employee, you can have your corporation pay all of your expenses, including deductibles and co-pays, and get a full tax benefit.

TAKEAWAYS

There are some economic advantages to organizing your business as a corporation, but not as many as in the past. Corporation owners enjoy small advantages over the owners of other business forms for health care and life insurance costs.

ADMINISTRATION AND PAPERWORK

Set up a sole proprietorship and you'll have to get a business license, set up a bank account, sign a lease, and perhaps do a few other things, but you're off to the races quickly. Set up a partnership and you'll need a partnership agreement covering terms and conditions of how much partners will contribute to the business, who will make what decisions, and what happens if a partner leaves or if the business ends. But it's still not too bad. Set up a corporation and you'll enter a whole new world of forms, filings, and business formality.

A corporation is a separate legal entity, or "person." As such, it must be clearly defined in the state's eyes and regular filings must be made to update the state on its status as a going concern. A for-profit corporation, by definition, needs a board of directors, a set of officers, and a defined body of stock with rules for ownership and clearly defined roles and responsibilities for each officer. The corporation must develop and file a set of bylaws documenting all of the above and providing general governance guidelines for required regular officers' meetings, stockholders' meetings, and other communications both to the state and to shareholders, as mandated by state statute. These requirements apply to both C and S corporations.

It can also be expensive to form, register, and manage a corporation. Filing fees range from a few hundred to thousands of dollars, depending on the state and the complexity of the business. There are legal fees and annual renewals, plus the cost of additional accounting and tax preparation. These costs are trivial for a large business but are obviously a consideration for small businesses.

The laws governing LLCs vary by state. Most states have made it simpler to set up and administer an LLC than its full corporate brethren. LLCs don't have stock; they have memberships. While members and their interests are tracked for the state, the filings and legal requirements are much simpler than those for corporate stock. Operating procedures are spelled out by a more freeform operating agreement, much as for a partnership, instead of formal bylaws. The LLC structure typically requires no formal minutes, resolutions, or filings with state authorities. It's generally inexpensive to form an LLC, but the owners would probably still benefit from some legal advice.

KEEPING CONTROL

And so why did you decide to "do this entrepreneur thing"? You saw an opportunity to take charge of your life, do something you wanted to do, while of course making money along the way. So how does the organization structure affect those ambitions?

Clearly, you have more control of any business that you own 100 percent. Of course, that control works two ways—you control the good but also the bad. You have nobody to help if things go sour. You have the most control in a sole proprietorship, as there are no partner or shareholder stakeholders and there is relatively little government intervention. (Nonetheless, many small sole proprietors grouse about having government at all levels as "partners," always involved through regulation, licensing, and taxation!)

When you're in a partnership, you lose some control, proportionate to the partners' stake and how you design the partnership agreement. There are provisions for *limited partners*, partners with an investment stake but little or no delegated authority and

more limited liability exposure. Entrepreneurs seeking to retain control but still attract partner investments may consider this alternative, retaining control for themselves or fully empowered *general partners*.

In traditional corporate forms, your control again is determined by your stake, this time in shares, but also by the formalities of the bylaws and delegation of responsibilities. Many entrepreneurs set up corporations in which they and their families own 100 percent of the stock; the control here is absolute but must still follow state requirements. C corporation owners can issue two *classes* of stock—*voting* and *non-voting*. The voting shares have a full share of profits and a vote in corporate decisions; the non-voting shares share profits but not necessarily control. C corporation owners can thus attract additional capital but retain control, if investors are content to relinquish that control and it's worth the administrative work to do so.

With an LLC your control is as established in the LLC charter, but an LLC allows for distribution of profits in a flexible manner not necessarily governed by the percentage invested. This so-called *flexible profit distribution* allows LLC owners more control over their companies.

ATTRACTING INVESTORS

C corporations entail a lot of formality and procedure and typically afford their owners less flexibility and control over how the business is managed and how profits are distributed. That may seem like an unnecessary bother, but it does create one distinct advantage: it makes it easier to attract capital upfront and down the road.

Just as owners want control, so do investors. Potential investors are much more likely to invest in an entity with a formal charter, clearly delineated ownership and lines of authority, and financial statements formally filed in accordance with state laws and federal securities laws. So a C corporation has much greater potential to attract capital from the general public (i.e., not just friends and acquaintances).

The investment potential for S corporations is a little less; to most outside investors, they look like partnerships. Also, there are shareholder limitations—there can be no more than 75 shareholders and no shareholder can be a corporation.

LLCs have more difficulty attracting capital because of less formal structures, the lack of defined shares, and lack of permanence: an LLC automatically dissolves if a member dies and must be formed again. Sole proprietorships and standard partnerships, of course, have the most difficulty attracting private capital, again because of informality and lack of permanence but also because of liability exposure.

COMPENSATION

When you own a sole proprietorship or are partner in a partnership, you get paid, at least on paper, the profits generated by the business. As a proprietor or partner, you may decide to leave the cash in the business or take it as a draw, but from a tax standpoint it is *all* business income subject to normal income and self-employment taxes. You may decide to hire family members and pay them, reducing taxable income somewhat while keeping income "in the family," but otherwise there are few knobs and levers to control.

Establishing a corporate entity gives you some flexibility into deciding when and how you pay yourself. Corporations can pay wages to compensate you and your cohorts for services provided. Corporations can also pay profits, which come after the wages are paid, as *dividends*. As we've seen, C corporations can also retain their earnings. You thus have choices about how you want to be paid, when, and how you want to be taxed. The S corporation is unique in that you can pay yourself wages and then collect dividend income on top of those wages not subject to self-employment taxes, so long as your

wages are reasonable compensation for the services you performed. (You don't pay self-employment taxes on C corporation dividend income, either, but unlike S corporation income, it has already been taxed at the corporate level.)

An LLC is a standard flow-through entity from a taxation standpoint, so you will pay full income and self-employment taxes on earnings. But the flexible distribution structure allows you to distribute bonuses and income as you and your member-partners see fit, not necessarily in proportion to the original investment.

Finally, C corporations, since they issue stock, find it easier to use stock and options on that stock as a form of pay or performance incentive. It is harder to motivate performance with a "someday" promise of a share in a partnership, an S corporation, or a LLC.

IT'S STOCK, BUT THAT MAY NOT MEAN MUCH

We've mentioned the lure of C corporation stock as a way to attract capital and to pay or motivate employees. However, it is easy to get carried away with this idea. We aren't talking about stock in GE or ExxonMobil; this is stock in your little company. It may have value now and probably considerably more in the future, but that value is hard to ascertain—and hard to convince others of. Don't forget this as you consider forming or migrating toward a C corporation.

CONTINUITY

For both business finances and personal finances, *continuity*—that is, what happens to the business if a partner or an owner dies or is otherwise unable to carry on—is very important. Corporate entities are more permanent, while proprietorships, partnerships, and LLCs technically dissolve when an owner or a partner dies. If that happens, the business or share of business automatically transfers to the decedent's estate. If it's a partnership, the dying partner's assets are first used to settle liabilities and then distributed proportionately to other partners. The proprietorship can be sold by the estate or re-formed by an heir; the partnership or LLC can be re-formed by a new agreement. In any case, the business ceases to exist as set up.

A corporation's life is perpetual: the company continues to exist as long as its directors decide it should. Obviously this makes a corporation more attractive to investors and more attractive to suppliers, clients, and customers with a long-term stake in its success. If you buy a new car from a sole proprietorship, what happens to that five-year bumper-to-bumper warranty if the owner dies?

LONG-TERM SALE AND TRANSFER

Eventual sale and transfer of the business—or part of the business—is another aspect of continuity. How easy is it to sell a proprietorship, a partnership, a corporation, or an LLC? The answer is generally that it is easier to sell a corporation and specifically a C corporation, simply by selling some or all shares. This can be done gradually or in a single event. Corporate charters may define when and how shareholders can elect to sell their shares.

Partnerships and LLCs must form again after being sold and must change their partner or member agreements to sell part of the business to outsiders, effectively adding the buyers as partners or members. Upfront agreements usually govern when and how a partner can sell his or her share; in many cases, the consent of *all* other partners is required. Sole proprietorships in effect sell assets, including intangible assets like brand names and customer bases, but not the business itself—there is no "form" to a proprietorship to sell.

TAKING A CLOSER LOOK

We've examined some of the important issues to consider in establishing a business structure, mainly from a personal finance point of view. In this section we take a "vertical" look at each business organization form, examining from top to bottom the features, advantages, and disadvantages of each. We look at its tax and personal finance consequences and its upsides and downsides.

SOLE PROPRIETORSHIP

Start conducting business as an individual (or a married couple) and you've by definition created a sole proprietorship. There are no forms to fill out, aside from state and local licensing requirements. You can give the business a name but don't have to do so. If you do, you may have to file for a *fictitious name* with your local government authority.

From a tax standpoint, business and personal finances are the same. But from a practical viewpoint, you should separate the finances by creating a business checking account and a separate set of records for the business. That will help you at tax time, for the results of the business will funnel into one line of your personal taxes. But it will also help you keep aware and maintain control over what's happening in the business and will make you appear more businesslike to customers, suppliers, and, of course, the IRS, should the need arise.

From day one, you own the business and are in control. Business income is taxed as part of personal income and it is yours to do with as you please. You can leave income in the business or draw it off for personal use. There are no tax consequences to taking a draw. Likewise, losses travel straight into your taxes as net operating losses and can generally be used, for actively managed businesses, to offset other income.

Liability and Risk

The tight financial connection between your business and your personal finances also comes with its drawback. You personally have unlimited responsibility for any debts or damages attributable to your business. A business creditor can, in theory, go against your personal possessions, including savings, a car, a home, or investments. (Retirement plans are usually exempt.) The business creates risk exposure for your personal finances. Event-based risk, like injury or property damage, can be mitigated by buying insurance. But there is no insurance, aside from what you might place in a savings reserve, for financial risk.

Tax Time

Sole proprietor taxation is simple. Form 1040, Schedule C, tabulates business revenue and expenses, giving a bottom line net income to carry over onto the Form 1040 individual return. (See Figure 4.1.) All reasonable business expenses can be deducted as costs of doing business, although major assets will have to be depreciated and expensed over time. (See Chapter 7 for more about expenses and asset recovery). Home office expenses, if applicable, are included in Schedule C. Once net income is entered on Schedule C, taxes are done much like for any other individual return. Health insurance and qualified retirement and health savings contributions can be taken as a "for AGI" deduction. For all benefits, it doesn't matter if you pay out of the business or out of personal accounts; it all comes out the same. Sole proprietors pay self-employment tax on their *business* income and income tax on *all* income, including business income. A sole proprietor with more than one business will fill out more than one Schedule C.

Best for What Businesses?

Sole proprietorships are best for truly small, individually run operations where anything more complex simply isn't necessary. They are best when no employees are involved and for businesses with relatively minimal business and financial risk. The wealth and income of the entrepreneur may be a factor, as direct flow-through taxation can be at high rates and a C corporate form might allow the company to retain some income. Proprietorships are good when starting out because losses may be written off against other income; however, the C corpo-

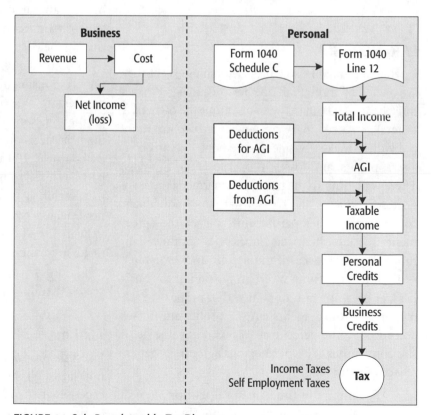

FIGURE 4.1. Sole Proprietorship Tax Diagram

Sole Proprietorship	
• Single owner (or married couple) • Business and owner are one • Income, expenses flow through to owner • Owner pays self-employment taxes on income	
Advantages	**Disadvantages**
• Easy to form • Simple bookkeeping • Can deduct losses, start-up costs • Owner in control	• Little to no liability protection • Business responsible for owner's liabilities • Owner is responsible for business liabilities • May be hard to find capital

FIGURE 4.2. Summary: Sole Proprietorship

ration form can allow the company to retain funds to be reinvested without paying higher individual tax rates. It will be harder for the sole proprietor to attract new capital or new investors.

PARTNERSHIP

Partnerships are like sole proprietorships except they are owned by more than one person and agreements must be worked out between or among the owners. A general partnership is created when two or more individuals make a business agreement to jointly own assets, profits, and losses in operating the business. There is no limit to the number of partners; there are no restrictions on the type of partners (individuals, corporations, other partnerships). Once the agreement is established, the business is conducted in much the same way as with the sole proprietorship.

Each partner funds a certain portion of the business, either with cash or some other property. Each owner is entitled to a share of profits and losses according to the percentage of business value he or she contributes. The partnership agreement generally covers the following:

- the amount of time, financial, and/or physical resources each partner will contribute

- how business decisions will be made
- how and when cash distributions will be made
- continuity: what will happen if a partner leaves, dies, or becomes disabled
- when and how the partnership will terminate
- when and how each partner can withdraw from the partnership

Liability and Risk

From a personal financial perspective, a partnership is in some ways riskier, in some ways less risky than a sole proprietorship. Partnerships somewhat reduce the financial risk for the individual because there are other owners; you as an individual don't have to provide all the money (and time and expertise) to run the business. You lose some control over the business as a result of sharing the risk.

As pointed out earlier in this chapter, partners are fully responsible for the debts and liabilities of the partnership *and each other*. If your best friend and partner hits someone with the truck or makes a bad financial decision on behalf of the partnership, you can be held 100-percent responsible. You and all partners are "jointly and severally liable" for the partnership; if you are the only partner with any personal assets, a creditor can come after you individually for all debts of the partnership. Before you make a partnership agreement with anyone, it's a good idea to understand his or her finances to ensure that he or she can share the risk.

Tax Time

Like sole proprietorships, partnerships are taxed as flow-through entities, except that income and expenses are divided up proportionally according to ownership. Revenues and expenses of the business

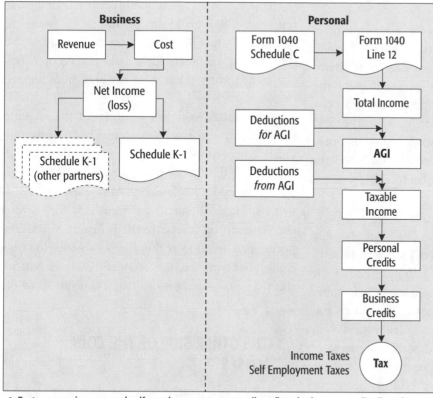

1. Partners pay income and self-employment taxes on all profits whether or not distributed.
2. Partners' share must match investment share.

FIGURE 4.3. Partnership Tax Diagram

Partnership
▪ Multiple owners, partnership agreement
▪ Assets, profits, and losses pass through according to amount invested
▪ Owners pay self-employment taxes on income share
▪ Income, expenses flow through to individual

Advantages	Disadvantages
▪ Relatively easy to form ▪ Sharing of capital, investment ▪ Can deduct losses, start-up costs against other income	▪ Little to no liability protection ▪ Each owner is responsible for all business liabilities ▪ May be harder to find capital ▪ Partners must stick to terms of agreement

FIGURE 4.4. Partnership Summary

are all summed at the business level, then divided, giving all partners their shares on a Schedule K-1. That share then flows to the individual partner's Form 1040 through Form 1040 Schedule E. The partners each pay full self-employment taxes on their shares of partnership income and income taxes on their total income, including partnership income. Business credits arising from the partnership can be claimed by individual partners on their Form 1040. There is no benefit to paying employee benefits out of the partnership; the taxes are the same. An individual involved in more than one partnership will receive more than one Schedule K-1 and flow all net partnership income into his or her Form 1040.

Best for What Businesses?

Like proprietorships, partnerships are best where simplicity is best and where liability and risks are known and reasonable. Partnerships often evolve when one individual doesn't have the money, time, or expertise to conduct a business alone. Partnerships work best, of course, when partners get along and have the same business and personal financial objectives.

C CORPORATION

As described earlier in this chapter, a corporation is considered a separate legal entity formally formed under state law. The owners are known as shareholders and they are not personally liable for the debts, losses, or risks of the business under most circumstances. It is possible to form a corporation and retain 100-percent ownership by owning all stock, although the corporation is usually required to have more than one director and officer. (Family members will suffice!)

Forming a corporation requires a lot of paperwork and some legal footwork. The business must have a name, usually followed by "corporation," "company," or "incorporated." Filings must list the number of shares to be issued and sold, the number of shares bought by each owner at the outset and what will be contributed (cash or property) in exchange for those shares, and some statement of the business in which the corporation will engage. The officers (President, Vice President, Secretary, Treasurer at least) must be identified, as well as the directors, who ultimately make the corporation's decisions. A set of bylaws and articles of incorporation cover such topics as meeting dates, the responsibilities of officers and directors, and rules for selling or reselling shares.

As a separate legal entity, the corporation *must* have separate bank accounts and records. All financial and other assets pledged to the corporation in exchange for shares and earned subsequently by the corporation are the property of the corporation. The shareholders get payments as the directors decide. In fact, the directors ultimately decide everything done by a corporation, although in practice much of this authority is delegated to the chief executive officer (CEO). Directors must meet at least once a year (this can be over a beer and a sandwich at the corner bar, but it must happen). The shareholders vote in proportion to shares owned to elect the directors. Any shareholder possessing 51 percent or more of the outstanding shares has ultimate control over the corporation. Although most operational decisions can be made by the CEO, bylaws normally require that the directors or shareholders make certain decisions, like merger, consolidation, or dissolution of the corporation.

Owners may work as employees of the corporation, receiving normal wages and benefits as provided. Corporations may also pay dividends to its owners, but the authority to pay dividends lies solely within the board of directors. An owner is not entitled to a cash dividend payment just for owning shares; again, all assets are the property of the corporation. The value of the shares owned is the only thing appearing on the owners' personal balance sheet. The personal pickup truck committed to the

THE OTHER SIDE OF THE COIN: LOSSES

We've been focusing on corporate income, but it's important to mention the other side of the coin—losses. The corporation is a separate entity for losses as well as for income. A C corporation's losses *do not* automatically become your losses, because the corporation is a separate entity.

This discourages business owners from setting up C corporations from the start. Congress didn't want that to happen, at least for small businesses. So they set up something known as Section 1244 stock, named for the section of the IRC code that describes it. Corporations issuing section 1244 stock at the outset can sell it to original corporate owners, for cash or property only (not for services) and for a total of $1 million or less in initial capitalization. Holders of such stock can write off initial losses. If you are starting a small business and are interested in the C corporation for other reasons, you should learn more about Section 1244 stock.

corporation by an owner is owned by the corporation and no longer belongs to that owner.

Liability and Risk

By now it's clear that one of the major advantages of the corporate form is liability protection. Unless criminal acts are committed, shareholders share no responsibility for debts, losses, or other obligations of the corporation. Creditors can go after corporate assets, but not those of the shareholders. The risk of any shareholder is limited to his or her investment in the corporation. There are some exceptions: owners can be tapped for past-due employment taxes, for

example. Also, many small corporations find it necessary for the owners to co-sign or guarantee loans, so the owners can be liable for such obligations. If a shareholder lends funds to the corporation and the corporation fails or runs into hard times, the claims of outside creditors come first; owners cannot pay themselves back before paying creditors.

Tax Time

Taxes and tax planning can be intricate and complex for corporations. In discussing taxes, we make the greatest distinction between C and S corporations. The S corporation is substantially like a C corporation except that it is taxed as a flow-through entity.

The C corporation is taxed at the corporate level. A corporate tax return is filed, Form 1120, *U.S. Corporation Income Tax Return*. As an owner, you can receive wages for your services and dividends to distribute your profits. The Form 1120 tax return lists revenues and costs of doing business, including your wages, in the calculation of net income. Corporate income tax is calculated on corporate net income, which is what remains after your wages and other expenses are removed.

Corporate income taxes are high once you reach the $50,000 level, but start out at a modest 15 percent. (See Figure 3.3 for federal Corporate tax rates.) This affords a tax planning opportunity: you may want to pay yourself and other shareholders just enough to leave $50,000 in the corporation as retained earn-

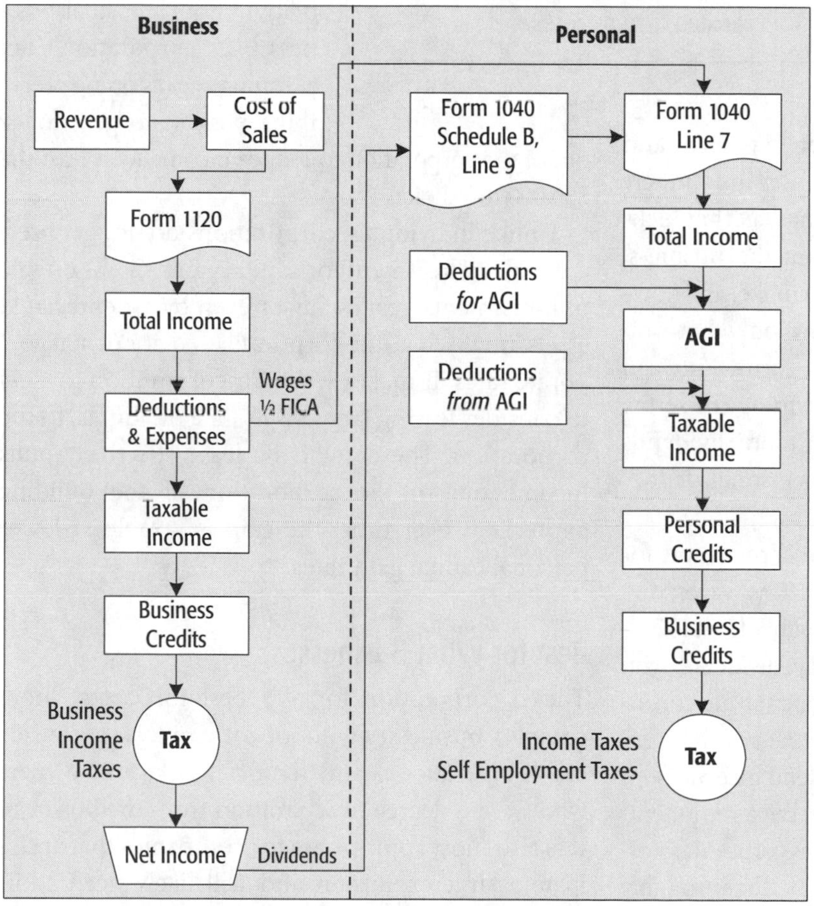

1. All reported profits are taxed at Corporate level using Corporate rates
2. Wages paid to owners are taxed as W-2 income with FICA tax split 50-50
3. Owner/shareholder dividends are taxed only if paid out.

FIGURE 4.5. C Corporation Tax Diagram

C Corporation
▪ One or many owners, separate legal entity, shares issued to owners
▪ Corporate tax return filed, taxes paid at corporate level
▪ Investors may receive dividends and may be paid wages by the corporation

Advantages	Disadvantages
▪ Strongest liability protection ▪ Earnings can be kept in corporation, lowering or deferring taxes ▪ Easiest form to raise capital, add new investors ▪ Can deduct some fringe benefits, not taxable to employees ▪ Easy to transfer ownership	▪ Most complex administration, tax planning, expensive to register ▪ Double taxation ▪ No preferential capital gains tax treatment ▪ Can't pass through start-up or operating losses (unless Section 1244 stock used) ▪ Owners may have some liability in limited circumstances

FIGURE 4.6. C Corporation Summary

again when you receive a share of it as dividends. You may also choose to hire and pay family members. As mentioned earlier in the chapter, corporations can pay medical expenses and some life insurance premiums, deducting those expenses from its taxes without providing corresponding income to you personally. Corporate contributions to retirement plans also reduce corporate income and tax liability. Bottom line: small business C corporation tax planning means doing everything possible to get money out of the corporation to reduce income to at least the $50,000 threshold.

Unlike individuals, corporations do not get preferential tax treatment for capital gains. Gains on sale of investments, real estate, or even over-depreciated assets are taxed at the corporate level at normal corporate rates. It makes sense for corporation owners to consider leasing large assets, like buildings, to the corporation. The cost of the lease effectively pulls income out of the corporation; if the building appreciates over time, the gain is taxable at lower personal capital gain rates.

Best for What Businesses?

The C corporation form is best for larger, more complex businesses with lots of employees, considerable operational and financial risk, and owners who want a degree of separation from the business. It is also most appropriate for companies that anticipate a large expansion and will likely need additional infusions of capital; it is easier to attract more investors. Construction and manufacturing companies are prime candidates, but almost any business

ings. Those earnings will be taxed at 15 percent and you can leave them in the corporation indefinitely (subject to an excess retained earnings tax that kicks in at $250,000) or reinvest them in the business, with modest tax consequences. Unlike in flow-through entities, you pay tax only on what you receive, not on what the business earns. You can control what you get paid in order to optimize tax results, for instance, paying yourself more dividends in a year in which you have more personal deductions or less other income.

Compensation received from the corporation for work is reported on the individual 1040 as wages; dividends are reported on the 1040 through Schedule B—Dividend and Interest Income. Any dividends you receive are effectively taxed twice—once at the corporate rate, once at your rate. But you pay no self-employment taxes or FICA on dividend income, so it doesn't matter much whether you receive remuneration as wages or dividends—so long as corporate profits are below $50,000—because the tax take is roughly the same. When those profits rise, it makes sense to pay yourself more in wages; otherwise, the resulting higher corporate income will be taxed at a higher rate—and that can justify the administrative efforts and cost to set up a C corporation should consider it.

S CORPORATION

Congress created the S corporation to give small business owners the veil of liability protection while still allowing them to operate and pay taxes largely as a partnership. They wanted business owners to make sound business decisions (i.e., choose a form affording liability protection and giving formality to the business) without the undue influence of tax considerations, namely, double taxation. The S corporation is essentially a C corporation that has elected flow-through tax treatment. It is a corporation that desires to be taxed like a partnership.

As such, S corporations carry many of the advantages of C corporations—permanent structure, liability protection, relative ease of adding owners and investments and eventually transferring ownership. S corporations have some advantages that we'll highlight in a moment. On the downside, S corporations require most of the same administrative effort to set up and maintain, including bylaws and incorporation fees and a regularly filed corporate tax return.

While the ownership composition of a C corporation is almost unlimited, there are specific restrictions on ownership to qualify as an S corporation status. These are designed to make S corporation status work only for smaller, domestically owned businesses:

- All shareholders must be U.S. citizens.
- All shareholders must be individuals (not other corporations).
- There can be no more than 75 shareholders.
- There can be only one class of stock.
- The fiscal year must match the calendar year.

Liability and Risk

Effectively, the S corporation structure provides the same liability and risk umbrella provided by the C corporation. Owners are separated from the business in terms of business and financial risk. A creditor cannot collect corporation debts from an owner. Shareholders are not liable for acts committed by other shareholders or corporate employees in the pursuit of business.

Tax Time

The S corporation is required to file a corporate tax return, Form 1120S (see Figure 4.7). Like the C corporation, the S corporation gathers all normal business revenues and costs and reports a net profit. Included in those costs is any compensation paid by the corporation to you for services or work performed. The rules say that if you work actively in your S corporation you must take some compensation as salary if the business is profitable. You pay employment taxes on that income. But the definition of "some" is vague and presents a tax opportunity described below.

IS AVOIDING EMPLOYMENT TAXES *ALWAYS* A GOOD IDEA?

Whether FICA on wages or self-employment taxes on self-employment earnings, avoiding the 15.3 percent employment tax on your hard-earned income sounds attractive, no? Well, to a point. When you finally retire (and you may think, as an entrepreneur, that you never will!), your Social Security payments will be based on the income you earned—and thus, the taxes you paid—by a complex formula that uses your highest 35 years of taxable earnings. So if you go too far in finding ways not to report employment income and thus avoid employment taxes, you may pay for those efforts in retirement. If you already built your Social Security basis through employment before you decided to become an entrepreneur, you may not have this problem.

Otherwise, in terms of taxes the S corporation behaves more like a partnership. Aside from certain capital gains or income from passive activities, it pays no corporate income tax.

Each partner gets a Schedule K-1 for his or her share of revenue and expenses and the net income and losses that result. The share is based on the percentage ownership and is not flexible. The income, of course, is net of any wage compensation paid to the partners. Ordinary income taxes are paid on that income, but as the rules stand now, *no self-employment taxes are paid on this income.* Here, the S corporation has an advantage over the C corporation: although no self-employment taxes were paid on C corporation dividends either, they

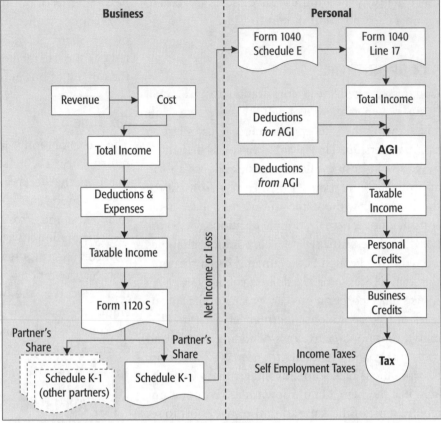

1. Employment taxes are only due on paid compensation.
2. Net income does not have to be paid out to be taxable.
3. No tax at corporate level except for certain gains or passive income.

FIGURE 4.7. S Corporation Tax Diagram

WHAT ARE AT-RISK LIMITATIONS?

To avoid excessive write-offs of flow-through business losses against other personal income, Congress created "at-risk" rules to limit those losses. At-risk rules effectively limit the amount of loss to the amount of investment capital you have at risk—that is, paid into your business. So you can't invest $500 to buy a 1-percent partner share, then write off $2,000 on your taxes when the business blows up big time.

were subject to corporate taxes of at least 15 percent.

The split of wage compensation from net income and dividend payments presents an interesting tax planning opportunity. S corporation owners will take as much in dividends as is reasonable, but need to be able to show the IRS that they took adequate income as wages, too.

The flip side is also important: S corporation owners, unlike C corporation owners, can take losses and use them against other income on their personal returns, subject to *at-risk* limitations.

Best for What Businesses?

The S corporation structure works well for a broad

S Corporation	
▪ One or many owners, separate legal entity, shares issued to owners ▪ Income and expenses pass through to owners for taxation, no tax on ordinary income at corporate level ▪ Owners may get both compensation and profits passed through	
Advantages	**Disadvantages**
▪ Strong liability protection ▪ Owners can write off upfront expenses against other income ▪ Owners may avoid self-employment tax on some profits ▪ Easy to transfer ownership ▪ Capital gains taxed at individual rates	▪ Some restrictions for eligibility ▪ More complex administration, tax planning ▪ Must pay taxes on earnings even if left in corporation ▪ Less attractive to outside investors, not as easy to raise capital as C corporation

FIGURE 4.8. S Corporation Summary

range of small businesses where flow-through taxation is preferred. It affords the formality and continuity of the C corporation form while avoiding double taxation and offering somewhat tax-advantaged treatment of profits and losses. Still, it is complex to set up and administer and is relatively inflexible. Recently, small businesses looking for the advantages of S corps have migrated into LLCs.

LIMITED LIABILITY COMPANY (LLC)

The limited liability company (LLC) is relatively new on the scene and, like the S corporation, combines features of corporate and partnership structures. It is not technically a corporation, despite often being called a limited liability *corporation*. Owners are called *members*. LLCs are set up using laws of the state; laws for LLCs vary more by state than do other corporate forms. For instance, some states do not allow a single-owner LLC.

The advantages of an LLC are primarily *not* tax-related. LLCs offer simplicity and flexibility of ownership that make them attractive to smaller businesses, especially those starting out. To form an LLC requires filling out forms and registering with

the state, but that process is relatively simple compared with the process for corporations, and there are many "do-it-yourself" kits for registering LLCs. Most states require an operating agreement similar to a partnership agreement and require filing a *certificate of formation* with the state. These certificates are often only one page and many states charge only $50 to file. Some states require publishing a notice in a newspaper. Most localities require a business license. Annual meetings are typically required and some formal protocol makes the business more "legitimate" in the state's eyes. But LLCs avoid some corporate complexities of directorships and complex filings associated with S and C corporations.

Liability Exposure

LLCs offer substantially the same liability and creditor protections for members as C and S corps do for shareholders, so long as the business really acts like a business.

Tax Time

Similar to a partnership, taxation for an LLC is flow-through, with each member receiving a share of revenues, costs, and net income or losses. If it is a single-member LLC, taxation will resemble taxation of a sole proprietorship. There is no such thing as a dividend, so all distributions are subject to self-employment taxes, a disadvantage that's a key difference from S corporations.

LLCs differ from other multi-owner flow-through entities in that distributions don't have to

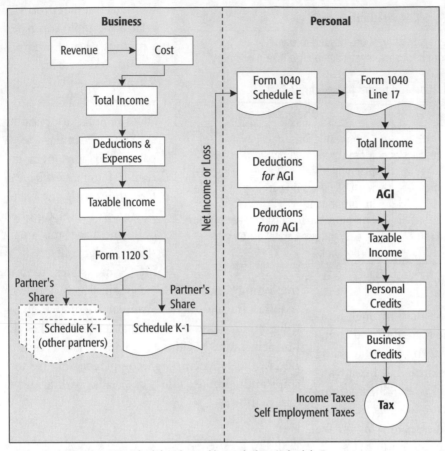

1. If a single member LLC, Schedule C is used instead of K-1/Schedule E.
2. Partner s share does NOT necessarily match share of investment.
3. Self employment taxes are payable on entire income share.

FIGURE 4.9. LLC Tax Diagram

avoidance of double taxation, liability protection, and straightforward taxation are all attractive. It may be harder to sell the business or raise capital someday, but these issues don't matter in many knowledge-based small businesses. And it just sounds a bit more sexy to have "LLC" after the name of your business.

CAN I CHANGE THE STRUCTURE SOMEDAY?

While choosing your business structure is an important decision with a number of possible effects on your personal finances, it should not be looked at as a "forever event." Entrepreneurs generally are better off to

be made in accordance with investment shares or percentages. Income and losses can be divvied up any way the LLC chooses, so long as permitted by the agreement. So a member making a huge contribution to the business or who is in a better tax situation that particular year can get a "special allocation" of profits.

Best for What Businesses?

LLCs have become very popular for small and start-up business. They seem to have the best blend and set of trade-offs between good features and bad features of business structures. Simplicity, flexibility,

use a flow-through entity in the beginning, to take the greatest advantage of initial losses. Then, as the business evolves, it is quite typical for the business structure to evolve, although many remain flow-through entities.

Start as a proprietorship and grow to the point at which you need partners; then it's easy to form a partnership or an LLC if you desire the liability protection. Add employees and grow into a larger business with more business and financial risk; at that point you may want to incorporate. You may want to form an S corporation or make yourself more attractive to investors with a C corporation. As the LLC is relatively easy to form, many entrepreneurs, especially those not going solo, are starting out with

Limited Liability Company	
▪ Set up according to state statutes ▪ One or many owners, separate legal entity, owners are members ▪ Income and expenses pass through to owners for taxation, members pay self-employment taxes	
Advantages	**Disadvantages**
▪ Strong liability protection ▪ Owners can write off up-front expenses and losses up to at-risk amount ▪ Few ownership restrictions ▪ Can set up flexible ownership shares	▪ Must pay taxes on earnings even if left in corporation ▪ Must pay self employment taxes on all earnings ▪ Not as easy to raise capital as C corporation

FIGURE 4.10. LLC Summary

the LLC form. The LLC is probably the most popular destination for small businesses "migrating" out of liability-prone proprietorships and partnerships and more complex S corporations.

One consideration to watch out for: migrating to another structure may create a taxable event, especially if migrating "backwards" from a corporate form. Changing from a corporate status requires a formal closing and liquidation of the corporation. This is a taxable event for both the corporation and the owners, as their stock is effectively sold. In so doing, C corporation owners will incur double taxation on retained earnings and capital gains and will pay higher tax rates on capital gains, including those realized through depreciation recapture. This can be a steep price to pay. Creating a C corporation is more of a one-way decision than the others. It is easier to migrate an S corporation to an LLC or some other form because there is no double taxation on most income, although the owners must still deal with some capital gains. These taxation issues are less important for a corporation with few assets or that has not been in business for long.

BUSINESS STRUCTURE IN THE REAL WORLD

The machinations, thought process, and results of real-world business owners trying to determine their best organization structure could fill a complete separate chapter. We won't go that far, but we'll look at the examples of our model businesses described at the end of Chapter 1.

DG Commercial Photo

Dave Green is a classic sole proprietor. As a professional photographer, for all intents and purposes, he *is* his business. He has a customer base and about $50,000 in photography equipment, but no employees and no major financial requirements other than to meet the working capital needs of his business. He has little in the way of business risk; it's hard to injure someone by taking a picture on a paid assignment. Of course, there's the company van (which also serves as his personal vehicle) that he uses to travel to assignments, but that risk is adequately covered through insurance. His home is his studio, but most of his shots are on location and the home studio is covered by a business rider. There is little to gain by using a corporate or LLC form, as there is little to protect, continuity isn't a big issue, there isn't much to grow, there are no partners, and taxation would likely not be affected.

Wheeler Dealer

Henry Wheeler started the business as a partnership. His partner John brought in some capital and, more important, expertise, as he was already in the bike business. But over time, John wanted to move on and two families were a little too much to support with the small town bike shop. So they dissolved the partnership and Henry had a decision to make.

He chose to run the business as a sole proprietorship. Now, in the bike business there are arguably more risks than in the photography business. Assemble a bike incorrectly or botch a repair and someone could be injured. That event could wreck the business—and Henry's personal finances. But again, he chose to insure the risk and keep the business simple.

Over the years, Henry has had the chance to buy some competing bike shops. He also got a great deal on a building and bought it to house the store today. He has five employees and has grown to become the biggest shop in town and a rather large area. He is now thinking about migrating to an LLC or an S corporation, at least to protect against liability issues and to establish his company more legitimately in the banking community to buy other businesses. He is also looking at the C corporation for all of the above advantages, plus to own his building personally in a leasing arrangement and to make it easier to sell the business when he retires in 15 years. For now, he has leveraged his reputation and his good relations with town bankers, customers, and suppliers to do business with sole proprietor status. He wants to keep it simple, but a change lurks in the back of his mind.

MicroMetal Precision Machining. Tim Cutter started off as an individually owned S corporation to shelter against potential liabilities incurred in the relatively dangerous metal-cutting process and because he would have employees. With substantial investments in capital equipment and a highly variable business cycle, Tim was worried about exposing his personal assets to loss and liability. The S corporation status worked well, providing protection and sheltering some income from self-employment taxes.

As the firm recently grew and began to migrate toward the more expensive laser machine tools, it became more attractive to change to a C corporation to raise capital, get favorable terms from suppliers, and make himself more attractive in the business community as a possible acquisition. He changed to a C corporation two years ago, is now paying himself enough to keep corporate annual income under $50,000 a year to avoid higher tax rates, and is seeking more investors to open a plant in another city near the Los Angeles market.

CHAPTER 5

The Art and Science of Budgeting for Entrepreneurs

OK, TAX TIME IS OVER, FOR NOW. CHAPTERS 3 and 4 were heavy on taxes because they provide such an important framework for maintaining business and personal finances. As we've noted, few things influence the linkage between business and personal finances as much as taxes.

Now we move on to address the less daunting topic of budgeting. A shorter, kinder chapter this will be.

Yes, it's the "B word." Business people worldwide shudder when they hear the word *budgeting*. Here come those accountants again. Days upon days of pulling numbers, scenario building, what-if analysis, and belt tightening to make everything fit. You just want to get it over with and resume business as usual.

It's even worse for most individuals and families. They run for cover when they hear the word "budget." That means figuring out all the expenses and putting a limit on each. Discipline. Restrictions. Keeping track of every penny spent on every latte or soda at the corner gas station. Getting that so-telling glare from the family financial head when you spend more than you

should have. Nobody wants to live with a limit. You work hard to get everything you have, so why so tightly regulate how you enjoy it?

It's hard, but it doesn't have to be *that* hard. Why? We'll soon see.

THE IMPORTANCE OF BUDGETING

In Chapter 2 we introduced a trio of personal characteristics and habits leading to successful personal finance: awareness, commitment, and control. Budgeting is the tool by which we create and maintain all three of these attributes. Successful entrepreneurs, and successful people in general, abide by the well-traveled wisdom, "Say what you're going to do, then do what you say." Budgeting is a big piece of the "say what you're going to do" part, and it also provides a basis—a reference or source if you will—for doing what you say.

Budgeting is planning. It is part of an overall business plan. It is the part of the business plan that involves money, or cash—the lifeblood of your business. Unlike a business plan, it is repeated and refreshed as often as necessary. It is, in business parlance, a living document.

Numbers, For All to See

Plans help you operate successfully. To use a little more business jargon, a budget provides a *framework* for ongoing business and personal financial activity. The framework provides a reference, sort of a "user's guide" for making many decisions, both in the business and the personal financial spaces. It adds a bit of formality to your work and helps you *communicate* your plans and expectations. You didn't expect your production manager to spend $10K on a new piece of equipment? The best way to make that clear is to be able to show that it wasn't in the budget. It saves a lot of surprises—and a lot of conflicts—later on. Or at least it *should*.

Budgets are important communication tools within your business and within your personal finances. But they also help deliver a message of solidarity and credibility to the outside world. When you meet with bankers, potential investors, or partners, there is hardly anything more important than your financial situation and projections. The numbers are important, of course, but the impression that you are in control and not just flying by the seat of your pants is equally important.

Budgets Don't Always Bring Bad News

As we suggested at the outset, the concept of budgeting brings fear. Fear that your every move will be controlled. Fear that budgets will say something negative about the current or future state of your business. It's the fear of "no"—no, you can't buy that piece of equipment; no, you won't be able to expand the office or hire more folks; no, you won't have enough cash to get through the slow part of your year.

There is a silver lining. First, of course, a good budget can make you feel good about what's happening. Although most likely you had a notion of this anyway, a budget tells you that, yes, you can spruce up the cafeteria or buy those new store displays or expand local radio advertising. It's nice to have those "yesses" with clearly documented rationale for them. Some things in business actually help you sleep better at night.

Even beyond those pleasant "yesses" delivered by your budget upfront, a budget provides an excellent opportunity for a reward system. Entrepreneurs and family financiers alike tend to overlook this benefit of budgets. Spend less than you said—either in the business or at home—and the rewards should flow. Employees and others who "make it happen" in the business should be rewarded. Likewise, family members should be rewarded for achieving family budget goals. It's pretty simple: people who are rewarded by good performance tend to perform well. Budgets provide the standard to determine that performance, at least financially.

Managing the Invisible Wall

A budget also provides vital information to manage the linkage between business and personal finances. Your business budget determines cash needs and cash available from the business, which become a driving force in your personal budget. It's a two-way street, as individual or family budget needs can affect business plans and ambitions. Budgeting not only helps you figure out how the business and personal financial spaces connect, but also helps you keep them separate. All too often business owners reach into their own pockets to buy something for the business. That shouldn't happen if the item purchased is part of a business budget.

Kinder, Gentler Budgets

To all of the above we must stop and add a few words of philosophy about budgeting to "stop the bleeding," to make budgeting less painful and onerous than it sounds. People get worked up of the idea of budgets—the time, effort, and pain to construct them and then the time, effort, and pain to live by them. Although budgets do take time and effort and although a poor budgeting effort will invariably lead to a poor budget result, we advocate a budgeting process and mindset that could be called "budget light."

Stated briefly, our "light" budget mentality gets the important stuff right while not beating you up for every detail of every expense. A budget, for business or personal use, should be less than one page.

The business budget is important and should be done with care and precision, for unknowns and surprises can trip up even the savviest and most aware owner. Adverse effects of such surprises to the business are likely to become family budget problems, either directly or through overtaxing business credit facilities. The business budget can be built at a high level or by going line by line, expense by expense; we expect you'll end up using a combination of the two. But it doesn't require as much detail as most think. Software tools make it easier.

Although the personal budget requires care, it can often be simplified to the point where it may not need to be written down. We do think it's important to document the business budget, for it is usually more complex and needs to be shown to more people. But especially for the personal budget, common sense—and awareness, commitment, and control—can substitute for grinding budget detail. How? We'll soon see.

DIFFERENT KINDS OF BUDGETS

Stick a foot into the waters of entrepreneurship and you'll soon realize there are (at least!) three kinds of budgets. For some kinds of businesses there will be more. The three basic types of budgets are *start-up*, *operating*, and *personal*. For some businesses, capital, labor, and inventory management budgets will become important supporting documents for the higher-level budget forms.

START-UP BUDGET

The start-up budget lays down all the expenses you'll incur to get the business started. Many of these are one-time expenses. Some are recurring but are part of the total launch picture. The start-up budget determines how much cash you need to get the business off the ground. Whether the amount comes from your savings, a bank loan, or other investors, you'll need this plan to get started. A sample start-up budget is shown in Figure 5.1. (A copy of this worksheet for your use can be found in Appendix C.)

This sample identifies major categories of expense (Legal, Accounting, Materials and Equipment, and so forth) and some specific details within each. The layout provides not only a place to identify cash outlays but also a checklist to make sure everything is covered, not unlike a flight checklist used by pilots. The sample is a template: every business owner will include some different items or some items he or she wants to show in more detail. The start-up budget generally is done only once and covers a short time period at opening. Similar plans can be prepared to open a second outlet or otherwise expand the business.

THE OPERATING BUDGET

The operating budget is, as the name indicates, a budget or plan for the operation of the business. We won't go into too much detail in this discussion; the finer points of business budgeting are a topic better covered under business planning. (See *Business Plans Made Easy*, 3rd Edition by David H. Bangs, Jr., Entrepreneur Press, 2006.) At our level, the important thing is to understand the importance of creating and documenting an operating budget and to develop clear linkages between the operating and personal budgets. In what follows, we discuss more the *wisdom* of operational budgeting, not the mechanics.

Income and Cash Flow

For most businesses there are two versions of the operating budget: one that projects income and one

BUDGETING SOFTWARE

There are budgeting software packages and templates provided by Intuit QuickBooks for businesses and Quicken and Microsoft Money for personal budgeting. These tools are well packaged with plenty of planning tools and offer the advantage of tying projections and plans to actual figures generated by check registers and, in the case of QuickBooks, individual account activity. While these tools have their advantages, good old-fashioned spreadsheet software, like Microsoft Excel, works well for budgeting. You can set up your worksheet as you wish and adjust it as you wish. It's easy to do "what-if" scenario planning. It's also easy to print budget summaries and incorporate budgets into other documents, like business plans. Entrepreneurs should become familiar with Excel; it is great for all kinds of numbers stuff and for designing forms that use numbers.

that projects cash. Recall from Chapter 3 the difference between cash and accrual accounting: accrual accounting records business activity as it happens; cash accounting records cash as it is received or paid out. For smaller businesses or businesses without a lot of inventory, a cash-only system might suffice. For other businesses, the accrual basis generates an income statement recording accounting-based earnings, which may be different from actual cash flows, but will also more accurately reflect the economic viability of the business. This is important for you to know, of course, but also for potential investors and creditors.

For your own financial planning, the cash-basis budget is very important. It determines what is available to put into your pocket—and what must come out of your pocket or someone else's to fund the business. Especially for businesses with large inventory requirements or that need to fund accounts receivable (that is, offer deferred payment or payment terms to customers), it is extremely important to understand cash needs and the timing of those needs. Likewise, for capital equipment-heavy businesses, cash outlays and the timing of those outlays must also be well understood. It is probably a good idea to have a separate capital budget with a time horizon longer than one year.

Structure

There are a lot of ways to create a budget document. Over time you'll find a model that best suits your business and personal needs. A good starting point is the structure of the IRS Form 1040 Schedule C, which calculates profit and loss from a business. Schedule C provides a good high-level framework for the categories of income and expense. Figure 5.2 shows an example. (A copy of this worksheet for your use can be found in Appendix C.)

You can see that the time horizon is one year. This example shows each expense category "rolled up" into a summary, as is done for Schedule C. There may be substantial detail beneath each of these lines. For instance, "Supplies" can consist of many kinds of supplies used in different areas of your operation. Typically you (and your accountant) can figure out how to "roll up" individual business accounts into each of these categories.

This example is set up to manage either a cash- or accrual-based budget. Much of what is important for personal finances comes in at the bottom:

- **Net Cash Flow from Operations** for a cash-basis budget is the amount of cash expected to be left over or needed to run day-to-day business operations.
- **Investments and Capital Expenditures** captures significant cash outlays to acquire assets that will be used generally for longer than one year, e.g., vehicles, equipment, some computers, and building improvements.

- **Commitments to Reserves.** It's always a good idea—in both business and personal finances—to save some extra cash for a "rainy day." Such cash is simply left in the business and earmarked for a lean period or some expected future outlay not yet well defined. Note that you will generally pay taxes on this "surplus," even if you don't move it into your personal finances. "Commitments to reserves"—and its analogous "rainy day fund" on the personal side—is an area of the budget often overlooked, exposing companies to financial surprises later on.

- **Cash Paid to Owners** is just that—draw or dividends designed to become "top-line" earnings or income for your personal budget. Of course, if this number is negative, that signifies cash you will have to get somehow.

These last four lines of the operating budget are all telling for how the business will affect personal finances—and vice versa. Obviously a business cash crunch can cause a personal cash crunch, but likewise a personal cash crunch can starve the business just when it needs to expand, purchase inventory, buy a piece of equipment, or bring a vital customer on board. As a result, it becomes critical for the entrepreneur to understand—and manage—these last four lines.

Bob's Bagels Start-up Budget		
Revision 1.0	Date: 10/01/06	
Category	**Item**	**Amount**
BUSINESS PURCHASE	Business or Franchise Cost Professional Fees	$ $
LEGAL	Partnership Agreement Incorporation Business Name Search Zoning Compliance Business License and Registration	$ $ $ $ $
ACCOUNTING	Business Structure Advice Business and Tax Process Setup	$ $
INSURANCE	Property Liability Health Disability Life	$ $ $ $ $
BUILDING/OFFICE	Initial Lease or Rent Deposit Remodeling Costs Fixtures Rent for Storage Space or Other Deposits for Utility Connections, etc.	$ $ $ $ $
MATERIALS AND EQUIPMENT (M&E)	Production Equipment Computers and Software Communications Equipment Deposits for Phone, etc. Furniture Tools Vehicles	$ $ $ $ $ $ $
INVENTORY	Initial Stock Purchase	$
SUPPLIES	Production Supplies Office Supplies	$ $
MARKETING	Brochures, Cards, etc. Yellow Pages Ad Initial Advertising Campaign Web Site Design and Build	$ $ $ $
Assumptions 1. 2. 3.		

FIGURE 5.1. Sample Start-up Budget Form

The Devil Is in the Detail

In a minute, we're going to describe why and how you should avoid getting into too much detail with your personal budget. But for the business, the devil is often in the detail, so you should make some effort to understand detailed expenses and assumptions that roll up into the final numbers. This is, after all, one of the main things that business *management* is all about.

**Bob's Bagels
Operating Budget**

Category	Item	Jan	Feb	Mar	Apr	May	Jun	Jul	Aug	Sep	Oct	Nov	Dec	Total
Revision 1.0	Date: 10/01/06	Cash Flow												
INCOME	GROSS SALES	$												
	Returns and allowances (% or $)	$												
	Cost of goods sold (% or $)	$												
	GROSS PROFIT	$												
	Other Income	$												
	NET INCOME	**$**												
EXPENSES	Advertising	$												
	Car and truck	$												
	Commissions and fees	$												
	Contract labor	$												
	Depreciation (not for cash flow)	$												
	Employee benefits	$												
	Insurance	$												
	Interest	$												
	Legal and professional	$												
	Office expense	$												
	Pension and profit sharing	$												
	Rent or lease	$												
	Repairs and maintenance	$												
	Supplies	$												
	Taxes and licenses	$												
	Travel, meals, and entertainment	$												
	Utilities	$												
	Wages	$												
	Owner compensation	$												
	Other expenses	$												
	TOTAL EXPENSES	**$**												
	Net Profit or Cash Flow from Operations	**$**												
	Investments to Capital Exp.	**$**												
	Commitments to Reserves	**$**												
	Net Cash Provided or Required	**$**												
	Cash Paid to Owner(s)	**$**												

ASSUMPTIONS

1.
2.
3.

FIGURE 5.2. Sample Operating Budget

While it isn't important to capture the cost of every roll of paper towels used in your enterprise, you should be aware of the major *cost drivers* of your business. If you're running a coffee cart, the cost of coffee and the mix of sales (and thus, the mix of ingredients required) are important. If you're running a photo studio, you should pay special attention to photo-finishing costs, delivery, studio rental, and overhead costs. If you're running a bike shop, your attention should be on inventory costs, setup costs, insurance, and building overhead. If you're in the metal fabrication business, you'll want to look at raw metal costs, electricity, labor, workers' comp—you get the idea.

The operational budgeting process, especially for a large business or one with many sectors or departments, usually includes a "top-down, bottom-up" reconciliation process. That is, a combination of intuition and experience is used to develop a high-level "top-down" budget at a level of detail similar to the budget example shown above. Then the entrepreneur, often with an accountant's help, dives into the detail to project major and some minor cost drivers based, again, on recent history and intuition. How much coffee will we need and what will the price be? What will next year's rent be? How many workers, how many hours, what kind of raises will we give? What do we expect liability and workers' comp insurance to cost? These items are laid out in as much detail as possible and summed up into a high-level "bottom-up" picture. Then, in a planning meeting with your staff or partners at a nice restaurant or resort near where you live, you reconcile these two versions into a final budget—and make a commitment to make sure it happens. (We've noted that it's common to use such meetings to *build* the two versions of the budget—not just reconcile and commit to the final version!)

Tips and Traps

You'll develop a budgeting process over time that best serves your business and personal needs. As stated, we can't prescribe exactly what to include or how it will work, only that the outcome is important for both you and your business. There are a number of tips—good practices—and traps—bad practices or overlooked items—that can trip up a business budget. Without going into too much detail, here are a few.

- **Start with knowledge.** It's natural for entrepreneurs to fly by the seat of their pants, to "just know off the top of their head" how much coffee they used last year or whether that big photo shoot really made money or a particular line of bicycle clothing was profitable. But again, the devil is in the detail, and sometimes there's a gap between appearances or impressions and reality. Maybe a lot of clothing was sold, but the profits were eaten up in the cost of inventory to keep each size in stock or in delivery costs. Maybe the large photo shoot looked good on paper but ate up a lot of time and travel. Any entrepreneur is well advised to have as many facts in hand as possible, supported by previous financial statements.

- **Garbage in, garbage out (GI-GO).** A natural follow-on from "start with knowledge," always *be wary* of oversimplifying or guessing too much. It's your business and you're the expert, but it's easy to get overconfident and assume you know what you don't. A budget created on erroneous figures will be erroneous. Sure, some errors cancel out; if you're high on one item and low on another, you get lucky. But sooner or later errors will trip you up.

- **Be realistic.** Pursuant to the GI-GO theme, it never helps to put together a budget that's overly optimistic or overly pessimistic. Budgets that don't come true, at least to some degree, people tend not to follow next time. Budget credibility is important: although absolute precision may be a lofty goal not worth the time and effort to pursue, the budget must look, act, and ultimately be realistic.

- **Watch irregular expenses and income.** Where the art and science of budgeting really shows its stuff is in how well you capture and manage irregular items. On the income side, you will have spikes and troughs through the year due to business seasonality, the Christmas season if you're in retail, or major accounts that tend to do business with you at particular times of the year. Small business owners who don't understand these irregularities fret the weak months and "live big" in the strong ones, only to be surprised later on. Expense irregularities—or "regular irregularities" like the annual insurance bill, yellow pages ad bill, and so on—can likewise cause headaches for the unwary. Good budgeting is as much about capturing and planning for irregularities as the "regular" items.

- **Zero-based is best.** It's a common instinct, especially in government, quasi-public, or non-profit agencies, to automatically start this year's budget with actual figures from last year. Take last year's photo-finishing cost, adjust for inflation, and that becomes this year's cost. Such complacency can lead to surprises. It can also, especially in the case of multidepartmental businesses, lead department heads to spend just to reach a number upon which next year's allocation is based. While last year's figures are a good place to start, don't rely on them totally.

- **Contingency planning.** No forecasting method is perfect. You don't know what you don't know—and that applies to all of next year. Smart budgeting commits an amount to reserves, sometimes as a special line item, for unforeseen events or expenses.

- **A small cushion is OK.** We've stressed rationale and realism over hype and guesswork, but it's wise to plan conservatively; that is, to range your sales expectations a little lower than you think they might be and run your expenses a little higher. That gives you the satisfaction of beating goals and some protection in case you don't achieve the rosiest of scenarios.

- **Do the what-ifs.** Take the time to do at least some scenario planning. What if a competitor sets up shop next door? What if you lose a major client? What if you gain a major client and have to invest a lot to deliver for that client? What if interest rates or payment terms with your suppliers change? Smart entrepreneurs know the scenarios and their implications.

- **Get commitment.** No budget is worth the paper it's printed on if the folks affected by it or delivering its promises aren't bought into it. This includes your partners—and you. We have seen so many entrepreneurs do a business plan—and then fly completely by the seat of their pants. Clear buy-in at the outset, followed by good communication and regular updates, is important, to keep everyone in the business aware and working from the same financial plan. Retailers give daily agendas specifying the day's financial goals and actuals from yesterday and last year. This is a way of giving a regular budget update. It also avoids surprises—both for you and your business cohorts.

- **Create rewards.** We'll stress this over and over, both here and with personal budgeting. Again, a budget to which people are not committed isn't worth its paper. There are two ways to cause people to really commit to a budget. One is to involve them in designing and creating it, so they don't feel that it's just handed down to them. The other is to create a reward system. A budget or plan that is executed successfully should lead to a reward for those who have a stake in it. It doesn't have to be big—a gift card for a coffee shop may be enough. But such a reward motivates the kind of behavior needed to run a successful business and, as we'll see, to run personal finances successfully.

WHERE OPERATING BUDGETS GO WRONG

The best-laid operating plans—and budgets—go wrong for a variety of reasons. Certainly, unexpected revenue or cost "events" and the general uncertainty of business will affect even the most carefully prepared budget. Most often, budgets fail because of poor or complacent research and assumptions, lack of commitment on the part of stakeholders, or both. Budgets that don't get updated to reflect new realities also fail. Budgets that are created without enough effort tend to fail— although we aren't advocating spending half your working hours on budgets. The best advice is to be honest, realistic, and transparent and to reward those who are helping you. Not surprisingly, we also advocate keeping a tight grip on your *personal* budget and the flows between it and your business.

THE PERSONAL OR FAMILY BUDGET

Budgeting for the personal or family "enterprise" is just as important as budgeting for the business, but for most families the process doesn't have to be complex or involved.

As mentioned in the opening chapter, it is far too common for business owners to pay attention to their business finances at the expense of their personal finances; budgeting is one area where that tends to happen frequently. Some business owners fly by the seat of their pants in both arenas; it's just the way they operate. More commonly, we've seen owners do fairly detailed and precise business budgets and yet neglect their personal finances twisting in the wind. Here too we advocate a gentler, simpler personal budgeting process, capturing many of the elements of the more precise business budgeting and planning process while eschewing much of the detail and leaving responsibility—awareness, commitment, and control—to each individual family member.

It's not always easy to get this system to work within families, particularly when the members

> ## ▼ A HANDY BUDGETING REFERENCE.
>
> The budgeting methodology and wisdom presented here is drawn from the author's experience captured in a book that he co-authored, *Pocket Idiot's Guide to Living on a Budget* (Alpha Books, 2nd edition, 2006). We highly recommend this little book (not that we're biased) if you want more information or a guide to share with family members.

have vastly different approaches to money, spending habits, and life in general. It takes work and practice and, as we'll see, some of the same communication and rewards practices that make business budgets more effective.

Personal Budgeting Wisdom

The essential wisdom of family budgeting lies in two main areas.

First, it is important to understand the irregularities of income and expenses and to build reserves to handle problems in the cash flow. Unexpected car repairs? Twice yearly auto insurance payments and annual homeowner's insurance payment always catching you unaware? Christmas gifts or a $150 wedding gift got you searching the bottom of your pockets—or going into debt? You can and should plan for these "budget bombs"—and it isn't that hard once you develop a solid understanding of your personal finances.

The second pearl of wisdom goes right to the heart of avoiding detail. Nobody wants to track every latte or movie rental or toll charge or magazine or newspaper bought on the newsstand. It's too much work and it's too much loss of control for most family members. It causes people to lose focus on the big picture and, sooner or later, most tire of the process and give up on budgeting altogether. So our version of personal budgeting calls for grouping things into categories and creating allowances—a *personal allowance*, a *family allowance*, and something we call *Taschengeld*, pocket money, to cover the "small stuff" of personal and family finance.

As you read on, you'll recognize other principles common to business budgeting: careful analysis of income and expense ups and downs, creating reserves or savings "off the top" to handle contingencies and unplanned events, getting commitment, and creating a reward system for good performance.

Personal Budgeting Goals

Not surprisingly, the primary goals of personal budgeting are to know where you are and where you are going and to provide some framework for your daily, weekly, and monthly spending activities. But there are more "big picture" goals to bring to light. Personal budgets do the following:

- **Keep families out of debt.** Debt is the invariable result of poor budgeting or no budgeting at all. Unplanned expenses or expenses exceeding income mathematically must turn into debt that must be repaid later. The average U.S. household has $13,000 in *consumer debt* in addition to household mortgages, student loans, and other big-ticket items. We consider that figure appalling—and it's largely avoidable with good budget habits and discipline.

- **Save for future needs.** We're all now increasingly more responsible for paying for our own retirement, college needs, more of our own health care, and ever more expensive housing. The only way to meet these financial responsibilities, aside from winning the lottery, is to save—and the only way to save reliably is to build a budget that provides for savings.

- **Ensure family peace and harmony.** While the term "budget" is infrequently used in the same sentence as "peace and harmony," especially in the beginning, life is happening faster and most

family members are tending to do more and more on their own. We work two jobs. Kids are out and about more and earlier with friends, doing more things that cost money. A budget provides at least some financial "connective tissue" among family members and it really works once the initial hurdles are overcome.

- **Manage the connection between personal and business finances.** You saw this one coming. Family finances are hard enough to keep in alignment, but it's worse when there is a business, with all of its variations and uncertainties, sitting on top. Good planning helps ease the flow of financial resources in both directions and helps to avoid surprises.

Personal Budget Framework

Figure 5.3 shows our conceptual framework and worksheet for the personal budget. (A copy of this worksheet for your use can be found in Appendix C.)

Like the business budget, the "master" personal budget covers a time horizon of one year, important to capture irregular income and expenses. But most families will want to create a monthly version to use each month. It's simpler and captures the latest expectations for income and expenses. Family members tend not to want to be tied into something set in stone nine months prior; it's best to be flexible in a way that balances current needs and resources with the longer-range plan. As a result, it's perfectly OK—and we've done it and seen it many times in practice—to simply scratch down this month's budget on a napkin or piece of scrap paper—or to not write it down at all. That "back of the napkin" budget includes the critical stuff, what's needed to meet current *obligations* and *necessities*, plus the allowances that get people what they want within reasonable limitations. We'll show how this works.

It's worth noting the basic structure of this document. First comes income, as we'd all expect, with a line for deductions of amounts for taxes and

Bob and Mary Bagelmeister Family
Family Budget

Revision 1.0	Date: 10/01/06														
Category	Item	Jan	Feb	Mar	Apr	May	Jun	Jul	Aug	Sep	Oct	Nov	Dec	Total
INCOME	Wages, Mary	$												
	Bonus and Commissions, Mary	$												
	Business Income, Bob	$												
	Interest and Dividends	$												
DEDUCTIONS	Mary, FICA, other taxes, misc.	$												
SAVINGS RESERVE	401(K), Mary	$												
	SEP-IRA, Bob	$												
	Rainy Day Fund	$												
	Big Purchase Fund	$												
	TAKE HOME	$												
OBLIGATIONS	Mortgage/rent	$												
	Property/renters' insurance	$												
	Property taxes	$												
	Property dues or fees	$												
	Day care	$												
	Private school tuition	$												
	AVAILABLE	$												
NECESSITIES	Groceries	$												
	Utilities: gas and electric	$												
	Utilities: water, sewer, trash, other	$												
	Phone/communications	$												
	Gas	$												
	Cable	$												
	Medical expenses	$												
	School lunches, expenses	$												
	Home maintenance, cleaning	$												
	dry cleaning, laundry	$												
	Pest control	$												
	Other maintenance, cleaning	$												
	SPENDABLE	$												
DISCRE-TIONARY	POCKET MONEY ("Taschengeld")	$												
	PERSONAL ALLOWANCE	$												
	FAMILY ALLOWANCE	$												
	NET BALANCE	$												

ASSUMPTIONS

1.
2.
3.

FIGURE 5.3. The Personal Budget

other normal payroll or self-employment deductions. The next figure is a "savings reserve," which in our construct is taken "off the top," that is, before other expenses are met and allowances are provided. Why? We'll get to that. Then we get to expenses. There are two kinds. "Obligations" are the fixed and uncontrollable items, like mortgage payments, utilities, association dues, day care, and monthly bills that we have little to no control over. "Necessities" are items like food and clothing, that are necessary but for which we have some control over how much is spent and when. Once income, off-the-top savings, obligations, and necessities are calculated, we arrive at "spendable" income, that is, what you and family members can spend on what you want. We create three forms of allowances to guide roughly what is spent, but basically what is provided for in those allowances can be spent by family members as they please. Finally, we arrive at the net balance; if it is negative, we must go through the process again until the net balance is zero (or positive).

These are the basics. The following are steps and pieces of wisdom to help you make this budgeting work for your household.

FINANCIAL FORENSICS

Are you ready now to start constructing the annual budget and then monthly budgets? Not quite yet.

The first principle in sound personal budgeting is to develop a solid understanding of where you are *financially*—what you're earning and what you're spending. We are trying to capture not only facts and figures but also financial *habits*.

We call this process *financial forensics*. As the phrase implies, it is about investigation. It's investigation into your past—past income patterns, past spending patterns. And yes, it's about exhuming the dead bodies of financial mistakes, often just buried in unmarked graves or thrown together into a pit marked with the four-letter word "debt." If you have

debt (and most of us do), what caused it? When did that unexpected expense happen and why? Could you have planned for it? Could you have avoided it with a little more financial awareness, commitment, or control? Getting a family budget together means figuring out what you have, where you are, and *what you do* on a regular basis.

The Ups and Downs of Income

One of the first steps in any budget is to figure out the "top line," the income. Nowhere is a close look at income more important than for the small business owner and entrepreneur, for there is no operating business that doesn't have at least some variation in monthly income. Business income variations can be amplified by business costs and needs; for example, a slow month of sales may mean more advertising purchases and still less net income. In any event, a downturn in business can reduce cash flow into personal finances and even a cash *outflow*. Any household budget must observe the variations in income inherent in the ownership of the business.

The Ups and Downs of Expenses

Financial forensics must uncover irregularities in normal expense patterns, resulting from natural irregularities in billing cycles, seasonal needs (like utilities in summer and winter), or irregularities in spending habits. The best way to investigate expenses is to simply look at a year or two's worth of bills, including credit card statements, and, if feasible, bank statements or cancelled checks. If you don't have this information, it is likely that your bank, utilities, credit card companies, et al. can help out if you ask nicely. While we advocate a "big picture" approach to personal budgeting in general, the phrase "the devil is in the detail" applies here. Time spent upfront will pay off in better budgets from now on.

Spending Habits

It should be possible to reconstruct the ins and outs of your personal finances fairly well if you have sufficient data from the past. What is trickier is to capture the nuances of spending habits. Do you and/or family members keep track of what you spend? Are you or they aware of what they spend, in rough numbers, each month? "I spend between $10 and $20 each month at the coffee shop" isn't OK if the real number is closer to $50. You get the idea.

The same goes for impulse spending. Do family members tend to pick up that extra bottle of wine or a magazine on routine trips to the grocery store? Can they pass up a "sale" sign at the mall or an outlet mall when they travel? If not, we're not saying that's a bad thing—but you must account for those impulses in your budget and create sufficient allowances to make them fit. We stress that the purpose of the "financial forensics" stage is not to criticize habits, but to capture facts.

PERSONAL BUDGET FEATURES

The one-time investment in financial forensics will pay off in making the budget easier to construct and live by. The rest of the budgeting process is a "common sense" meshing of income availability, savings requirements, expenses, and other needs of the family. What follows uses the worksheet in Figure 5.3 as a basis, although, as mentioned above, this exercise is also done monthly to provide each month's spending guidelines.

Income Plan

The income plan incorporates all regular and irregular income brought in by family members. If husband and wife are both in the business, the income line can be brought in as a single figure or separately. More typically, one spouse has a wage and the other has the irregular business income. (The wage earner may also have income irregularities from bonuses, commissions, and so forth.) Finally, there may be *unearned* income from investments, including interest, dividends, and rental income.

Once again, it's important to capture income variations and it's important to understand the "big picture." Why? To avoid the tendency to "live fat" when things are going well, only to come up empty a short time down the road. It happens all the time.

From income we must eliminate normal deductions for taxes, FICA, and so forth. Some budgeters think in terms of gross income; others bring gross income down into a net wage or a business income less self-employment taxes. You can do it either way. It gets trickier where an S or C corporation structure is used and tax treatments might vary depending on the mix of wage compensation and dividend or profit distributions from the firm. It's a matter of planning; once again, if it doesn't make that much difference, it isn't important to sweat the details here. If anything, be a little conservative with income planning; an upside surprise here never hurts.

Savings Reserves

Once income is figured from all income sources, the next step—and a very important one for sound budgeting and personal financial management—is to figure out savings requirements and take them "off the top" before expenses and allowances. We are desperately strong proponents of off-the-top savings because those having the discipline to salt savings away first are more likely to make it happen. If you plan to save after spending, it's not likely to happen.

For most, "savings" breaks down into several components:

- **Retirement savings.** These are amounts allocated for contributing to retirement savings plans— to 401K plans and similar for wage earners and into self-employment retirement vehicles for entrepreneurs. Both wage earners and entrepreneurs may have separate or additional retirement savings in IRAs or other vehicles. The detail here isn't important, but you need to get the right figure, stick to it, and make sure funds budgeted actually get into the accounts (a common failing among entrepreneurs, who must take the initiative to contribute on their own).

- **Rainy day fund.** This is analogous to the *reserve* or *contingency fund* we set up for the business. The rainy day fund consists of liquid (always accessible) savings to handle unexpected bumps in the road, either in income or in expenses. Credit card debt is the typical result of *not* having such a fund. Financial planners recommend three to six months of wages as a cushion for most households; we think that the cushion for entrepreneurs should be a year or more, given the ups and downs of business income and expenses. Of course, that's an aspirational goal; it doesn't mean you should close down the business if you don't have that much set aside already.

- **Big purchase fund.** This fund is intended to build savings in advance of an expensive purchase, like a home, a car, remodeling, or a major vacation. A family should save at least something in advance of these purchases or they simply flow straight into the "debt" column.

Taking savings "off the top" gives you what we refer to as "take-home pay." This is the amount you have available to allocate to known and required expenses and the more discretionary things you might want to do, yourself and as a family, with your money. At this point we're not done with savings; if we can't meet the following requirements, we *may* have to adjust savings to make everything balance—but only as a last resort.

Obligations

Now we move on to expenses. The first category of expenses is the least controllable and, for most families, the most threatening: *obligations*. These are expenses we cannot control or change much. If your mortgage is $2,000 a month, then you must pay that,

rain or shine. You can't pay only $1,800 because you're having a lean month. These costs are relatively fixed in the short term: of course, you can look for a cheaper mortgage some day and perhaps reduce the payment to $1,800, but that's not going to happen overnight or any time soon. For obligations, all you can do is understand them and be prepared to write the checks. These are some common obligations:

- mortgage or rent payments
- property or renters' insurance
- property taxes
- property dues or fees
- day care or private school costs
- car payments
- car insurance
- some health care costs

The net result, after deducting obligations, is *available income*—available for the expenses over which you have more choice and control.

Necessities

Necessities are things that you need or cannot do without. However, you have some latitude in controlling the *amount* and *timing* of those expenses. Take groceries as an example. You have thousands of choices at the grocery store and you have choices among grocery stores. For a typical family of four, a weekly grocery bill can range from $75 to $200, depending on what you eat, what brands you buy, and where you shop. So every budget must include *something* for food, but you have latitude in determining the amount and the timing through the course of the month.

Necessities include (but aren't limited to):

- food, groceries
- utilities (some control)
- communications—phone, Internet, wireless
- school lunches and activities
- home maintenance and cleaning expenses
- pest control

- some clothing and clothing care expenses
- some health care costs

The income left over after obligations and necessities is *spendable income*. It might be oversimplifying a bit, but spendable income is the amount you can spend on things you *want*, as distinct from things you *need*.

Now we move forward in the budget to cover these "wants." However, just because they're wants, don't think that they aren't subject to some planning diligence. Many people end their budgeting exercise after taking care of needs, only to blow it by not carefully planning their discretionary expenditures.

▼ **DO I *REALLY* HAVE A CHOICE?**

Some of the items labeled "necessities," like cable TV or wireless phone, will seem like "obligations" once you sign up for them. You have a contract that requires a monthly payment. But the original short-term choice was still yours. If, for you, cable TV or the cell phone is indispensable and fixed, you're free to move it into the "obligations" category. It's your budget.

Discretionary Expenses

Hallelujah! We've reached the part of the budget where good things happen—that case of wine, nights out at the movies, trips to restaurants, that new pair of jeans, those visits to the specialty coffee shop. We all work to live, but life is much better if we have some money left after we pay for basic living expenses.

Here is where we depart from much of the traditional wisdom of budgeting. Pick up most budget books and you'll see separate line items for clothing, snacks, video rentals, specialty coffees, and the like. We won't do that to you—that's too much detail and it's too constraining and threatening to your sense of control. So the approach we take is to create three

kinds of allowances to cover such expenses.

Allowances

When you were a kid, you probably got an allowance—five bucks a week to do anything you wanted: buy candy, save for a skateboard, whatever. In our simplified personal budgeting scheme, we take the same approach. Why? Once again, to give you and each family member a sense of control and to avoid obsessing over too much expense detail.

To give a clearer picture of ownership and responsibility, we break allowances down into three categories:

- **Taschengeld.** It's a German word: *Tasche* means "pocket" and *Geld* means "money." Each family member gets a "pocket money" allowance each week or month to cover the really little stuff—sodas purchased at the gas station, an occasional bagel here and there, a magazine. For us, it's "ATM money"—that $20 or $40 you withdraw each week and keep in your pocket to handle little stuff. In fact, a weekly fixed ATM withdrawal is a good way to manage this part of the budget.
- **Personal allowance.** Once the *Taschengeld* is established for each family member, the personal allowance, or "PAL," comes next. The PAL is a more substantial sum of discretionary money allocated to each family member (usually the adults). The amount can be $100, $200, $300 per month. The PAL is often managed by giving that family member a personal credit card; the balance is paid off each month and should never exceed the amount budgeted. The PAL is for all the individually desired "stuff"— books, clothing, personal entertainment, refreshments with co-workers, etc. Again, there's no need to budget or track these items separately. Note that bigger expenses—like education, personal vehicles, etc.—should be covered above, most likely under "necessities."

■ **Family allowance.** But what about things the family does together—eating out, weekend trips, planting spring flowers, going to a movie or a musical performance? Such discretionary expenses taken at a family level come out of the family allowance (FAL). This item comes last, intentionally. The FAL has the lowest priority; it is obviously important to take care of savings requirements, obligations, and necessities first. But we think that, to get full family buy-in, each family member needs to get his or her allocation *first*. So the size of the family allowance is dictated by how much room there is left over from the rest of the budget: restaurants, movies, entertainment, weekend trips, etc. happen only *after* other needs are met.

MAKING ADJUSTMENTS

Did it all come out right the first time around? Did your personal budget yield a positive net balance? If you're like most people, we doubt it.

A negative balance on the first pass doesn't mean you've done something wrong. It only means that you have to make some adjustments. Those adjustments will most likely start with discretionary items, starting with the FAL, but not necessarily. *Anything* can be adjusted with family agreement. For entrepreneurs, it's even possible to adjust the top line—the draw or dividend paid by the business—so long as it doesn't conflict with business needs.

Naturally, there are a few "sacred cows" that should be left untouched if at all possible. Retirement savings is one. Naturally, many obligations also fall into this category. You can adjust the rainy day fund to the extent that rainy days are already covered—for you and for the business.

The adjustment process may be painful, but is entirely necessary. Many see the negative bottom line and simply give up or get negative about their personal financial situation—which only makes it more

THE $800 WEEKEND AND OTHER "BUDGET BOMBS"

Families have a lot of ways of "blowing it" financially—with or without a budget. One of our favorites, and we see it again and again, is the short weekend trip gone out of control. Sure, buy two tickets cheap on Southwest or some other carrier for a three-day jaunt to some sunny place: just $99—great! But those two "cheap" tickets end up costing more with taxes. Then you pay for a rental car, two nights in a hotel, meals in restaurants, and souvenirs for the kids you left home with grandma and grandpa—or, worse, a baby sitter. The price tag rapidly balloons to $800, $1000, or more—just for a short getaway. It all adds up—and many people neglect to add it all up. You can and should manage such "budget bombs"—which are more likely to occur when you own a business. A business can hurl ever so many more kinds of budget bombs your way.

negative. Adjusting budget items in such a way as to "share the pain" equally among all commitments is more art than science and it's the hallmark of a good and well-disciplined budgeter.

GETTING FAMILY COMMITMENT

Getting commitment from family members can be the hardest part. We're talking about real commitment—not just saying "yes" at the family dining table, but really executing the budget as designed. If they have a $300 PAL, stick to it. If you have a $40 *Taschengeld* allowance, stick to it.

Part of sticking to the budget is that family members know where they are, in rough numbers, at any given time. No, we don't expect each member to know his or her exact credit card balance or to dial the 800 number or go on lineeach day to check it. But they should have a pretty good idea of where they stand month to date. They should know how much pocket money they have left and spend accordingly.

We've found the best way to get commitment—at least in our modern, capitalistic society—is to create rewards for good performance. "Stay within your PAL and you'll get to order something special from the next Saks Fifth Avenue catalog." "If we do a good job as a family, there may be a trip to Disneyland at the end of the year. Or a bigger holiday gift buying budget." Smart budgeters use year-end gift giving as a tool to say "thanks" for the commitment and a financial year well done. It's good to lay out some of these offers in advance, so folks know about them. But—as in the business you run—the unexpected bonus or gift can mean even more. Be creative.

WHERE PERSONAL BUDGETS GO WRONG

There are as many budget traps as there are individuals or families living on budgets. Here are a few of the more common and dangerous:

- **Budget bombs.** These big expenses can be discretionary, like the $800 weekend, or unexpected, like the $1,200 car repair. Either way, if there is no preparation in the form of savings, it means debt—and playing catch-up for a while.
- **Unforeseen business needs.** Unique to the entrepreneur, business "budget bombs" or unforeseen cash requirements for working capital (inventory or receivables), capital improvements, etc. can wreak unexpected havoc on family finances
- **Inadequate rainy day fund.** The fund must be big enough for the amount of rain. If not, you could get soaked financially.
- **Failure to capture income fluctuations.** People tend not to understand their incomes clearly enough.
- **Tax problems.** Entrepreneurship expands the chances of underwithholding for taxes, especially with self-employment tax requirements.
- **Uneven family commitment.** If one family member sticks to the budget and another doesn't, the effects are obvious. No two people view money the same way.

CHAPTER 6

Finance It: Cash, Credit, and Capital

Particularly in the early start-up phases of a business, "Where can I get the money?" is probably heard more often than any other question. To start a business, it usually takes not only a good idea or a good market but also a sizeable amount of capital—that is, cash. You probably already knew this.

You probably also knew that most likely some of that money will come from your own pocket—your own personal finances. You remember that we connect the start-up phase in the business financial life cycle to the investment phase in the personal financial life cycle. And some of your start-up capital will come from other sources, like banks, credit facilities, suppliers, or other investors. All of these capital sources have a common denominator: they are more willing to lend to you and work with you if your personal finances are solid.

Your capital needs don't stop with the start-up. Many entrepreneurs overlook this. Throughout the life of your business, it will need capital infusions from time to time. True, most times of need come in the early phases of a business, when growth is most rapid and the business is expanding. But capital needs can arise at any time—to replace equipment, to buy a competitor, to manage a brief business down-

turn. Your ability to retain capital in the business and get capital from outside sources will build the business while protecting your personal wealth.

Most entrepreneurs use both their own capital and capital from outside sources to run the business. The mix of capital sources—*financing strategy*, if you will—is one of the more important aspects of managing business and personal finances together. In this chapter we summarize the sources of capital—including those already within your own personal finances.

THE IMPORTANCE OF CASH, CREDIT, AND CAPITAL

Simply, capital is the amount invested in assets that make the business work. It can come from you or your partner or investors or shareholders—that is *equity*. It can come from a lender under contract for repayment with interest due as a price for using the capital—that is *debt*. Regardless, unless your business is based purely on your knowledge or intellect, some capital is required. (Even if all you have is a personal computer: that's purchased with capital.)

Capital, or cash, is thus described as the lifeblood of a business. Cash pays the bills to acquire the inventory and pays the labor so that you can produce or sell something—for cash (hopefully more than you've spent). That cash circulates through all corners of the business, but, unlike the blood in the human body, it may stay in certain areas of it for quite some time, as in the case of large fixed assets like buildings and equipment. If too much cash stays out of circulation for too long or if there isn't enough to supply certain parts of the business, your business starts to starve. Suddenly you can't buy enough inventory to fill your store shelves or can't afford a trip to see a client or can't afford to offer 30-day payment terms to attract a new customer. Cash-starved businesses invite trouble. The situation usually gets worse before it gets better, for it's obvious that revenue streams are at risk, which, of course, starves the business for more cash.

You will need capital—cash—at all times to run a business.

Investment Phase

Whether you buy a business or start one from scratch, you will need to come up with an initial investment before your first dollar of revenue rolls in. When buying the business, the initial investment pays the previous owner and usually, but not always, acquires enough assets to keep the business going. When starting from scratch, you need a location, equipment, inventory, marketing collateral, cash to pay for various services upfront, cash to pay employees—you get the idea. Your pockets can get pretty empty before that first dollar rolls in. And unless you have some magic source of capital, it's your personal finances that filled or helped fill that pocket.

Capital Assets

Capital assets are generally defined as those items lasting more than a year: buildings, machinery, equipment, vehicles, computers, furniture, and fixtures are typical examples. These items are large

enough that an entrepreneur can plan for them with some accuracy as the business gets off the ground. A capital spending plan, or *capital budget,* details spending for capital assets. This should be part of every start-up budget, and it can usually be developed with a fair degree of precision. Capital spending requirements should be detailed as part of the overall business plan to give clear understanding and provide credibility for lenders and potential investors.

Working Capital

Working capital is more abstract than capital assets and more often misunderstood. Technically, it's the difference between *current assets* (like cash, cash equivalents, accounts receivable, and inventory) and *current liabilities* (like accounts payable, short-term loans or debt, and other obligations to be paid within one year). That's how you calculate it, but many entrepreneurs still don't understand it.

Using the lifeblood analogy from above, working capital is the "blood" that routinely circulates through the body of the business to feed its current needs. Those needs are fed by current assets, such as cash, accounts receivable, inventory, and consumable supplies—like photo paper in a photography business. Any business requiring any of these items (and we can think of very few that don't) requires an initial working capital investment.

Even with these definitions and analogies, the concept of working capital may still be difficult to grasp. Perhaps the best way to illustrate working capital—and the problems caused when insufficient—is by example.

Our model sole proprietor, Dave Green of DG Commercial Photo, ran into working capital problems almost immediately after acquiring the business. Dave had a plan to acquire the $50,000 it cost him to buy the business assets—cameras, fixtures, customer base. The owner lent him half; he came up with half out of his own pocket. So why did he end up $30,000 in debt (on a high-cost American Express card) a mere four months after starting the business?

The answer was a tough and poignant lesson in working capital financing. The previous owner collected on most of his accounts before transferring the business. Then Dave did a lot of work for clients and invoiced them normally with 30-day terms. In the meantime, he had to pay large photofinishing bills and normal overhead—rent, utilities, vehicle costs, supplies, etc. He paid his bills on time. Unfortunately, most of his clients did not. A short tour through his finances revealed almost $40,000 in accounts receivable, half of which was past due. He didn't plan for the working capital required to finance this gap between inflow and outgo, so he was caught in a high-cost debt that took several months to resolve through a combination of additional capital and collecting on the late accounts.

This problem happens in many small businesses. If it's not the more abstract accounts receivable that cause trouble, it's the more concrete and obvious accumulation of inventory. If you sell a physical product, you have to buy something first in order to have the product on hand to sell (in most cases, anyway). That accumulation of inventory requires capital—cash—upfront. The amount invested never goes away: instead, it is (or should be) tied to the level of business, with new inventory replacing what you sell. Rising business levels imply rising inventories and thus rising working capital requirements. Well-managed businesses figure out how to keep inventory from growing as fast as the business, so that proportionately less working capital is required and the return on investment is improved. Poorly managed businesses, in contrast, let inventories go out of control, growing too fast or becoming too variable. Such unmanaged growth or variability produces a lot of working capital surprises in the form of expensive debt or unplanned digs into personal resources.

DOES A KNOWLEDGE BUSINESS REQUIRE WORKING CAPITAL?

Suppose you start a consulting business. You think, "This doesn't apply to me. I'm a knowledge business. I'm immune to most of this inventory and accounts receivable stuff. I don't need to invest anything in upfront working capital because I don't have to buy anything to sell, I don't have any overhead, and I don't have to pay anything else to outside sources for the services I provide."

Wrong. Sure, a knowledge business won't invest as much initially. But in all likelihood, you're still going to have to buy airplane tickets, rent cars, and stay in hotels. And you'll need telephones, Internet connections, and office supplies to produce all of those nice reports. And you'll hire an accountant and perhaps an attorney. And you'll have some accounts receivable, unless you can convince your clients to pay you in cash as you leave their premises. It's a natural tendency in *any* business to underestimate—and underfund—its working capital requirements. Put *this* knowledge to good use and you'll be better off for the long term.

Short-Term Shortfalls

Unless you have a "miracle" business *and* you're a "miracle" business manager, you will inevitably run through short stretches where your bottom line is negative, even as your business matures. All businesses have cycles, both in revenues and in costs. Most businesses have irregular income and irregular costs; even those fairly regular business will have irregularities as customers don't always pay on time. You will go negative from time to time. Unless your suppliers are willing to take the hit for you and let their businesses run negative to save you, you'll need some capital reserves available to make up the difference.

WHAT MAKES DELL WORK SO WELL?

Much has been written about the stunning success —at least until recently—of Dell Computer. There is no need to repeat the entire story here. But one of the most important secrets to Dell's success is working capital management. We just expressed doubt that your suppliers would be willing to come up with working capital to spare you. In most businesses, that idea would be preposterous. But Dell didn't follow that rule. Its business model calls for a real-time build-to-order manufacturing. Using its size, brand prestige, and effective negotiating, Dell convinced its suppliers to hold parts in their inventories until Dell needed them. This effectively pushed most of the inventory-driven working capital requirements up the channel. It also further reduced the risks of obsolescence, a big deal in the PC business. Dell reduced both obsolescence costs and working capital requirements. Also, since the company sells primarily on credit cards, it has little in accounts receivable. It's safe to say that Dell's success story, especially its financial success, is driven as much by minimizing working capital and obsolescence as by its product or brand name.

CAPITAL SOURCES

So where does all of this vital capital come from? Where do you get it and how? How does capital you acquire for the business work in conjunction with your personal finances?

Clearly, every entrepreneur has two objectives when it comes to finding capital. One is to get enough to avoid some of the problems just highlighted that result from underfunding the business. Two is not to put too much strain on his or her own personal finances. Not surprisingly, these two objectives are often in conflict.

VISA OR MASTERCARD?

Many small businesses—especially those outside the retail space, where it is almost mandatory— are dogged by the question of credit cards. The case for taking credit cards is clear for retail bike dealer Wheeler Dealer, but what about DG Commercial Photo, MicroMetal Precision, and that consulting business you dream of starting? Of course, the fees are daunting—1 to 2 percent of revenue or higher. But if taking credit cards reduces working capital needs and smoothes the flow of business with your customers or clients, it still may be worth the price. Remember that paying 1 to 2 percent upfront is better than 18 or 21 percent on the back end if a shortage of working capital forces you to get expensive short-term financing, not to mention the effort in collecting overdue accounts. Put more simply, taking credit card payments on the front end of your business will create less strain and variability on the back end—and your own personal finances.

A Question of Balance

Every entrepreneur has to get enough capital to fund the business without draining his or her own finances. Good entrepreneurs know all possible sources of capital and use them effectively and in good balance.

Capital comes from three sources: personal capital, capital furnished by other investors as equity, and capital borrowed from individuals or institutions in the business of providing capital, otherwise known in business circles as *credit*. Each source has its advantages and drawbacks; the smart entrepreneur taps each source for different amounts at different times.

▼ IT TAKES A SOUND BUSINESS PLAN

If you as entrepreneur are conductor and the various sources of credit are members of your orchestra, then your business plan is the sheet music. Sheet music tells each performer what is going to happen and when and shows how everything fits together to reach a desired outcome. The business plan does the same for potential investors and lenders as well as any partners, any employees, and you as conductor. We won't go into the details of business planning here; you can find them in many of the books on small business already out there. But here, adapted from the MasterCard small business Web site (*www.mastercardbusiness.com*), are "Five C's"—areas or topics most capital providers want to see addressed:

- **Cash flow.** Capital providers and especially lenders are looking for a secure return on their investment. They need to feel sure that the business will generate enough cash consistently enough to pay interest and loan principal and to pay a sufficient return. Cash flow projections should not only cover the expected scenario but also the what-if scenarios if things don't turn out as expected.

- **Collateral.** Cash flow projections are forecasts and capital providers realize there's uncertainty in any forecast. So they want to know that the business is buying quality assets with the funds and that there are more financial assets available to smooth out the ups and downs. Business plans should say something about the assets or property of the business and the finances of the owner(s).

- **Capital.** Investors want to know what others, particularly the owners, have invested. Naturally, investors and lenders will get behind a business when the owners have a substantial stake and stand to benefit or suffer personally. Good business plans provide some detail on owner stakes.

- **Conditions.** Capital providers and especially lenders look at overall business conditions and at conditions in the industry in which the business operates. They look at credit risks and the successes and failures of other businesses. What they want in your business plan are key features highlighting why your business is different from the others—and *better*.

- **Character.** Lenders want to know that an entrepreneur (or a team of entrepreneurs) has the ability to run the business successfully. They look for a combination of experience, honesty, and integrity as shown by background, by business and personal endeavors.

What Determines Your Capital Mix?

Many factors determine your capital mix, your capital structure. First is your type of business. A business with a sure-thing business model and a proven track record, perhaps a business that you're buying or a franchise business, will be more attractive to outside investors and lenders, while a "wild hare" idea will attract less from the outside. Also, size matters: you simply don't need that much outside capital to start up a flower stand, for example. Your personal business experience and the credibility and trust engendered will also be a factor. Your credit background and that of the business—your record for paying back borrowed capital—is a big factor, for determining both how much capital you can acquire this way and how much it will cost, i.e., the interest rate. A final factor in your capital mix is the quality and soundness of your business plan, as just described.

From here, we examine the major capital sources: personal capital, banks and banking, more general forms of credit, and equity and other capital sources, for their features, upsides, and downsides. Knowing that they are tightly related, we will examine these capital sources from both business and personal finance perspectives.

PERSONAL CAPITAL

Start a business and sooner or later you'll have to open your wallet, unless you're one of those "miracle" entrepreneurs we talked about earlier. You have to put your money where your mouth is. Why? Because unless you've just invented an automobile that runs on water or you have a rich aunt or uncle completely devoted to your every enterprise, nobody will buy into your idea so completely as to fund 100 percent of your journey down the yellow brick road of small business.

As a rule of thumb, you should be prepared to finance your business at least 30 to 40 percent from your own pocket. Of course, this figure varies according to the type and size of the business venture and the extent to which others buy into your idea. If you really have achieved "walk on water" status by inventing a car that runs on water, the size and certainty of success of the venture likely will cause a mad "gold rush" of capital from people eager to jump onto the bandwagon—and relatively small (in percentage terms) investments on your part. That's probably even less likely to happen now, after the Internet boom of the late 1990s. Simply, too many people jumped onto too many bandwagons with too much capital for entrepreneurs whose business ideas were not so solid. A car that runs on water has a lot more upside than a Web site that sells dog food.

Personal Savings

Starting a business will require at least something from your personal nest egg. Again, it's unlikely that someone is willing to provide a 100 percent stake up front. It's possible to fund a business with personal loans, but lenders will get nervous about funding anything when they see that you are funding nothing. According to a Small Business Administration study, about 80 percent of all new businesses start without the help of commercial loans. This fact underscores the role and importance of personal savings—and the role and importance of other potential investors and partners.

The common question, of course, is "How much can you afford to take out of savings?" The financial planning rule of thumb is for households or families to have a contingency fund of three to six months' worth of normal running expenses to handle unexpected short-term potholes, both in income and in expenses. Arguably, the entrepreneur should have a larger contingency fund, as the potholes can be larger.

You probably have been saving over time for the purpose of starting a business. However, we realize that most are unable to accumulate much, what with the costs of buying a home, providing for college educations, and building a nest egg for retirement. We also realize that the imperative to start a business can arise suddenly from career changes, layoffs, or business ideas or opportunities that materialize rapidly. Dave Green wanted to start a photo studio eventually; he did not expect his boss to offer to sell and his opportunity arose sooner than expected. Henry Wheeler had a similar experience when the bike shop that became Wheeler Dealer was put up for sale. Nonetheless, to show good faith to other capital providers and to preserve at least some funds for these other worthy purposes, you should make a point of setting aside at least some carefully invested savings to start the business. (The meaning of "carefully invested" will be discussed further in Chapter 9.)

Friends and Family

Formally or informally, many entrepreneurs tap the resources of family members and good friends. The advantage here, of course, is that they know you and you aren't likely to disappear from their sight if they invest in your business. Generally they want you to succeed and, of course, want to profit from your success too.

Whether or not friends and family sources are good for you depends, of course, on your relationship with them. That and their personal financial objectives will determine what kind of participation they want, that is, whether they want an equity stake or to make a loan. Best of all, of course, is if a family member is willing to simply give you the funds. But if that happens, watch for strings attached and also for gift and estate tax consequences, for gifts exceeding $12,000 per year per donor and recipient may be subject to gift taxes. (See Chapter 11.)

There may be emotional complications arising from borrowing money from family members; should anything happen and you can't pay them back, it could become part of the family history, to your detriment, forever. If family members or friends are willing to lend you money, make sure you write a formal agreement and pay interest on the loan; otherwise the IRS may consider the loan a gift, which could bring adverse tax consequences. The same consequences may result if you fail to make the required payments on the loan.

Friends and family members may want to become partners in the business; however, you should do the same diligence on them as you would any other partner. Will they really contribute to the business? With effort and knowledge or just capital? Bringing a friend or relative in as partner just for his or her capital contributions can lead to the same complications as accepting a loan (except for the gift tax issues). A limited partnership, where the partner gets a stake but no decision-making powers, can be an effective solution, but it requires a well-written contract and adds to administrative work at tax time.

Finally, you can incorporate and sell shares. For many entrepreneurs, this is the best choice, for investors (shareholders) get a well-defined role in your business. They won't share your liabilities directly and their control is limited to their ownership percentage as shareholders. Some corporations may issue two classes of stock, one voting and one non-voting, to further define control. Shares are something your friends and family capitalists can buy and sell to each other, back to you, or to someone else as your corporate charter allows; many friends and family contributors take comfort in the relative solidarity of their investments. But, as examined in Chapter 4, corporate forms are more complex to set up and administer.

Retirement Savings

By the time you get around to starting your own business, you've probably worked for somebody else somewhere and built up a qualified employer-based retirement plan. The 401(k) is the most common form. If you have a 401(k), is it a good source of capital to start a business? A successful business can create a better retirement than any savings plan, but there are drawbacks to using a 401(k).

If you tap any retirement savings plan before age 59½, you'll generally incur a 10 percent penalty on the amount you take and you'll have to pay federal and state income taxes at your current rates on the amount. Keep in mind that those rates may be much higher than your ordinary rates, for a large one-time withdrawal can kick you upstairs into a higher tax bracket, a higher *marginal* rate (the percent for the portion of your income above a bracket threshold). So withdrawing funds can be very expensive. Of course, you're also losing the tax-free compounding interest on the amount that you withdraw.

Many entrepreneurs prefer the security of starting their business before they leave employment. If they remained employed and they have a 401(k) plan, they may *borrow* funds from the plan, subject to the specific rules of their employer's plan. If you're in that situation, then you should know that there are some merits to this idea. First, you don't have to convince anybody of your creditworthiness. Second, you generally are not required to pay principal, only interest on the outstanding loan balance. Third, the interest you pay on the loan is accrued to your retirement account, not going to someone else, so the net interest cost to you in the long run is zero.

There are, however, two significant downsides. First, the funds you borrow are removed from your investment pool, so you forgo tax-advantaged returns on those funds. (Actually, it should be noted that the returns are not tax-free. You pay taxes when you withdraw them during retirement, likely at lower rates. Technically, these returns are tax-*deferred*.) Second, and critical to your decision whether to borrow from your 401(k), the rules specify that any amount borrowed from a 401(k) plan must be paid back upon termination. So if you start a business and leave your employer—expectedly or unexpectedly—you will have to pay whatever you've borrowed from the 401k—when it's probably the worst time to have to pay back.

We generally do not advocate using 401(k) funds to start a business unless you can well afford to do so because you've sufficiently provided for your retirement needs. (See Chapter 10 for more about retirement needs and retirement savings.)

Home Loans and Equity Lines of Credit

If you own a home and have equity in it, that may be a good source of short-term capital to fund your business. You can borrow against this equity through either a fixed home loan or a home equity line of credit or "HELOC" for short.

A fixed loan provides a fixed amount, usually at a fixed interest rate, to be paid back within a specified period of time, usually with regular payments. A fixed home equity loan—often called a *second mortgage*—is usually a secondary loan; that is, it comes

after the primary mortgage in priority if you default on either loan.

The HELOC is a line of credit set up with a lender—a bank, a credit union, or a mortgage company. You don't actually borrow the funds when you set up the HELOC; rather, you make the funds available. You can tap them as needed, usually with a special checkbook or even a debit card. You pay interest on the outstanding balance. Most lines of credit have variable interest rates; that is, the rate is set by some standard reflecting overall long-term interest rates. Most have an annual fee of $50 or so and most have a life of five to ten years, after which they can be renegotiated. Some require principal payments; for others, payments are interest only.

What are the advantages of home loans?

First, since the loan is secured by a fixed asset, interest rates are relatively low. In contrast with the unsecured rates of 15 or 20 percent or higher for unsecured personal loans or credit cards, the rates are normally only 2 to 3 percentage points higher than long-term government bond securities. In recent years, this has meant rates between 5 and 7 percent. With variable-rate loans, like the HELOC, the interest driver is short-term interest rates, giving effective rates as low as 4 percent. These rates have risen to 7 to 8 percent recently, but are still attractive.

Second, with home loans, you retain full control of the business. There are no outside investors, relatives, or friends sharing their opinions with you and imposing their demands. Especially with the HELOC, you can borrow what you need when you need it. It's a cardinal rule of borrowing that it's harder to do when you most need to, when you're out of money or having a bad month. Home equity financing generally allows you to avoid this problem.

Of course, there are downsides.

First and foremost, you are putting your home on the line. If things really go sour in your business, you still must pay back your loan. If you don't pay, if you default, you could lose your home, a terrible price to pay for starting a business.

Second, and more subtle but also important— your home equity is a foundation block supporting your personal finances. For many, home equity is the largest asset in their personal portfolio. It can provide retirement funds. Also, if you retire without paying off your home, retirement will be harder financially. So it is important to build home equity while working; those who borrow excessively against their home will have a harder time doing so. Further, that home equity is often the best emergency reserve for personal finances—unexpected medical expenses, college education, braces for a child's teeth. Tap too far into it for business purposes and you become more vulnerable.

Securities Loans

Do you have savings invested in stocks, bonds, or other investments through a broker? It's possible to borrow against these securities by using *margin*, that is, funds borrowed from your broker. While margin interest rates are usually 2 to 3 percentage points higher than home equity loan rates, mainly because of the volatility of the underlying securing interest (your stocks), such financing can be helpful, especially for short-term needs. Of course, a downturn in the economy could hit you with a double whammy: it could reduce the value of your collateral and reduce the inflows into your business. If your equity value drops below 35 percent of the amount borrowed (this figure, known as the *minimum maintenance requirement*, can vary by broker), you might receive a *margin call*, that is, a demand from your broker to deposit more funds or else sell some or all of your investments. This can happen at the worst time, for you're least likely to have funds available from your business to pay back the loan and the prices of your investments are likely to be at their lowest.

BANKS AND BANKING

Every entrepreneur will, sooner or later and more or less, deal with a bank, both for business and personal finances. It's virtually impossible to live without a bank. Banks provide a safe repository for funds you own, a place to borrow the funds you need, and the ability to transact with your suppliers and your customers. Banks make money handling these transactions and "marking up" the funds they acquire through account deposits and from "wholesale" credit sources like the U.S. Federal Reserve. The point here is not to describe the banking system and its economic role, but to offer some pointers on how to use it to manage business and personal finances effectively.

Business and Personal Banking

You've probably noticed that banks come in all shapes and sizes, from gigantic national "money center" banks like Bank of America and Chase Manhattan to small corner banks with perhaps one, two, or three branches in your area. As banks have grown and consolidated through mergers, they have come to offer a full array of services for both business and personal finances. Before this consolidation, most banks specialized in business or commercial banking services, while many consumer-oriented services like home mortgages and savings accounts were offered through savings and loans. Today those lines have blurred; most banks offer a wide variety of consumer services. And the line between pure banking and other financial services like investments and insurance has also become blurred, as legal and regulatory barriers to an across-the-board financial smorgasbord have been removed.

Business Banking

For businesses, banks offer not only checking but an assortment of lending products and business services. Such services include merchant services like credit card processing, payroll processing, advisory services, electronic payment, and tax services.

Lending products include assortments of loans and loan types, including credit lines, equipment loans, loans for working capital and general purposes, and federally guaranteed Small Business Administration (SBA) loans.

Banks have included more and more in their business service packages, including insurance, retirement plans, and financial planning services, as illustrated by the "Small Business Financial Services and Resources" Web page of national banking power Wells Fargo & Company (*www.wellsfargo.com/biz*) (Figure 6.1).

Business Checking

Most banks oriented to business and commercial accounts offer an assortment of checking services. The choice depends on the size of your business and how many checks you write. Larger businesses may be able to take advantage of interest-bearing checking accounts, earning perhaps 1 to 2 percent if they maintain a minimum balance. Business checking accounts have a monthly fee, usually $10 to $15, and a modest per-check fee. Both fees may start to disappear if the account balance reaches specific levels or if a business purchases other services as part of a package. The choices may be complex and confusing, as again illustrated by Wells Fargo (Figure 6.2), which offers eight checking plans. Your best course of action is usually to talk with a commercial

banker; he or she can find the best fit for you after learning about your circumstances.

Business Lending

Banks are in business to make money. They do it in two ways: by charging fees for services like checking, credit card processing, and business service packages, and by lending money. In lending money, they "buy" an "inventory" of cash at low rates from depositors and wholesalers like the Federal Reserve and lend it out at higher rates. Often they are playing the "yield curve," trying to buy at lower short-term rates and lending for longer terms at higher rates. When the yield curve inverts, as it did in early 2006, that strategy backfires.

Our point here, again, is not to describe how banks make money but instead how you can use lending products to your advantage. There are four basic kinds of business loans, with many variations:

- **Revolving.** A revolving loan works like a credit line, like a HELOC as described earlier. You set up a limit up to which you can borrow at any time for any need. Interest rates are usually based on the *prime* lending rate, the rate the bank charges its best customers. You may pay prime or up to 1 or 2 percentage points above prime; the interest rates are *variable*, adjusting over time. Payment schedules vary by loan and

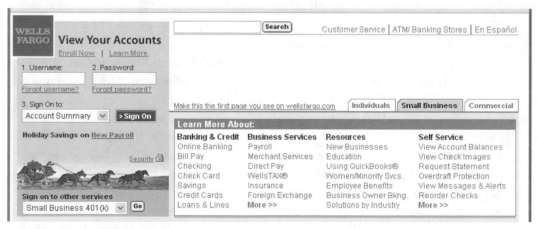

FIGURE 6.1. Wells Fargo Small Business Home Page

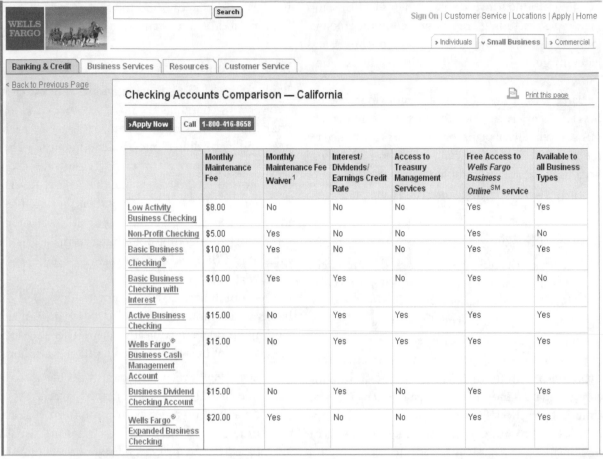

FIGURE 6.2. Wells Fargo Small Business Services Screenshot on Checking Accounts in California (www.wellsfargo.com/biz/products/accounts/checking/comp_chart)

bank. There are usually some modest fees involved to keep the line open. Small business credit lines typically vary from $10,000 to $100,000. Convenience and rapid access are the main benefits: you can write a check, use a debit card, or transfer funds by phone or online. These loans are typically used for short-term working capital requirements, like buying inventory, or for managing short-term shortfalls.

- **Equipment financing.** Equipment financing loans are designed for just this purpose—a relatively long-term loan for the purpose of buying fixed equipment or vehicles. Typically they are fixed-rate loans with a payment schedule

and often secured by the equipment being purchased, so the interest rates are lower than for unsecured loans. For convenience, business owners may prequalify for a certain amount when shopping.

- **Small Business Administration (SBA).** If you qualify, federally insured SBA loans may be right for buying large assets or even a business. The details of the SBA loan program are beyond our scope here, but generally the SBA provides a guarantee for up to 80 percent of the loan, enabling you to borrow more than you might otherwise qualify for and at lower interest rates. SBA requires good credit standing, a sound business plan, and a significant equity stake in the business, typically 25 to 50 percent. SBA loans are made by the bank, not the SBA, in amounts typically ranging from $10,000 to $500,000, although some go up to $2 million. The loans come in different forms, including basic fixed-amount loans, equipment purchase loans, and "microloans" for working capital requirements. See your bank or the SBA Web site (*www.sba.gov*) for details.

- **Signature.** If you need a fixed-term loan with predictable payments but don't want to tie up collateral, one choice—more expensive than either of the above—is a signature loan, where a fixed amount is committed to nothing but your signature (and credit history). Signature loans are best when other options don't work and are often used to buy things that don't collateralize easily, like a competing business, or to open a new location. Signature loans may also help initially if you're buying a business.

These options all vary by bank. It's a good idea to build a relationship with a bank and get familiar with its products and their costs.

Personal Banking

Personal banking services are similar to business banking, but typically the range of products and services is narrower. Most people use a bank for routine household checking and perhaps a loan for buying a car or a house. Some use a bank for savings: it is possible to get higher "money market" rates of return on deposits and, of course, to buy certificates of deposit. Many banks offer a broader assortment of personal financial planning services, like insurance, retirement planning, and estate and trust planning and management.

Shopping Your Bank

You could spend days shopping the banks in your area, large and small, for features and services to meet your business—and personal—needs. Essentially, like buying anything else, it comes down to products, features, service, and cost. Any bank decision should take into account the assortment of services offered, the price of those services, and the accessibility and helpfulness of the personnel.

Convenience is also an important factor. When you're in business, time is of the essence, and the "one-stop shop," where payroll, personal financial, merchant, loan, and transaction services are all under one roof, may be attractive, even if it is a little more expensive. Entrepreneurs can beat their brains out looking for the best deal for each part of their banking needs.

A Word—or Two—About Fees

Banks make good profits buying money at wholesale and lending it at retail. But with lower interest rates and competition from a lot of places—credit unions, brokerages, online banks, etc.—banks have had to find other ways to earn money. As a result, they are becoming more aggressive in charging fees for the services they provide, for both business and personal accounts. Here are a few to watch out for:

- **Checking account fees.** Most charge a monthly fee plus a per-check charge, which may be waived if you maintain a minimum balance. You should look carefully at what you could save; a bank that waives fees may be a good idea if your business writes a lot of checks. Also, you may be able to use business funds to waive personal checking fees and vice versa.
- **Overdraft charges.** Overdraw your account and your bank will charge you $25 or $30, in addition to a similar charge by the entity to which you wrote the check. Overdraft protection is a must, but beware of the fees that a bank charges per overdraft for protection.
- **Stop-payment fees.** If one of your suppliers

KEEPING THINGS SEPARATE—HOW AND WHY

We've discussed the "invisible wall" by which, at least to a degree, you should separate your business finances and your personal finances. In banking, most experts suggest separating business and personal checking and cash reserve accounts, even for very small businesses. We concur. There are three reasons:

- **Record-keeping.** Keeping good records for tax time and other reasons is hard enough, but it gets harder when your business expenses and the fees for Johnnie's tuba lessons move through the same accounts. It's also easier to keep track of draws and cash infusions into the business.

- **Business legitimacy.** Especially if your business is very small, the IRS may question whether you are really operating a business or just conducting a hobby. Show them your separate checking account and business loan and it should alleviate or dispel these concerns.

- **Business credibility.** Even if your business is established and/or larger, it simply looks better to suppliers, customers, and potential investors if you have a business name.

If you're really serious about your business, it's worth the $100-200 a year to get separate accounts.

doesn't deliver and you need to stop payment, you'll pay $10, $20, and maybe more to do so.

- **ATM charges.** If you use an ATM that's not part of your bank's network, you might pay that bank $2 and your bank another $2—a hefty price for a $20 withdrawal. Also watch for fees for excessive ATM withdrawals in a month and plan accordingly.

- **Savings withdrawals.** Beware of fees for excessive transfers or withdrawals from savings accounts.

- **Balance inquiries.** Some banks charge $1 for a detailed balance at an ATM. Online banking may be an alternative.

- **Online banking fees.** Banking on the Web saves time and postage. But many banks still charge exorbitant fees to pay bills online. Know how your bank handles online services.

- **Late payment fees** or other adverse consequences of not quite keeping up.

CREDIT—AND OTHER KINDS OF CARDS

Whether or not you're in business, you've almost certainly used credit cards, so we don't need an explanation here. If you are in business, you've probably received a deluge of solicitations for "business" credit cards. These cards have evolved rapidly as a convenient way for businesses to do routine procurement, manage records, and get special benefits. We'll summarize those cards as well as the ones you're likely to use in your personal finances.

Personal Cards

A credit card is really nothing more than a transaction tool, usually with an attached credit facility. They come in several flavors:

- **Major credit card.** Major credit cards come with the familiar VISA and MasterCard franchise brand names and can be issued by any bank or financial institution licensing the brand. Major credit cards are all revolving credit facilities: you run a balance and pay as much of it as you wish each month, incurring interest on average amounts outstanding if you don't pay in full. Interest rates typically run from high to exorbitant. There may be annual fees and

LARGE BANK OR SMALL?

Should you use a big multistate banking colossus like Bank of America or Wells Fargo or should you use a local institution for your business and personal accounts? It's a tough choice and a trade-off for most entrepreneurs. Large banks share their overhead among many branches and handle everything from consumer accounts to giant corporate accounts. The smaller banks, which don't have enough branches to attract many customers, are typically geared to small businesses in their area. The value proposition of a large bank is to offer a wide variety of services and handle banking needs no matter where you are. Smaller banks compete by offering you better and more personalized service. Smaller banks are likely to give more advice, be more flexible in lending, and provide a more comfortable experience in general. Banks that operate only in your city or town are likely to be more supportive of your business, for it makes them look better and—who knows?—you may become the next Procter & Gamble or Coca-Cola. New entrepreneurs may find it better to go with the local bank until the need to expand outside the area necessitates broader coverage.

Should you put your business and personal accounts at the same bank? We've seen little reason other than convenience to do so. Personal accounts are usually best at a larger bank with a broader geography, if for no other reason than to save on ATM fees when you travel. However, as commerce migrates ever more to debit cards, that advantage may go away.

there are numerous and increasingly expensive fees for late payments, exceeding credit limits, and sometimes even for help from call center agents. These cards are accepted almost anywhere for almost anything, which is one reason why you, as a business owner, should consider accepting them.

- **Debit card.** Debit cards aren't credit cards. They carry the VISA or MasterCard brand name and are almost universally accepted, but that's where the similarity ends. Debit cards are tied to an account with a balance, like a checking, savings, or brokerage account. Whenever the card is used, funds are immediately debited from that account; there's no credit, just convenience.
- **Charge card.** Charge cards are like regular credit cards, except that balances must be paid each month in full. American Express is the classic example, although lately, especially for business accounts, AMEX has programs to run balances and pay interest on them. The main draw of charge cards is convenience and usually higher credit limits. Instead of interest, they make their money by marketing other programs to you and through higher merchant fees.
- **Reward card.** Reward cards act like ordinary major credit cards, except that they accumulate airline miles or points, "cash back," or merchandise credit to reward cardholders for using them. Classic airline cards include United Mileage Plus and AA Advantage, giving thousands of miles for regular users and special benefits when used to buy airfare on that airline. The classic cash-back example is Discover, which returns in cash up to 1 percent of what you charge each year. But the interest rates are higher and the cards are not accepted everywhere. But reward cards can make a lot of sense for those who pay their balances each month.
- **Affiliate card.** Now you can get a VISA or MasterCard from Starbucks, LL Bean, or

Nordstrom, or probably your alma mater, or maybe your favorite organization—you name it. Not only do you get a cool-looking card, but you can get special offers, free shipping, free lattes, and so on.

Business Cards

It has always been possible to use a traditional credit card in a business. For years entrepreneurs have been using a mix of ordinary cards and business-oriented charge cards like American Express. Recently, as credit card issuers have broadened the search for profitable customers and as the number of small entrepreneurs has boomed, we've seen a big push into business credit cards.

Today, practically every bank and lending institution has its version of a business card with such names as "Advanta Platinum BusinessCard," "CitiBusiness Card with ThankYou Network," and "MBNA Platinum Plus Business Rewards MasterCard." These cards bundle services already available on many major credit cards but oriented more toward small business needs. Typical are discounts at office supply chains, travel service providers, and periodic special offers through the year. Most cards provide detailed quarterly and annual account statements to make it easier to track expenses and to improve accountability among employees with the cardholding organization. Higher credit limits are common. Many cards boast "small business specialists"—really a special set of agents available with shorter wait times. Most charge annual fees, up to $70 for American Express (we still don't know how the company gets away with this!), but some now are free. Interest rates are variable and often based on prime rates but typically 5 to 7 percent higher. Be sure that you'll be bombarded with all sorts of advertising related to small businesses.

Are business credit cards a good idea? It depends. They help by separating your finances and giving more detailed info about expenditures. Many small businesses use them for all procurement needs, so they have a one-stop record of what's been spent and save hours in accounts payable processing—that is, paying bills. They also help establish a credit history *for the business*. Taken together, these advantages probably outweigh the disadvantages for all but the smallest businesses.

Using Credit Cards Strategically

We've only scratched the surface in guiding you through the many choices among credit cards and advising you on those choices. Here are a few tips:

- **Use cards to manage allowances in your family.** In Chapter 5 we introduced the concept of personal and family allowances—PALs and FALs—to manage monthly discretionary expenses for family members and the family as a whole. Each family member can get his or her own major credit card (one only). Each month, the balance should be less than or equal to PAL and it should be paid off. Using the credit card improves discipline and you can call or check online for current balances. For the FAL, using a cash-reward Discover has worked very well for us, especially for home improvement, restaurants, and most travel items. The one percent back each year is free money available for a family reward.

- **Don't get too many cards.** There's more on this caution to follow, under "Managing Credit," but the point is to get the cards that you need—and no more. "Need" should be defined by the need to track something, not by the need for credit. If you have too many cards, it becomes difficult to manage them; eventually you'll find yourself in debt and with a poorer credit rating.

- **Don't fall for status.** We see it over and over. American Express Platinum. VISA Extra Super Duper Gold. Such cards are not just for buying things but also for showing others how important you are. We laugh. Sure, there may be a few extra services offered, but we see little in the way of true value for the $50, $60, $70, and more in fees charged for these "vanity" cards.

- **Get cash rewards if possible.** We love Discover. Instead of airline miles and free lattes, we get cash—hundreds each year—that we can spend anywhere. We don't understand why more people don't do this....
- **Don't borrow on cards when you can get loans.** Borrowing on credit cards pretty much guarantees the highest interest rates possible and, for your personal finances, there's no tax deduction to cushion the blow. Further, it's just too easy. When you have to walk into a

bank and talk with a loan officer, that requires at least a little discipline.

- **Use only as a convenience, to capture good deals, or for emergencies.** No need to explain this advice.

Managing Credit

It's extremely important for a business owner to build and maintain a good credit history. Why? Because sooner or later, you'll need to borrow for your business, establish credit with a vendor, or buy something important like a house or car for your family. As a business owner, your needs for credit— even if you don't borrow or otherwise use it much— are greater and more diverse than people who do not own businesses.

Credit Is Not the Same as Debt

Here we get to one of the most important lessons of personal finance, especially when a business is involved. Although the terms are often used interchangeably in conversation, *credit* is not the same as *debt*. Far from it, in fact. *Credit* is the potential to buy something; *debt* is the result of buying something but not yet having paid for it. Credit is important for personal finances and is *vital* for business finances; otherwise you won't be able to get the funds you need to grow, to establish a new supplier, or to get out of a pinch. Good credit is a necessary positive; debt is a negative to be avoided if possible.

Credit Scoring

In the old days, your credit was as good as your relationship with your local bank and banker. Your name was known to the bank and, if you were in good standing, known to the community beyond your bank. That was about all you needed until about 1960. With the broad proliferation of credit devices, including credit cards, the "nationalization" of the business landscape, and the automation of the

---

BEING A "GOOD" CREDIT CUSTOMER

If you're frugal like us, you'll stay out of debt and pay off balances each month. You'll acquire a good credit standing for yourself and your business. That's really the place to be. But realize that banks and credit card issuers are working to make money off you. You might think you're a great customer, paying off your balance each month. But if you run small balances, avoid paying interest, and demand a lot of service, you might actually find yourself on the wrong side of the eight ball.

Banks and financial services companies have very sophisticated customer-valuation programs measuring your current and potential profitability. They may not give you a break on that late payment or waive a fee when you think you deserve it if you aren't profitable for them. So it might be a good idea to run a balance on your card once in a while or to borrow some money from your bank, just to keep the relationship working for them, too. Making money is a two-way street.

financial world, the evaluation of credit has become more of a science.

Credit evaluation is now done through an automated, computerized scoring process. Scoring is done by complex algorithmic computer models evaluating and weighing your credit history, including how much credit you have, how much you've used, and how well you've managed it over time. Credit scores are widely available and used for everything from qualifying you for a loan and setting the interest rate to such seemingly unrelated things as qualifying you for life or property insurance or getting you a job. Thus credit score has evolved into a quantitative assessment and reflection of your personality and character, not just your ability to pay—much to the chagrin of many observers.

You'll read a lot in the newspapers and financial media about building and maintaining your *credit score*. America is overall a nation of debtors and the average person's ability to finance purchases is directly tied to his or her available credit. As a result, credit scores have moved out of the back room of the finance office and become essentially financial "grade point averages" for consumers. And financial institutions, eager to seize on this growing interest, have capitalized by offering a myriad of services to give you your score, provide the history behind it, and offer services to help protect or improve it.

We won't take apart these services here; a full treatment would consume most of this book and would probably change before it got published. Here we'll highlight the gold standard of personal credit scoring, the FICO score, discuss emerging business scoring tools, and give a few pointers on how to maintain and improve your score.

Your FICO Score

FICO is an acronym for Fair Isaac Corporation, a New York Stock Exchange-traded financial services company best known for its three-digit FICO scores and the scoring model that creates them. Anybody

with any credit history can get a FICO score. FICO scores take into account credit history, employment, home ownership, and other financial history.

FICO scores can be purchased directly from Fair Isaac at *www.myfico.com*, for $14.95. Included in the score is a report of all credit history used in calculating the score, which enables you to see where you've been and to make sure all reported events are accurate.

There are three primary credit service bureaus collecting, tracking, and selling your credit history to pretty much anyone who wants it, including current and prospective lenders: Experian, Equifax, and TransUnion. Credit-reporting guidelines are fairly standardized, but there are variations. And especially as identity theft is a growing problem, it's a good idea to examine this history once in a while, even if you don't know of any credit problems. We recommend obtaining your FICO score and other credit agency scores annually.

The FICO score assesses an individual's creditworthiness and likelihood to default. The scale is shown in Figure 6.3.

Naturally, it's best to have a score above 700—the higher the better. To understand why, look at how the interest rates for 30-year fixed home mortgages in Figure 6.4 vary according to FICO scores.

Score range	Percentile Ranking	Delinquency Rate
Up to 499	Lowest 1 percent	87 percent
500-549	Next 5 percent	71 percent
550-599	Next 7 percent	51 percent
600-649	Next 11 percent	31 percent
650-699	Next 16 percent	15 percent
700-749	Next 20 percent	5 percent
750-799	Next 29 percent	2 percent
800 and above	Top 11 percent	1 percent

FIGURE 6.3. FICO Score Ranges

FICO Score Range	30-Year Mortgage Rate
760-850	6.01%
700-759	6.23%
680-699	6.41%
660-679	6.62%
640-659	7.05%
620-639	7.6%

FIGURE 6.4. Effects of FICO Score on Borrowing Rates

Improving Your Personal Credit Score

It's probably obvious that the best way to improve your credit score is to use and manage credit wisely, that is, pay your bills on time and don't borrow too much. But there is more to it than that, as the complex FICO algorithm considers a lot of things. Here are a few tips:

- **Keep debt ratios low.** Reduce debt loads so that monthly debt service, including home mortgages, car loans, etc., is less than 30 percent of your gross income.
- **Don't apply for credit cards**—unless you have a good reason to. Any application will cause a flag on your credit history; too many in too short of time will penalize you. Even if you cancel an old one, it still counts.
- **Don't cancel old accounts too soon.** Having old accounts in good standing can help.
- **Sign up for automated bill payment**—an additional sign of financial security and responsibility.
- **Identify mistakes and correct errors.** During your annual review, take the necessary steps to right any wrongs. Statistics show one in four credit reports has an error.

Remember that more is at stake here for business owners. Credit isn't just for buying clothes or a car—it may be necessary to keep the business going.

SCORES FOR FREE?

A lot of press was given in 2005 to a new law, the Fair and Accurate Credit Transactions (FACT) Act. One key provision was allowing customers to get a free credit report once every 12 months from one of the three credit service bureaus—Experian, Equifax, or TransUnion. We applaud the intent of Congress, but our legislators neglected to stipulate that the credit report should come with a FICO credit score. So it doesn't. Yes, you can get a credit report—the detail—for free, but with no score, so you don't really know where you stand. As fortune and the American Way would have it, the service bureaus are glad to provide your score—for an additional charge. (This charge cannot exceed $8 in California. There are similar laws in other states.)

As you're bound to notice if you go to MyFICO.com or any of the credit service bureaus, providing credit information and a vast assortment of credit "repair kits" and "protection plans" is big, big business for these companies. Suze Orman has a FICO kit and so does just about everyone else. The best "repair" is prevention—pay your bills on time and don't overuse your credit and you'll never need any of this stuff.

Business Credit Scores

If you are a typical non-corporate small business, your business credit score is for all intents and purposes the same as your personal credit score. If you go to borrow money to buy a piece of equipment for your construction business, the lender will start with your personal credit score and history. Some lenders will look at the cash flow you receive from the business as part of your income, but generally, it is you, not your business, applying for the loan. Similarly, if you are buying something for yourself

▼ DOES LOWER DEBT BRING HIGHER FICO SCORES?

In case you're curious, according to a study released by service bureau Experian, Inc., the average U.S. consumer debt in 2006 was $11,225. Here's the interesting part: 25 percent of people in this country have debt exceeding that amount and have an average FICO score of 695. The average FICO score for the 75 percent who owed less than that average amount was 671. So the point made by Experian is that using debt doesn't necessarily hurt your score—if you use it correctly. Or is it a chicken-and-egg question—the people with the lower scores couldn't get the credit to go into debt? We think it might be the latter.

personally, such as a new home, the income you earn from your business will be considered, but most lenders will not look too deeply at the credit-worthiness or profitability of that business.

For corporations, including LLCs, it's a different matter. They have separate taxpayer IDs and exist as separate legal entities. As such, business credit bureaus can monitor their transaction, payment, and borrowing history as well as their *trade credit* (credit given by other businesses) and establish a *business credit score*. Service bureaus include the aforementioned Equifax and Experian plus Dun & Bradstreet and Credit.net (formerly Business Credit USA). Business credit scores range from 0 to 100.

The problem is that, while this history can be tracked, there is no requirement to do so. Credit bureaus may not receive all or even *any* information about your corporation's transactions. As a result, a lender will either ask you to justify credit based on your corporation's financial merits, a painstaking task, or (more often) ask you as principal owner to cosign the loan.

Thus it's smart to establish a good credit history for your corporation, to effectively complete the separation between its finances and yours. Experts suggest these three actions: register your corporation with all credit service bureaus; get all licenses, phone lines, and other services in the corporation's name; and borrow and use trade financing actively in daily business (as it makes sense, of course).

OTHER CAPITAL SOURCES

Entrepreneurs aren't limited just to their own capital resources and borrowings to finance their businesses. If that were the case, many would be stranded with a good idea, a business plan, and no business. Even if they managed to get started, they would face additional hurdles ahead in finding the necessary capital—for fixed assets and working capital—to finance growth. If you have a good enough business plan, you should be able to attract capital from others, either as active partners or as more passive investors. Additionally, in the course of business you will buy many goods and services from others—companies that also want to develop and may help you through various forms of vendor financing. Never say "never."

Partners

As introduced in Chapter 4, partners are usually brought in to help fund the business, to share the workload, and to contribute needed skills, talent, and expertise. You can structure your partnership and the partner responsibilities evenly or any way you agree to do it. You can bring in limited partners principally as investors, with no active role or shared liability in the enterprise.

It is said that a partnership is the closest thing in business to a marriage. All must agree and there is the same sort of give-and-take you might find in a domestic setting. Partners are also more likely to be familiar with each other's personal finances, and maybe even involved in them, since trouble there spells trouble for the business and, ultimately, for the partners. Partnerships work best if the partners are good friends with common goals and interests, who would do things together even if they didn't have a business. A partnership based on common goals and interests and a well-written partnership document can provide the capital and stability you need, so long as you can deal with liability protection and other issues.

Venture Capital

Brought into the limelight during the dotcom boom of the late 1990s, venture capitalists have always been around but more in a background role. Venture capitalists (VCs) are private investors looking for a high return on some portion of their holdings. They usually work with placement firms (sometimes also called venture capitalists) that match investors with attractive business investments. In short, VCs are looking for an ownership stake in "the next big thing." They would like to get in on the ground floor of a strong business model, usually a new idea or strong niche in a good market. Occasionally they are also looking to take advantage of start-up losses for tax reasons.

If you're opening an espresso stand or a bike shop, you aren't likely to attract much VC interest, but if you have a new drink formulation or a new bike accessory, that might be a different matter. If you're in this latter category, it might be worth your while to network with a VC firm in your area. Your business plan and your ability to present it must be razor sharp. Be advised that most VCs are looking for exceptional returns on their investment, but some are also looking for a degree of control in your business.

Vendor Financing

Vendors aren't going to write you a check to help you start a business, but they may offer a lot of help financing certain parts of it. You can use trade credit—the normal "on account" business—to finance at least some working capital, as Dell has so famously done. (See sidebar at the beginning of this chapter.) But if you're buying equipment for your business, especially during weak economic times, you'd be surprised at what your vendors might do for you. Just as auto dealers advertise "zero percent financing" to get consumers into their showrooms and then into their vehicles, you can get similar packages on a vast assortment of big-ticket items for your business. Maybe you need a backhoe or a bulldozer for your business. t would be great to get zero percent for three years from Caterpillar, with an assortment of accessories thrown in. Remember: these suppliers want to help you, because to them you're worth business and good references down the road.

Leasing

The decision of whether to buy or lease will come up from time to time, mainly with vehicles but sometimes with other business assets. Leasing is basically a form of financing, usually for a new model of an asset: you make regular payments during the lease period and then turn in the asset at the end of a few years. At turn-in you may get an option to buy the asset for a predetermined price.

For personal assets, leasing is usually more expensive financing, as you are left with nothing at the end of the lease cycle; you have to start all over again. Additionally, there may be other catches, such as when you lease a car and must pay expensive mileage penalties for miles driven beyond the contracted amount. You still have to pay taxes and other operating expenses for most leased assets. Leases may help improve your personal balance sheet—and your credit rating—if you're in a situation where your personal finances are likely to be on the line for more credit-based purchases. Personal leases make the most sense when you know your needs are going to change, e.g., you need a minivan for your kids in three years or you need a new car to impress real estate clients.

For a business, leasing can make sense for assets needed for only a short time but also for tax reasons and to give a better impression of financial health. Corporations in a relatively high tax bracket can write off lease payments; it's simpler and often more tax efficient than capitalizing a purchased asset and depreciating it, especially for expensive assets. (Note: special rules apply for automobiles. See next chapter.) Also, the IRS doesn't consider most leases to be purchases but rather as overhead expenses, so leases don't hit the business balance sheet as long-term liabilities but instead flow through the income statement as periodic expenses. On the other hand, if your business is not a corporation, leasing certain qualifying asset may cause you to lose the lucrative Section 179 asset-expensing provision. Our advice: read the next chapter and check with your accountant before deciding to lease assets for your business.

PART III

Building Long-Term Wealth

CHAPTER 7

Keep It: How to Turn More of What You Earn into Wealth

EVERY ENTREPRENEUR HAS DONE IT—AND more than once. Left money on the table. Gave away the store to avoid a customer conflict. Made a Hail Mary desperation maneuver to make the sale and feel better about an otherwise lousy day. Bid too low on a job just to get that customer and because things were slow that week. Or threw in some extra accessories or services the customer would have bought anyway just to ice the deal. These things happen all the time: they're a natural part of the landscape of doing business. You can't predict the future and you don't know what a customer would have been willing to pay.

There is nothing quite like that queasy feeling you get when the customer leaves the store or signs the deal. Did I do it again? Could I have gotten an extra 5 or 10 percent out of this deal? Will I set a precedent so nobody else will be willing to pay my price? You don't quite know. While the feeling strengthens your resolve to avoid doing it again, sooner or later another set of circumstances will cause you again to leave trade cash on the table.

IT'S WHAT YOU *KEEP* THAT COUNTS

Entrepreneurs lose sleep nightly over whether or not they could have squeezed a few more dollars out of their business. While it's important for every entrepreneur to learn to maximize business revenue—and develop the discipline to do so—our focus shifts to the back end, what you *keep* from what you take at the cash register.

It hurts to sell a lot and succeed in your marketplace, work hard to become efficient, and then watch it all go out the window to taxes and/or poor cash management. It happens all the time. Hard-earned cash falls through the cracks or is swept into federal and state coffers. Entrepreneurs work their tails off to bring as much money as possible into the business, only to leave some on the table—or with the IRS—when bringing it home into their personal finances.

This chapter is not so much about business profitability and efficiency, including expense control, but about "bringing it home." Here, we catalog some of the many techniques used by entrepreneurs—and their accountants—to reduce the tax bite. The goal is to leave less money on the table for the taxing authorities. Effective tax planning *legally* reduces taxes and, in some cases, works backwards to influence the operational and financial decisions you'll make in the business. In this chapter, you will not learn about the entire tax system but rather how to use the tax system strategically to guide business and financial decisions so you get the most out of what you make.

BASIC AND ADVANCED TECHNIQUES

Some tax-planning techniques are simple and straightforward, while others are enormously complex, to the point of confounding tax professionals and even IRS agents. (Remember: the IRS *enforces* but does not *create* tax law!) We've divided tax-planning techniques into "basic" and "advanced" and grouped them accordingly in what follows.

Basic tax planning typically involves simple business expense transactions. Most of the items that follow involve fairly mechanical, "black and white" expensing of business items as allowed by the Internal Revenue Code. Often these are a matter of good record-keeping and expense recording as much as anything else, but some creativity can be applied in some expense categories. You're probably familiar with most basic expense deductions, but it doesn't hurt to review the list, for they do get missed, even by eagle-eyed accountants and entrepreneurs. Along the way we'll develop a better understanding and knowledge of what makes an expense deductible, for it isn't only a matter of lists but also making judgment calls in the ordinary course of business.

Advanced techniques involve retirement planning, benefits, and income-splitting techniques. We'll cover advanced planning techniques later in the chapter.

THE BASICS: OPERATING EXPENSES

Spend money in your business—or *on* your business—and you can write it off. Well, this is *almost* true. It's a good first thought, anyway. Dollars spent as valid business expenses usually can be written off,

effectively saving taxes at your marginal federal, self-employment (if applicable), state, and local rates. Spend a dollar on office supplies and save 45 cents, if the combined marginal tax rates are at that level. Your net cost is 55 cents. Not free, but a lot better than paying the full buck.

Not surprisingly, Congress didn't make it quite *that* simple. Buy an asset like a vehicle for the business and deduct $25,000 against this year's income? Probably not—but there are exceptions. That asset will be used over a period of years in your business, so the expense must be deducted in increments over its lifetime. Such assets are known as *capital* assets. And can you deduct a $200 dinner intended to convince a client to buy a $150 portrait? No. First, by law you can deduct only 50 percent of entertainment expenses. Second, such an expense is probably outside the realm of what Congress thinks is reasonable to attract that piece of business. Likewise, Congress doesn't want you to deduct all upfront costs of investigating a business before starting it or acquiring it. So, while many of these expenses are basic, it helps to know the rules.

What Makes an Expense Deductible

It may seem elementary: write a check, especially on a business account, and file the stub in a drawer or expense file for bookkeeping. The Internal Revenue Code considers just about any expense used to produce income as deductible. Oh, if it were only that simple. Most legitimate expenditures can be deducted, but there are a lot of rules. These rules are especially for the big-ticket items like vehicles and other that cross over into the personal financial space. Expenses that can look more like personal than business expenses—like travel, meals, and entertainment—have a number of conditions and get a lot of scrutiny.

As interpreted from the Code, the following general principles apply to any expense to be considered deductible:

- **Ordinary and Necessary.** The Code doesn't define this expression but leaves it mainly to common sense. If an expense is related to a typical or justifiable business practice required to produce income, it's OK. A country club membership isn't typical or justifiable to run a coffee cart business. (And it's specifically excluded by rule.) Nor is flying to the big island of Hawaii to examine coffee plantations—unless some specific business transaction is made requiring your presence.

- **Not Extravagant.** Your trip to Hawaii probably isn't a justifiable expense even if you bring back a couple of bags of coffee. Extravagance, like necessity, is also an exercise in common sense. The Code frowns on "lavish and extravagant" expenses, but doesn't define exactly what that label means.

- **Not Personal.** Here's where entrepreneurs are most likely to cross the line—and where the IRS does a whole lot of probing. Is the trip to Hawaii really a personal endeavor? It's sure going to look like it, so you better have a substantial business reason behind it to write it off, and you had better do business most of the time on the trip if you want to write it *all* off. The Hawaii example is a clear-cut red flag for the IRS, but that doesn't mean you should not do it if you really think it's justified. A great many other expenses fall into gray areas. Dinner with your business partners? Company parties? A digital camera or computer to use for family and business purposes? As we'll see, there are some opportunities for creativity. Some items that seem personal, like an on-facility exercise room, may actually be deductible.

These qualifiers are not intended to discourage you from taking *legitimate* write-offs. We've seen many an entrepreneur avoid expensing legitimate items for fear of waking the sleeping IRS tiger—and leave a lot of cash on the table. If your expense is legitimate, deduct it! If you go to dinner with a business partner and discuss *business*—business *strategy* or a hiring decision or an important business purchase, not just what it would take to make another $10 sale—it's probably OK to consider $100—plus tip as a business expense. Just document what you talked about, why and with whom, on the receipt if possible, and put it in the drawer for your accountant. If you can tell a friend or acquaintance about it without smiling or laughing, you can probably tell the IRS too and they will find it acceptable.

Capital vs. Operating Expenses

The goal of taxing authorities is to measure true earned income, to the extent possible. That means they want to time the accounting of a cash outlay with the use of the proceeds of that outlay, to the extent possible. That is, if the expense produces something you need this year to run your business, then it makes sense to recognize that expense this year. If the outlay buys something used in business over a five-year period, then it makes sense to allocate or prorate the outlay over that period. If the cash outlay is used to buy inventory to resell, it follows to recognize the expense at the time the corresponding revenue is produced—that is, at the time of sale.

So tax rules—and the accounting processes that support them—are designed to *time* expenses, and thus deductions, to match the business activity they support. They don't necessarily match the actual cash outlay, even if you run your business on a cash basis. In a cash-basis business, most transactions are recorded as the check is written, not as the event occurs. But that distinction affects only current expenses, that is, expenses for items consumed immediately, items with a useful life of one year or less. Items with a useful life of one year or more are *capital expenses*, expenses incurred to buy *capital assets*.

Capital expenses include such items as vehicles, equipment, buildings, and other, usually tangible assets with more than one year of useful life. Capital expenses include not only what is spent to acquire these items but also what is spent to substantially improve them or prolong their lives. Put a new electrical panel or a new break room in your business facility and the expense will normally be *capitalized*.

So in our quest to minimize the tax bite, we search for deductible expenses, especially those that we can deduct immediately. We also look at capital items for how large a deduction they will produce this year and for each year over their useful lives. Capital items are expensed each year through depreciation deductions. Accountants call this *asset recovery:* how much of asset's value will be *recovered*, or accounted for, each year in the income statement. Asset recovery through depreciation and the accelerated Section 179 expensing provision so beneficial for small entrepreneurs will be covered in the chapter.

BUSINESS START-UP COSTS

There is considerable confusion over *which* start-up expenses can be deducted and *when*. It would seem that Congress intends to make it as easy as possible to get into business. There's the Small Business Administration and the assortment of SBA loans. There are write-offs for operating losses and immediate deductions for many business assets through Section 179 expensing, which we'll get to shortly. You might think Congress would go the rest of the way and make pre-start-up expenses—like investigation and research, business plan development, and assets acquired in preparation for start-up—deductible.

Wrong. Apparently, the U.S. Treasury has been burned enough by dreamers stuck indefinitely in that "I'm going to do it someday" stage that they've wised up and made business expenses deductible only for businesses that actually exist. And at that, expenses exceeding a rather modest amount, $5,000, must be capitalized and amortized over 15 years. And if your start-up costs exceed $50,000, your $5,000 deduction is decremented by the amount your expenses exceed $50,000. So even if

you've decided for sure to take the plunge, be careful. You may also choose not to deduct start-up costs but rather include them in the cost basis of the business, which comes into play only when you sell it. Recently, Congress added another break for the expenses of organizing a business to counter the high legal and administrative costs of formally organizing a business. Legal fees, costs of drawing up contracts and agreements, and state and local filing costs can be deducted for corporations (C and S), partnerships, and LLCs. IRS Publication 535, *Business Expenses*, is a good source of additional information.

Investigation Expenses

Investigation expenses are incurred to determine the feasibility of entering into business or expanding a one. Such costs include travel, industry, business and market research, and professional fees related to evaluating the business. The tax treatment depends on what business the entrepreneur is already in, if any, the nature of the business being investigated, and whether or not the acquisition or start-up actually happens. Here are some guiding principles:

- **Already in the business.** If the taxpayer is already in the same business or a similar business, all expenses (even above the $5,000 limit) are deductible in the current year for the existing business. So when Henry Wheeler investigated buying the competing bike shop across town, those expenses were fully deductible.
- **Not in the business already, buys or starts investigated business.** Such expenses must be treated as above, i.e., as a new business with the applicable $5,000 limit or fully capitalizing the expenditures.
- **Not in business already and does not buy or acquire investigated business.** These expenses are not deductible in any business, but may be deductible personally as investment expenses subject to the 2 percent AGI floor. (See Chapter 3.)

CURRENT OPERATING EXPENSES

Current operating expenses are, as the name indicates, deductible against business income during the current year. Such expenses are incurred during the normal course of business during the year and are deducted on Schedule C for sole proprietorships, Schedules 1120C or S for corporations, and Form 1065 for partnerships and LLCs. For all business forms except C corporations, these expenses carry over directly into your personal taxes.

We explained capital expenses above as outlays for items having a useful life of more than one year. Occasionally the line between current and capital expenses is fuzzy, as when costs are incurred to repair or improve a capital asset. If the expenditure adds to the asset's value, substantially lengthens its useful life, or repurposes the asset for a different use, it must be capitalized and recognized over the asset's remaining life. Routine maintenance expenses or supplies, just to keep a piece of equipment running, however, can be written off immediately.

Normal Overhead

The largest category of operating expenses, for most businesses, is normal overhead expenses—expenses simply to keep the business and business facility running. Monthly rent, lease, utilities, and normal operating supplies like cleaning materials are ordinary expenses, as are services like cleaning, landscape maintenance, or pest control. The costs of Internet service, including broadband, should be deducted. With the exception of repair or improvement expenses as mentioned above, normal overhead expenses are straightforward and require little further comment, except that, of course, it is important to keep track of them.

Marketing Costs

Like overhead, marketing costs are straightforward and include such items as advertising, publicity, and

▼ **OUT OF THE CLOSET: HOME OFFICE DEDUCTIONS**

Home office deductions are more complicated. Your home is not 100 percent a place to do business. Typically, the formula is to take all home operating and maintenance expenses—utilities, insurance, taxes, interest, maintenance and repairs, and so on—and allocate expenses to the business based on the percentage of floor space used exclusively for the business. Be inclusive: bookshelf or closet space used for business storage can also be included. The IRS is quite specific about expensing only the business proration of basic telephone service, but additional lines, specific business-related long distance calls, and services like voice mail are fully deductible.

printed collateral (brochures, etc.). Many businesses include the cost of Web sites and Web site development in their marketing expenses. The cost of yellow page ads, Web addresses, and other "handles" are also marketing costs. The cost of sponsoring local community activities, like sports teams, can also be included.

Most deductions are basic, but there are ways to extend deductions. For example, if you put your company logo on a shirt, a jacket, or a pair of sweatpants, that is considered a promotional expense, whether you wear it yourself or give it away. Within reason, you can wear logo clothing most of the time and write off most of your clothing. But don't get carried away—if you deduct logo clothing for your entire family, the IRS might frown upon it. And don't try to write off personal parties as promotional or marketing expenses; sure, there may be a potential client or customer there, but the reason is primarily personal.

▼ DON'T FORGET ABOUT SAMPLES

Samples and other giveaways are also part of marketing. Be careful not to overlook these items. If your company produces 100 bars of gift soap, sells 95 and gives five away, it's easy to miss the cost of the five bars. Your accounting system will log the cost of goods sold for the 95 sold, but without a specific transaction to expense the five samples, you may fail to deduct the production cost as a promotion or marketing expense.

▼ SHARPENING THE PENCIL

Business owners get very good, after a while, and with the help of tax pros, at recognizing research and finding ways to deduct it. Like most other categories, there needs to be a connection to the business; the research should somehow improve the business or your ability to conduct it. If you have sound rationale and your deduction passes the "smell test" or the laughter test, then you have a good chance of being able to deduct it. The research event or acquisition must be both pertinent to the business and in reasonable scale to the need. Don't deduct the cost of a Disneyland trip to "research the use of color in clothing." Always remember that the IRS is looking for outright evasion, not avoidance of taxes. If you deduct expenses like research and the IRS disallows them, you may have to pay taxes due with penalties, but it's highly unlikely you'll be held criminally liable or face jail time.

Professional and Contractor Fees

Professional fees include sums paid to companies that help you produce your product or service and to accountants and attorneys who help you run your business. If you hire a writer or illustrator to perform a specific task, that expense usually is recognized as a contractor fee. If the cost is attributable to running the business itself, it goes into the "Professional and Legal Fees" line of the tax return.

Professional fees can also include amounts spent for trade association membership, trade show attendance, and subscriptions to trade-related publications. Alternatively, you can write these items off as "research."

Research

Depending on your business, it may be possible to deduct certain amounts spent for research. Research includes materials designed to help you, your partners, or your employees learn more about your business and how to conduct it. If you're a financial services professional, amounts spent for *Wall Street Journal* subscriptions, books, magazines, newsletters, investment research, and so forth would be clear-cut deductions. Dave Green of DG Photo can write off amounts spent for photo magazines or to attend a photo workshop; Henry Wheeler can write off the cost of bicycle industry trade publications, although the trip to Moab, Utah to test-ride a bike under field conditions might not fly. Field research may well be valid, however. If you're writing a book about personal health or spa treatments, an afternoon in a spa is probably deductible—but not three afternoons in a row! Research can also include market research, either done directly as studies for you or purchased outside, but you may expense it under "Marketing" instead. The cost of an experiment, such as selling bicycles on eBay, could also be deducted as research.

Education

Education expenses may be deducted from your business if they specifically maintain or improve skills required in your work or if they are required by law. So a three-day course on studio lighting would be deductible for DG Photo but not for MicroMetal Precision. Note that educational expenses incurred to qualify you for a new business are *not* deductible as business expenses.

There is a broad assortment of education deductions and credits available for *personal* education, including the Hope Scholarship and Lifetime Learning Credits, tuition deductions, and interest on student loans. These programs cover you *and* members of your family and are subject to income ceilings and other conditions. They are intended to *help* you pay for an advanced education, not cover the whole cost.

There is a degree of irony in these assorted educational tax "boosts": you virtually need a college education to understand them! It usually makes sense to deduct business-related education at the business level to save self-employment taxes. But when no other family members or relatively small costs are involved, the Hope Scholarship and Lifetime Learning Credits may work better because they are credits, not deductions. (Educational tax incentives are further detailed in Chapter 10.)

Insurance

All insurance costs related to the business are deductible as ordinary expenses except insurance targeted toward personal well-being, like health or disability insurance. Health insurance is handled separately as a tax item under employee benefits. Business insurance, casualty and loss insurance, and property insurance are all handled as ordinary expenses. For home offices, property insurance is prorated by percentage of use.

Health insurance for business owners is fully deductible on their personal returns; however, there are some notable restrictions:

- The amount paid cannot exceed the net profit of the business.

- Business owners must not be eligible for insurance coverage provided by an employer or through their spouse.

Travel

The expensing of travel opens up some useful tax-planning possibilities. Generally, all transportation, lodging, and incidental expenses related to business travel are fully and currently deductible. Meals and entertainment expense deductions, as we'll see below, are capped at 50 percent of the actual expense.

Travel gets interesting because it is common to mix business and personal travel interests. There are also different ways to handle the expenses. The IRS lets you deduct actual expenses or so-called per diem expenses to cover meals and incidentals. (See IRS Publication 463, *Travel, Entertainment, Gift, and Car Expenses*.)

Travel done as research is generally not deductible—unless you are producing something directly related to that travel. If you write travel books or provide relocation advice, travel to places covered in your profession is deductible.

Travel expenses incurred to attend something directly related to your business or profession are deductible. If you're a professional photographer and travel to a photography trade show, that travel is generally deductible, but if you own a bike shop, the connection would not be strong enough to deduct the expense. Travel incurred for education, where it can be shown that no similar education was available locally, is deductible.

It gets trickier when business and personal travel are mixed together. Generally, a trip *within the United States* must be more than 50 percent business, as determined by the number of days of business-related activity, to deduct transportation costs. You can, of course, deduct specific expenses related to those days on which business is conducted, even if you cannot deduct the transportation cost. So if you fly to Las Vegas for a week to attend a relevant convention for two days, you can write off the costs of those two days (lodging, meals, etc.) but not the airfare.

When traveling *outside the United States*, different rules apply. Transportation costs can be allocated between business and personal time if the trip is for more than one week and more than 25 percent of the time was spent for business. So you could go to Europe for ten days, spend four of them attending a convention, and deduct 40 percent of transportation costs, as well as actual outlays for the business days. Finally, if less than 25 percent of the time is spent on personal items, *all* travel expenses are deductible. If you are attending a convention, the IRS may want you to substantiate that you couldn't have attended substantially the same convention or meeting inside the United States.

Traveling with companions, including spouses, also brings opportunity with complexity. Travel expenses for a companion can be deducted if you meet these three conditions: if the companion is a business partner, employee, client, supplier, or agent with whom you regularly do business; if the travel has an inherent business purpose; and if you would otherwise qualify to deduct travel expenses. So you cannot bring your spouse and deduct the cost just so he or she can iron your clothes and help you stay organized. But if your spouse has a distinct business purpose in transacting commerce and/or attending trade shows or educational events, defined by his or her role in the business, the costs are probably deductible. Of course, costs incurred for shared hotel rooms, rental cars, etc. are fully deductible— you would have incurred these costs anyway.

The result: many entrepreneurs learn the ropes of mixing business and pleasure travel. Plan carefully and you can write off substantial portions of family travel expenses.

Meals and Entertainment

The main thing to remember about meals and entertainment (M&E) is that only 50 percent of the

> ### ▼ TRAVELING SPOUSES
>
> There may be a long list of good reasons to bring a spouse into a business, either as an employee or as a partner. One is travel: if the spouse is employed or set up as a full partner or owner in a business, it is much easier to deduct travel costs for the spouse.

expenditure is deductible. The IRS rationale is that you would have had to eat something anyway, whether on business or not. Unfortunately, the rule extends to meals prepared in your home for clients, employees, et al; even though you add value in the form of labor, the IRS still doesn't recognize that and allows only 50 percent of the cost of the food. There also must be some business purpose in the meal and entertainment and it must be in scale to the business being transacted. So you can't book a $500 trip in a fighter jet as a reward for your top coffee cart client and hope to write it off. The rules are tight. There aren't many tax-planning opportunities in M&E, other than to document and remember to write off what is legitimate.

Vehicle Use

Vehicles are expensive to own and to use. Their treatment within a small business can bring interesting planning opportunities, particularly where a vehicle is used jointly for personal and business purposes. Regardless of how you choose to expense vehicle costs, you must keep good records of both actual costs or mileage and the percent of mileage used for business purposes and not personal. You should record the trip date, destination, mileage, and purpose.

The tax code allows for one of two approaches to recognizing vehicle costs:

Standard Mileage Method. The simplest approach,

standard mileage allows you to deduct an IRS-specified per-mile rate for every *business* mile driven. In 2006, the rate is 44.5 cents per mile. You simply multiply your mileage by this rate and deduct the result.

The mileage rate is inclusive of *all* vehicle-related *operating* expenses, including gasoline, gas taxes, repairs, maintenance, insurance, and the cost of the vehicle. You may not deduct depreciation, the cost of new tires, or any other vehicle-related expense, but you may deduct additional *trip* expenses, like tolls and parking and any taxes and fees paid on the vehicle, such as registration and *ad valorem* (property) taxes.

The mileage rate works best for older vehicles, for which most depreciation has already been taken, and for fuel-efficient vehicles. Ostensibly, it doesn't really *cost* 44.5 cents per mile to operate these vehicles. The mileage method cannot be used when actual cost deductions have already been taken on the vehicle, including Section 179 special business asset expensing.

MAKING THE MOST OF 44.5 CENTS PER MILE

Discipline and creativity enter into making the mileage approach work for you. Smart entrepreneurs learn to bundle trips together to include some part with a business purpose. If you're headed to the grocery, a stop at the post office (for business) makes that trip deductible. If you're taking your kid to a Saturday soccer game, stop at the office supply store for that ink cartridge and that trip is deductible (at least for the round-trip mileage between your home and the store). If you're planning a family trip to Disneyland, Schedule a legitimate meeting with an LA-area client and write off the trip mileage for your family. You get the idea.

Actual Expense Method. This method, not surprisingly, requires you to record all actual vehicle expenses. Keep receipts for fuel, repairs, insurance, taxes, car washing, and similar expenses. To this list, add depreciation expenses, which are governed by a fixed and rather stingy IRS schedule (spelled out shortly below, under "Depreciation for Vehicles"). Percentage of use comes into play. Total expenses are prorated according to business and personal miles, once tallied.

The actual expense method is better when actual vehicle operating costs are substantial, typically the case with larger, more expensive, newer vehicles that consume a lot of fuel. Actual expense methods are also required for businesses operating multiple vehicles, i.e., a fleet.

Interest Costs

Interest costs for items purchased for business are in almost all cases deductible. The major planning opportunities arise in deciding, where given a choice, whether to finance a business or a personal asset and in the business use of a home.

Most personal interest, other than interest on a home mortgage, is not deductible. So it can make sense to borrow to purchase business assets and to use cash savings to purchase personal assets. This is especially true if business borrowing rates are lower than personal borrowing rates, which is quite often the case, especially when personal credit cards are the borrowing vehicle for personal items. The caveat: don't take too much cash out of the business to buy personal things or you may end up with insufficient cash or working capital in the business. Such shortfalls are hard to fix with that big-screen TV you just bought.

Mortgage interest on a home is deductible for personal income taxes. But to the extent you use the home for business, the mortgage interest can be written off against the business. If you can lower taxable business income, you can save not only on income tax but also on self-employment tax.

Taxes

Tax planning is, of course, the primary subject of this chapter. What we're talking about in this section is paying certain taxes to other authorities besides the federal government and the deductibility of those taxes.

Tax-planning opportunities for entrepreneurs arise from items like property taxes. Most jurisdictions bill twice a year for these taxes. There's flexibility in when you actually pay those bills, subject to established guidelines. If you're having a particularly good year, you can pay taxes early to get the most from the deduction—either for the business or for your personal property taxes. It may also be possible to time state and local income tax payments advantageously.

Careful capital gains tax planning is also important. Recent legislation has capped capital gains tax rates at 15 percent for *long-term* (greater than one year) normal capital gains, for investments and other normal capital assets. The cap doesn't apply to short-term gains or to depreciation recaptured by selling an asset for a price higher than book value.

Corporations enjoy no preferential capital gains tax rates, so if you're buying an asset with considerable opportunity for appreciation, like real estate, it might make sense to buy it in your own name (or through a separate partnership) and lease it to the corporation. Of course, there are other considerations, like whether you can afford or finance the asset personally. Most owners can't afford factories and it's easier for a performing corporation to attract lending capital. And the potential to reduce *corporate* income through acquisition and maintenance costs may outweigh the capital gains consideration; it requires careful tax scenario planning and a professional tax advisor will be helpful.

Sales, employment, property, excise, and fuel taxes are generally deductible. However, sales taxes on long-term capital assets cannot be expensed immediately but instead must be added to the cost basis and written off over time. Individuals cannot generally deduct sales taxes; however, recent legislation allows a *choice* between deducting sales and state and local income taxes. For most individuals, deducting income taxes is better—unless you live in Alaska, Florida, Nevada, South Dakota, Texas, Washington, or Wyoming, which have no income tax, or in New Hampshire or Tennessee, which tax only dividends and interest income. Aside from these states, the ability to deduct sales taxes in the business may motivate you to own assets like vehicles through the business. Finally, in a year with lean business profits, it might make more sense to deduct sales taxes.

Bad Debts

Every business has debts it can't collect on, sooner or later, although expanded use of credit cards has reduced that risk for most small businesses. These are some rules to be aware of:

- **Value of services cannot be deducted.** If you perform a service and the customer doesn't pay, you cannot deduct the value of the service.
- **Foregone profits can't be deducted.** If you sell something for $250 with a $100 profit margin and the customer doesn't pay, you can only deduct the $150 cost.
- **Bad loans must be legitimate business loans** and you must make some effort to collect.

As a matter of common sense, businesses run on a cash basis cannot deduct bad debts; there is no account receivable created nor any income recorded in the first place. *Business* bad debts, subject to the above rules, can be deducted in full during the year incurred. *Personal* bad debts are deductible, but are treated as short-term capital losses and thus subject to a $3,000-per-year maximum. It makes sense to shift bad debt exposure to the business wherever you can to get the full deduction and save self-employment taxes. But you can't use the business to loan $4,000 to your uncle to buy a car and expect to write it off against the business:

it's not a legitimate business loan.

Employee Benefits and Retirement Plans

Businesses get to deduct the full amount paid to purchase employee benefits or to fund retirement plans, both for employees and for you as an employee/owner. Retirement plans in particular are a big-ticket tax-saving opportunity and are covered further later in this chapter and in more detail in Chapter 10.

Gifts

You can give any gift you want to anyone and it is fully deductible up to a maximum of $25 per recipient per year. This is a rather stingy limit, but you should keep this deduction in mind at holiday gift-giving time. The $25 represents the value of the item itself, not the shipping, packaging, or wrapping, so you may be able to deduct a little more. Some day Congress will update this deduction to reflect current reality.

ADVANCED TOPICS

So far, we've covered the more basic expensing and deduction of ordinary business activities—spend it, write it off, spend it, and so on. Ordinary expenses track fairly closely to business transactions and the flow of cash into and out of the business. Keeping good track of such expenses is most important; there is relatively little tax-*planning* opportunity other than to keep those records and try to match expenses to income as closely as possible to avoid paying taxes at higher rates during "fat" periods.

As we move into more advanced topics, the tax-planning opportunities increase. Significant opportunities—and pitfalls—lie in the acquisition and expensing of assets, the use of home offices, retirement plans, and other benefits. These are big-ticket items, among the most expensive things purchased in many businesses. Non-cash expenses—or expenses you would have incurred anyway, as in the case of

home offices or many benefits—can be used to offset income and reduce the tax bill, improving your current income and cash flow as a business owner.

ASSETS AND ASSET RECOVERY

An asset is a piece of physical or financial property used in the business to generate income. Short-term assets—like cash, inventory, and accounts receivable—flow in and out of the business and support short-term sales activity. Long-term assets, on the other hand, are physical fixtures, machines, build-

▼ EXAMPLES OF CAPITAL ASSETS

It would be impossible to come up with an all-inclusive list of capital assets. The rule of thumb: capital assets have a useful life of more than one year, regardless of value. As a practical matter, many businesses expense items under $1,000 or under $500 even though it may not be technically correct. Also, the Section 179 asset-expensing provision covers many kinds of assets. We'll get to that in a minute. Here are some assets the IRS considers to be capital assets:

- Buildings
- Computers, network equipment, software
- Communications equipment—phones, cell phones
- Machinery and production equipment
- Tools
- Building improvements (even on leased or rented facilities)
- Office furnishings, lighting, decorations
- Vehicles
- Patents, copyrights, goodwill (usually, the cost of an acquired business in excess of tangible, measurable assets)

ings, and so forth with a useful life greater than a year and sometimes a great many years. The sum of money required to acquire a long-term (*capital*) asset is usually paid at once (either with owned or borrowed funds). But you cannot take that sum as a deductible expense when you pay it, for that asset doesn't produce in a current tax year all it was purchased to produce.

What Is Asset Recovery?

Tax issues aside, good business sense suggests you would want to allocate the portion of that asset's value corresponding to the portion of its value consumed each year. If you buy a $2 million laser machine tool, you should allocate (recover) the cost as you use the tool. Otherwise, your business shows a huge hit in the first year, then overstates profits in subsequent years, when you do not include any of the cost of the laser tool in determining net profit.

Asset recovery is the accounting approach to allocating portions of a fixed-asset cost to each year of operation. Essentially, a portion of the asset's value is expensed against income each year until the full amount of the asset is expensed (recovered) in the financial statements. Even though no cash changes hands in these subsequent years, an expense is recognized on the financial statements—and in tax calculations. For ordinary physical assets, the yearly allocation is determined by a process known as *depreciation*.

Depreciation 101

The calculation of depreciation—the annually allowable expense for a physical asset—is spelled out by the tax code. Depreciation rules break assets down into categories depending on their useful life and offer the choice of two basic formulas for determining the annual allocation. According to the asset category and formula used, you can plan or schedule the amount of depreciation you take each year for your asset base. Depreciation rules change fairly often; for better tax planning, it's important to track rule changes.

Depreciation Categories

The tax code groups assets into classes and categories and assigns useful lives for each category. Assets fit into one of eight categories: three-, five-, seven-, ten-, 15-, and 20-year property, with two more classes for residential real estate (27.5 years) and commercial real estate (39 years). Most ordinary business property falls into one of four classes:

- **three-year property:** some wear-prone manufacturing equipment, such as tooling
- **five-year property:** computers, peripherals, vehicles, construction equipment, lab or research equipment
- **seven-year property:** office furniture, permanent manufacturing equipment, fixtures, light structures—and anything else not listed specifically
- **real estate and improvements:** 27.5 years for residential property and 39 years for commercial property—applies to most improvements made to that property and applies to building value only (land is never depreciated)

Depreciation Formulas

There are four formulas for allocating annual asset recovery to an asset once you've determined the useful life. There are two primary approaches: accelerated and straight-line. Straight-line depreciation is straightforward: asset value is divided up into equal chunks to be expensed each year over the useful life. Accelerated depreciation front-loads the allocation to write off relatively more in early years. Anybody who has bought a new car understands the idea that an asset depreciates more, at least in terms of market value, in its early years. Accelerated depreciation puts this concept into practice and provides larger write-offs sooner, which is what most businesses want. Both approaches expense assets down to zero value at the end of their useful life.

Straight-line depreciation is simpler. It backloads deductions into later—and presumably more profitable—years. The ability to carry over net operating losses makes it less important to delay taking expenses, but planning depreciation to spread deductions over the long haul to realize lower tax rates over a number of years is still a tax-planning challenge and a valid exercise.

Accelerated depreciation is generally handled by the Modified Accelerated Cost Recovery System (MACRS, pronounced in the tax world like "makers"). MACRS is based on a "200 percent double declining balance" formula, the details of which are important only to accountants. MACRS assumes that no asset is put into service on the first day of a year, so it moderates the first-year depreciation deduction. The second year usually gives the largest deduction. Figure 7.1 shows the MACRS breakdown of five-year property over six years.

So, even with the attenuated deduction the first year, over 70 percent of the asset's value is depreci-

MACRS	Five-Year Property
Year 1	20%
Year 2	32%
Year 3	19.2%
Year 4	11.52%
Year 5	11.52%
Year 6	5.76%

FIGURE 7.1. Modified Accelerated Cost Recovery System, Five-Year Property

ated in the first three years. Most business owners prefer the early asset recovery and larger upfront write-offs of MACRS, while some may prefer the

simplicity and back-loading of straight-line. It's beyond our scope here to cover all depreciation formulas for different useful-life categories. IRS Publication 946, *How to Depreciate Property,* is an excellent resource. Most tax management software, like TurboTax, has easy-to-use depreciation calculators and planners.

Depreciation for Vehicles

So your plan is to start a business and, on Day 2, run straight out to buy a new 350 SLK to celebrate? With the ideas that the IRS will foot a big part of the bill by letting you depreciate the car using accelerated depreciation? "Accelerate" is a term often associated with cars, but not for the IRS.

Congress realized long ago the potential abuse of depreciation write-offs to subsidize expensive cars and put into place special vehicle depreciation rules that cap the amounts written off each year. The basic idea: you can depreciate a vehicle by using any appropriate formula, including MACRS, up to the cap (Figure 7.2).

So, although you use MACRS to depreciate it, that handsome $80,000 Mercedes, instead of giving a

Year	Cars	Trucks/Vans/SUVs
Year 1	$2,960	$3,260
Year 2	$4,800	$5,200
Year 3	$2,850	$3,150
Year 4	$1,675	$1,875

FIGURE 7.2. Depreciation Limits, Vehicles Placed in Service 2006

$20,000 write-off, saving you potentially $9,000 to $10,000 in taxes (federal, state, and self-employment taxes), yields a write-off of a paltry $2,960 the first year. Yes, you will get to deduct the entire vehicle eventually, although the IRS may consider it "extravagant" and not "ordinary and necessary" for your business. Also, depreciation amounts must be adjusted for the

ANOTHER LOOK AT LEASING

Vehicle depreciation caps would appear to make vehicle leasing more attractive in many situations. For vehicles up to $18,000, you can write off the entire monthly lease cost, which largely includes—and in some cases can exceed—the cost of financing and depreciation. You will still have normal operating expenses for the vehicle. The deprecation cap seems to make it more attractive to lease a more expensive vehicle. But Congress wised up to that one, too. There is an adjustment known as an *inclusion amount* mandated for leases costing over $18,000. The exact amount depends on the price of the vehicle and the amount of personal use; it also varies by the type of vehicle (car vs. truck/SUV) and the year of the lease. This adjustment tends to be *relatively* tame, so leasing may still work out best for expensive vehicles. Below shows a sample set of inclusion amounts for the third year of a car lease:

Vehicle Value	Amount Added to Income
$20,000	$114
$25,000	$225
$30,000	$332
$40,000	$545
$50,000	$758
$60,000	$981
$70,000	$1,194

There is no concrete rule for what works best in your scenario; it depends on your tax situation before you acquire the vehicle, how much you use the vehicle, what kind of vehicle you acquire, and how your business is structured. If a business uses vehicles at all, they usually offer significant tax-planning opportunities. Best advice: use your current vehicle to take your tax advisor to lunch to figure it out—and prepare by reading IRS Publication 463.

amount of personal use; i.e., if the vehicle is used only 60 percent of the time for business, only 60 percent of the calculated depreciation amount is allowed. Another special rule calls for using only straight-line depreciation for a vehicle used less than 50 percent in the business. For more detail, see IRS Publication 463, *Travel, Entertainment, Gift, and Car Expenses.*

In general, vehicle depreciation rules haven't kept up with rising vehicle costs. As covered earlier, you have a choice: either capitalize a vehicle and deduct actual expenses and depreciation or deduct a fixed mileage rate, 44.5 cents per mile in 2006. For older or less expensive vehicles, it probably makes sense to use the mileage deduction. For more expensive vehicles, ordinary depreciation will help defray some of the costs but doesn't work out as well as it first appears.

There is, however, some relief for certain kinds of vehicles and ownership strategies. The Section 179 provision allowing immediate expensing of business assets in some cases has a loophole allowing a large deduction for vehicles exceeding 6,000 pounds gross vehicle weight. (More on that in a minute.) Also, owners of a C corporation may in some circumstances be able to own an auto and take a full depreciation allowance, written off by the corporation, as a tax-free employee reimbursement.

Section 179

Finally, we entrepreneurs get a real break—and a good-sized one at that.

While most entrepreneurs won't recite tax code section numbers in normal conversation, this handy little gem does not have an easy "handle" other than its oft-used code section moniker. Simply stated, a small business (defined in 2006 as having less than $420,000 in revenues), no matter how organized, can expense up to $105,000 each year in newly purchased business assets as if they were ordinary operating expenses, sidestepping normal depreciation rules. So Dave Green wants a new $7,000 digital camera for his photo business? He skips the MACRS stuff and writes off the whole thing.

There are, of course, a few exceptions. Section 179 can't be used to depreciate real estate, inventory bought for resale, or assets bought from yourself (converted from personal to business assets). Assets must be used 50 percent or more for business. And the *big* exception you were waiting for—it can't be used to bypass the depreciation cap on vehicles.

Or can it? In one of the more controversial provisions of the tax code, you can expense a vehicle with gross vehicle weight (as determined by the manufacturer) exceeding 6,000 pounds. The original intent was to allow business owners to expense trucks used in the course of business. Congress of course was thinking that any vehicle exceeding three tons would not normally get much personal use.

But along came large SUVs. If you're not familiar with vehicle weights, this 6,000-pound-plus category generally includes the larger varieties of SUVs, the Ford Expeditions, GMC Yukons, Chevy Suburbans, and Hummers found in many an American driveway. Under current rules, you can write off up to $25,000 for a newly purchased member of one of the species. (Until 2005, you could write off the whole thing so long as you didn't exceed the Section 179 annual limit, which was then $102,000.) So, as a result—to the chagrin of tax code critics and environmentalists—many entrepreneurs have an incentive to buy such a larger-than-necessary vehicle, so long as the percentage of business use is high and the other costs of ownership don't wipe out the savings.

Entrepreneurs use this loophole quite frequently and maybe in time it will close. There is little controversy surrounding other Section 179 deductions

▼ A LARGE–AND FLEXIBLE–UMBRELLA

Section 179 may be even better than it looks, for you can use legitimate Section 179 deductions to offset income derived from other personal income sources, even employment. While Section 179 deductions can't exceed your total taxable earnings, you can offset wages earned by you or even a spouse in another job or income from another business. Section 179 deductions can also be carried over indefinitely into the future.

and it remains one of the biggest small-biz boosts the IRS has to offer.

INVENTORY

Inventory, for most purposes, is treated as being somewhere between a current expense and capital item. When it is purchased, it is not expensed but capitalized into the business. But it cannot be depreciated in the traditional sense; it's expensed against the sale of the item as cost of goods sold.

The IRS specifies how inventory must be valued. There may be some tax-planning opportunities in valuing inventory and especially expensing it as it loses value due to obsolescence. Entrepreneurs should manage inventory carefully to avoid tying up and losing more working capital than necessary. They should also work with a tax advisor to identify other inventory planning strategies. See Publication 334, *Tax Guide for Small Business*, or do a search on "inventory" at *www.irs.gov* for specifics.

BUSINESS TAX CREDITS

In Chapter 3 we discussed how the tax code has developed, among other things, as a set of incentives for individuals and businesses to act in the public interest. In this view, the government acts to redistribute income to areas of greater need and to motivate behaviors that benefit society as a whole. This greater purpose becomes most clear in the assortment of credits, most particularly business credits, available to the individual entrepreneur.

It is easy to overlook opportunities to take these credits in your business. In many cases, modest shifts in your business operations can work to realize a credit. Remember that credits are better than deductions, for they offset your tax liability dollar for dollar. Many can be taken against income outside the business, used to generate a tax refund, or carried over into future years.

There are also many *personal* credits, the most popular of which are the Child Credit, which can realize a tax savings of up to $1,000 per year per eligible child, and the Dependent Care Credit, which can bring a tax savings of up to $1,050 per child depending on your income level.

For this discussion, we'll shine a light on the more obscure general *business* credits and refer you to IRS Publication 334, *Tax Guide for Small Business (For Individuals Who Use Schedule C or C-EZ)*, for more detail. There are 27 credits listed in all. None will make you rich, but you can squeeze a bit more out of your business by taking advantage of them. Your tax advisor can help. Here's a quick snapshot of those more widely applicable:

- **Alternative motor vehicle credit** (IRS Form 8910). This covers hybrid vehicles and gives a credit of up to $3,150 (2006) for certain hybrids or other alternative fuel vehicles. The hybrid credit is also available for non-business individuals.
- **Biodiesel and renewable diesel fuels credit** (Form 8864). Self-explanatory.
- **Credit for employee Social Security and Medicare taxes paid on certain employee tips** (Form 8846). If you properly pay your portion of employment taxes on employee tips, this

credit gives it back—providing a not-so-subtle incentive to report that income and make sure employees pay taxes on it.

- **Credit for employer-provided childcare facilities and services** (Form 8882). Provide a day-care facility for your employees (increasing their productivity and desire to work for you) and the government helps out.
- **Credit for increasing research activities** (Form 6765). This is a 20-percent credit for a qualified increase in research.
- **Credit for small employer pension start-up costs** (Form 8881). This credit helps defray the costs of setting up an employee retirement plan (whether a "pension" plan or otherwise).
- **Disabled access credit** (Form 8826). Modify your facilities to accommodate people with disabilities and get a credit. You should consider this credit and the rules before undertaking any facility improvements.
- **Empowerment zone and renewal community employment credit** (Form 8844). Locate in a renewal zone and hire employees, and you might qualify. See Publication 954, *Tax Incentives for Distressed Communities*.

THINK GLOBALLY, PRODUCE LOCALLY

In 2005, Congress quietly initiated the Domestic Production Activities Deduction, ostensibly to boost onshore "manufacturing, producing or growing of tangible property," which is further defined to include software, sound recordings, and so forth. Those who claim this deduction must have employees, although you can be the "employee" under a corporate structure. This obscure little provision allows a deduction of up to 3 percent of income from qualifying domestic production activities. See Form 8903.

- **Energy efficient home credit** (Form 8908). If you're a building contractor, you may get a credit for installing certain energy-efficient features.
- **Welfare-to-work credit** (Form 8861) provides incentive for hiring recipients of family assistance. See Publication 954, *Tax Incentives for Distressed Communities*.
- **Work opportunity credit** (Form 5884) provides incentives for hiring for targeted high-unemployment demographic groups. See Publication 954, *Tax Incentives for Distressed Communities*.

ADVANCED TOPICS

Smart entrepreneurial financial planning involves understanding basic principles of money management, tax planning, and wealth building. Inevitably, some tax-planning strategies, like taking ordinary deductions, are relatively simple and not much more than a matter of record-keeping. Others are much more complex and intertwined with business strategy and long-term personal wealth growth goals and means. The rules and options on retirement savings plans, benefits plans, and various asset deployment strategies are complex and often require outside financial advice and administrative help. But they can offer powerful financial benefits for entrepreneurs.

Retirement Plans

Retirement plans and Section 179 deductions represent the biggest opportunities to save taxes and build long-term wealth from your business. Section 179 works in all phases of the business life cycle, but it's perhaps most important in the start-up phase; play this card right and you may pay little to no taxes whatsoever as your business grows. Retirement plans, on the other hand, grow in power as the business matures and throws off more cash and taxable income.

Retirement plans allow you to set aside large amounts of business income and defer federal and state taxes. The idea is to sock it away today without paying taxes on it, then withdraw it in the future at much lower tax rates. Generally, self-employment or payroll taxes must be paid on funds set aside for retirement, so they don't avoid taxes totally. However, the opportunity for retirement savings to compound and grow without being taxed more than compensates for this shortcoming.

High contribution limits are the real story of self-employed retirement plans. While the 401(k) plan available to most employees allows up to $15,000 (more if age 50 or older) to be set aside each year, retirement plans available for small businesses allow *far* more to be set aside. *Defined contribution plans*—where the amount going into the plan is specified but the payout amount is uncertain—typically allow for contributions of 25 percent of net income *up to* $42,000 per year. *Defined benefit plans*—where the payout amount is specified but the amount paid in can vary—allow a much larger contribution, up to $170,000 per year. If you own a business generating $200,000 per year, you can set aside almost 25 percent of it, and possibly a much larger amount if you choose the administratively and mathematically more complex defined benefit plans. This saves tens of thousands in taxes *each year* and puts compounding to work for your long-term personal savings in a big way. The key is to plan your finances to wait for retirement (for tax purposes, age 59½) before cashing in.

Chapter 10 examines retirement plans in more detail.

Benefits (Other than Retirement Plans)

Congress has cut off many of the preferred benefits in benefits programs—mostly by making expenses paid by owners personally just as tax-deductible as they are for the business. That is, there is no advantage to having the company pay.

There are a few lingering benefits, mostly for C corporations: life insurance (up to $50,000), full reimbursement for health care expenses, long-term care insurance. Getting insurance, especially health insurance, through the business may qualify for group rates, also a substantial savings. Bottom line: these savings won't make you rich but can add a little to your own personal bottom line, especially if you are principal owner of a C corporation.

There are some more obscure benefits that give you an additional tax break:

- **On-premise athletic facilities.** Club memberships—even athletic club memberships—are no longer deductible. However, Congress preserved at least a minor incentive to stay healthy and in shape—do so on your premises. You can deduct the cost of anything from a motorized jogger in a closet to a company gym and swimming pool. So far as we know, these deductions apply to facilities in a qualifying home office, too.

- **Day care.** Any business can deduct the cost of day care up to $5,000 per employee, so long as the employee qualifies and the benefit is offered to all qualifying employees (over 21, over one year of service). If you're a husband-wife C corporation owner, this benefit is easy to take, but you should calculate the benefits against the personal dependent care credit also allowed.

- **Education benefits.** A business can pay and deduct all education expenses, including travel and lodging, for education-related work. There is no upper limit so long as expenses are reasonable. Businesses can also deduct up to $5,250 per year for *un*related education. Again, this deduction must be measured against the various personal credits and deductions allowed, but often makes financial sense if you consider self-employment taxes and C corporation corporate tax.

Home Office

Many entrepreneurs, especially the smaller home-based variety, work the home office deduction to their benefit. Essentially, the costs of owning and operating a home can be deducted to the extent that your home is used for business. The portion of the purchase price attributable to the building (not the land) is included by way of depreciation.

There has been some question about whether taking the home office deduction was a good idea. Prior to 1999, the tax code and IRS enforcement were very strict on the issue of whether the home actually qualified as a place of business. If you conduct your business exclusively from your home and you have a place that is used "regularly and exclusively for business," there is no issue. It gets more complicated if you have another place of business—a plant or an office. Many entrepreneurs choose to conduct "administrative and management" activities at home; some may also meet with clients. If you set aside a dedicated space to run your QuickBooks and do other bookkeeping or transactional activities, for example, and there is no other "fixed location" to perform these activities, you may deduct your home office. It is also clearly deductible if these activities are conducted in a separate structure on your property. (See IRS Publication 587, *Business Use of Your Home.*)

The home office deduction may bring some tax consequences when the home is sold. Current tax law allows up to a $500,000 (married filing jointly) exemption for home capital gains for owners who made the home a primary residence for two of the last five years and have not taken this exemption within the last two years. When you sell the home, most likely for more than the purchase price, you will probably be liable for capital gains taxes on the depreciation recaptured on sale. The good news: the portion of the capital normally prorated to the business now qualifies for the $500,000 exemption, whereas it did not prior to 1997. (This little sticking point discouraged many entrepreneurs from taking the home office deduction.) The recapture portion, however, is *not* exempt and will be taxed at higher Section 1250 depreciation recapture rates, not the preferred capital gains rates. (See IRS Publication 523, *Selling Your Home.*)

Family Businesses

Many small businesses are family businesses; that is, they are controlled by the family, with substantial participation by more than one family member. Such arrangements offer unique tax- and income-planning opportunities, as well as presenting transition challenges that will be covered in Chapter 11, the final chapter.

Family businesses, like corporate structures in general, provide opportunities for *income splitting*. One type of income splitting involves hiring and paying family members who otherwise have lower or no income and are thus taxed at lower rates. A minor can earn $4,200 before owing any taxes. These payments are also exempt from FICA (payroll taxes) and FUTA (unemployment taxes) and reduce your self-employment taxes as well. It is also possible to transfer some ownership to other family members and pay them dividends, although such transfers may be irrevocable depending on how they're structured. There are some tricky tax rules. One is known as the "kiddie tax": dividend income to a child exceeding $1,500 per year is taxed at the parents' rate if the child is under 14. (Otherwise parents might become *too* aggressive in transferring ordinary investments and family business ownership to their kids just to save taxes!)

Use of Family and Personal Assets in Business

The strategic planning and use of family or personal assets can also generate tax savings and provide additional benefits. An asset bought by the family and leased to the business has at least four possible benefits, particularly for a business organized as a C corporation:

- **Business credit and credit rating** do not reflect debt incurred to purchase the asset.
- **Asset protection.** In case of default or bankruptcy, business creditors can go after the business only; your personal assets are protected
- **Lower capital gains taxes.** Capital gains are taxed at personal, not corporate rates—especially handy for real estate. (C corporations only.)
- **Flexible cash flow management.** You as owner of the asset can set the rent, lease, or per-use reimbursement price *reasonably*, subject to what the IRS determines to be reasonable. Collecting rent can be a good way to pull cash out of the business, but the IRS insists that such transactions be "arm's length"—that is, not wholly different from a similar free market transaction. Yet, there is some flexibility.

A RETIREMENT PLAN FOR YOUR CHILDREN?

It is also possible to set up an IRA for children and pay into this IRA. Just as for adults, up to $4,000 can be contributed per child per year for any working child earning wages—and deducted from family income. The money then belongs to the child, but it can make sense to use such a plan as a college fund, despite the 10-percent early withdrawal penalty provision. Why? The immediate tax deduction and the tax-free growth over a long period can outweigh the tax and penalty due upon distribution. It's likely that when these funds are withdrawn for college the child will be in a lower tax bracket and thus owe relatively little tax on the distribution.

The trick is not to overextend personal finances to buy assets for the business. Also, business owners planning to sell a business may do better if sizeable assets are included. Not surprisingly, professional tax advice is a good idea before considering complex asset ownership arrangements.

MANAGING CASH RESOURCES

We've seen a lot of examples over the years of business owners making mistakes or leaving money on the table simply because they don't manage their cash resources effectively. We showed earlier how pulling too much cash out of the business can leave it weak and vulnerable to shortages of working capital. On the flip side, many business owners leave too much cash in the business, thus earning little to no return or leading to poor spending decisions as people often tend to make when their wallets are fat. Further, family personal finances can also be starved, leading to personal debt and conflicts among family members.

Budget Your Draw

There is no hard-and-fast set of rules for managing personal draws from a business. When there's more than one owner, the rules are often specified in the agreement, but there's no governing rule or principle for how much should be left in the business or put into personal pockets.

Managing draws—and dividends—is best handled through planning and budgeting. Good business and personal budgets, better yet complete with scenario and contingency plans, will help manage the dividing line between business cash and personal cash. It's important to say what you're going to do and then do what you say, to keep business and personal interests in balance.

Where to Stash Your Cash

One final error we commonly observe is the generation of insufficient returns on cash resources. While business cash flows and on-hand balances can fluctuate considerably, it's common for businesses to hold too much cash in accounts that generate no interest, such as checking accounts. Usually there are two reasons: fear of needing that cash short term and failure to take the time to examine alternatives.

Fortunately today's all-in-one banking and brokerage accounts reduce the size of these pitfalls. Today's money market accounts and brokerage-related asset management accounts (like Charles Schwab and E*TRADE) make it easy to achieve money market returns while preserving flexibility. They are easy to use and come with other features, like debit cards, that can make business cash management easier.

Additionally, the recent rise in short-term interest rates has made short-term cash management more important—and lucrative. Suppose your average business cash balance is $20,000. If you put that into a money market account paying 4 percent, it would generate $800 per year. Now that doesn't seem like much, but if your business before-tax profit margin (net profit/gross sales) is 10 percent, you would have to generate $8,000 in sales just to make the same amount. For most businesses, putting funds in a money market account is less work.

Cash management strategies, of course, must consider safety. Particularly for large amounts of cash, at least some depositor insurance is a good idea. Businesses with larger or predictable cyclic cash holdings may want to use *laddered* CDs or bonds—that is, with maturities planned to coincide with cash needs—to achieve the best returns. Again, it's important to make sure you can access the cash if things don't go according to plan.

CHAPTER 8

Protect It: Risk Management for Entrepreneurs

YOU'VE WORKED HARD TO START AND MANAGE your business. But life happens. Stuff happens—to you, your loved ones, your business partners, and your property. How do you protect your family's assets—that you have worked so hard to build—from risks? We've talked about how to get wealth; now we'll switch gears to focus on how to keep and preserve it.

The story begins the concept of risk management. We'll define the term and offer some basic principles and processes for doing it. After the basics, we'll move forward to cover specific risk management tools. Many people equate risk management with insurance—and a major portion of this chapter is devoted to the assortment of specific insurance products designed to transfer the risk of loss to others—but there are other ways to manage risk.

Among all the financial tools we'll use (and pay for) from time to time, some consider insurance the least desirable of all. Why? Because we hope we'll never use it. Sure, it hurts to send off those premium checks all those years and never collect a dime. But the peace of mind gained and protection from the unexpected—no matter how unlikely to occur—are worth the cost. And if you happen to suffer a loss in your business or personal life, you and your family will most likely thank your lucky stars that you're covered.

RISK MANAGEMENT FOR ENTREPRENEURS

Risk is the potential for loss or, in the rather flowery language of risk management and insurance professionals, the "probability of an adverse outcome." As business owners we certainly know about risk. Risk is a constant concern as we start our businesses and while we're developing them. We wouldn't be doing what we are doing without being comfortable taking on and managing risk. As a business owner, you certainly have some natural ability to identify and manage risks—or you most likely wouldn't be in business.

Although somewhat different than business risks, the risks you take on in your personal life are an inherent part of your personal finances. Like many other areas of personal finance, it is easy as an entrepreneur to get caught up in managing risks for the business—at the expense of attention to personal and family risks. Many of the risks are similar, so naturally the risk management thought process and many of the tools are similar as well. In this chapter we take a balanced look at both business and personal risk and risk management.

Risk Management as a Concept

We live in a world of uncertainty. Being aware of risks and taking steps to avoid, minimize, and manage them are crucial for the business owner as well as anyone who wants to protect his or her personal assets. Peter Bernstein, in *Against the Gods: The Remarkable Story of Risk* (John Wiley & Sons, Inc., 1998), identifies the importance of risk management and how it has evolved into modern times:

> The revolutionary idea that defines the boundary between modern times and the past is the mastery of risk; the notion that the future is more than a whim of the gods and that men and women are not passive before nature. Until human beings discovered a way across that boundary, the future was a mirror of the past or the murky domain of oracles and soothsayers who held a monopoly over knowledge of anticipated events.

OK, that thought might be deeper than necessary at this juncture. But as entrepreneurs we seek opportunity and, at the same time, must work to minimize anything that can get in the way of our business financial success and (in the context of this book) personal financial success.

So, let's stop to define *risk* and *uncertainty*. Some might think these words are interchangeable, but they're not. *Uncertainty* is the probability of an outcome different from the one we expect. As a practical matter, we don't mind when the outcome varies from our expected outcome on the favorable side. Thus arises the definition of *risk* mentioned above—the probability of an *adverse* outcome. It is really only the downside that worries us. The goal then becomes to *eliminate* it or—if we can't eliminate it—to *minimize* the downside. How do we do that? By *managing* risk.

Identifying and Controlling Risk

Risk management is the process we use to *identify* and *control* risks. The "identify" part is critically important and is the part often omitted, especially in personal finances or in critical points where personal and business finances intersect. If you run a home-based business, are you covered if a FedEx or UPS delivery agent slips and falls while making a delivery to your business? Maybe, maybe not.

Part of the "identification" process involves determining the probability of the adverse outcome and then the cost. Sure, there is a probability that you'll drop this book in a puddle of water when you get off the bus on the way to your office, but what is the cost of that event? Not a lot. But if you're driving a delivery truck, you can cause millions in damages, losing your business and in many cases your personal net worth as a result.

Very few risks can be eliminated completely. The goal is to identify them and categorize them in terms of probability and cost, and then to put together a risk management program to deal with them. The program works to keep the risk within probability and loss parameters with which we feel comfortable.

By definition, risk management is part of the financial planning process. As outlined in Chapter 2, the process of personal financial planning begins with goals and then develops plans to achieve those goals, including navigating obstacles in our path. So, risk management is a defense mechanism crucial to achieving your personal financial success. We think it's natural to use management skills you've already applied in your business to build a good risk management program for your personal finances.

RISK MANAGEMENT AS A PROCESS

Risk management is an organized process that begins with your goals, establishes exposures, identifies assets that may be exposed to risk, and methodically controls those risks. If you have an established broad risk management process in your business, you can adapt that for your home and personal use. However, if your business does not currently have an established risk management process, it's a good idea to develop one for business and for home. Many business consultants, insurance agents, and financial planners have established processes from which you can draw.

Let's consider managing risk in six steps.

Develop Objectives

Think about how broad you want your objective to be for a particular risk management review. You may want to start with one specific aspect of your business or household finances or you may take a more global overview. Whatever the scope, establish your objectives for that review.

A complete review for your business might include:

- Physical assets and property
- Ability to produce income, including:
  - Physical, financial, human, and intellectual capital
  - Contracts, warranties, products, and services
  - Critical operations and processes of product and services delivery

A comprehensive risk management review for the household would take a similar approach, treating the house as an enterprise and looking at all its assets (both financial and non-financial) and the applicable risk exposures. The two largest categories of personal or household risk would be assets—property, investments, etc.—and income—your ability to provide income now and going forward to maintain the household.

Identify Risks

Now within the context defined by the risk areas identified above, identify the risks faced. For a total personal risk management review, you might find it helpful to separate business exposures and household exposures. Business and household exposures might be further separated into financial and non-financial assets—and don't forget the value of your *human capital*—how well would the business or the household get along without you? You begin to see that a risk management process is more contemplative than just buying insurance or reviewing existing coverages.

Identify Risk Management Tools

Many people jump immediately to the conclusion that they must buy insurance. Then they get the quote—too expensive—and do nothing. Wrong! There's more than one way to manage risk. (Read carefully—this is important! See Figure 8.1.)

- **Avoid risk.** Risk avoidance means simply staying away from risky activities. When the probability of an adverse event is too high, the cost of that event is high, or you are unable to deal with that risk in some other way, you should *avoid* it altogether. For example, you will not die from rock climbing if you do not engage in that activity.
- **Reduce risk.** You may not be able to eliminate risk completely, but you may be able to reduce it by eliminating the likelihood or cost of an adverse outcome. If you rock climb only with the most qualified guides or with the best equipment or on the best-known rock faces, you will *reduce* risk.
- **Retain risk.** We suggested earlier that not all adverse outcomes—like dropping this book in a puddle—are costly. Retaining risk is accepting responsibility for the risk and deciding to absorb potential losses yourself. The cost of an adverse outcome may be low. The probability may be low also. You can decide to self-insure or to insure partially by having deductibles or waiting periods. This is sometimes called *risk sharing*—more to come later.

■ **Transfer risk.** Now we get to the one with which you're probably familiar. Risk that you cannot avoid or don't wish to retain can be transferred by contract or other instruments. *Insurance* is the most commonly used contractual risk transfer method. In business, other ways also can be used, like subcontracting work to others or purchasing a surety bond or using options, futures, or derivative securities to lock in prices. *Diversification*—not putting all your eggs in one basket—is another form of risk transfer. In the investment field, diversification is well known and documented, but diversification of other assets is also feasible. By having more than one household income or having business partners or acquiring multiple business skills, we lower risk through diversification.

Evaluate Exposure

Now let's look at types of exposures that a household may face and consider the tools appropriate to those exposures. *Human capital*—your skills, experience, and ability to provide for your family—is usually the most significant asset class in the portfolio of a business owner's household. Human capital can also include *entitlements*—income streams like Social Security, Medicare, pension assets, gifts, and inheritances to which you might be entitled.

Risk management professionals use the term *longevity risk* to talk about life and lifespan risks. Longevity risk can be broken down into two separate risks: we will not live long enough to produce the income necessary for our household and we may live longer than our resources may sustain us. Life insurance is used to manage the former, while savings, pensions, and annuities are the best protection for living too long—*superannuation* in risk management parlance.

Sickness and disability also impair the capability to produce income; savings and insurance are the appropriate risk management tools. Risk reduction and avoidance techniques such as diet, exercise, and stress management should all be considered in the proper context.

Economic risks are inherent in any business activity. Macroeconomic risks in the general economy are to be expected. Business cycles and inflation will affect not only our businesses concerns but also our households in many ways. Microeconomic risks associated with individual industries or companies can also have a major impact. Inflation, covered more in the next chapter, is another notable risk. Savings, rainy day funds, government incentive programs, and diversification can manage these economic risks.

Relationships—business or personal—can also bring risk. Good supplier or customer relationships, not to mention relationships with partners or shareholders, can be vital to a business. And of course, there are risks inherent in those relationships. Maintaining a good relationship with one's spouse can save a business from being liquidated to satisfy the demands of a divorce decree (not to mention the obvious primary benefits from maintaining the relationship).

Aside from these risks, perhaps real property and other tangible assets come with the most obvious risks. Risk managers call these *property and casualty* risks. At business or at home, your automobiles and other vehicles or vessels, furniture, tools, and personal property are subject to fire, theft, and other damage. Many assets, like vehicles or features of your property, also create liability exposure. Risk avoidance and reduction through safety measures, training, and maintenance are the starting point. Eventually, you'll probably transfer risk, although sharing some risk through deductibles is probably prudent. Risk transfer—buying insurance—is legally required in most states unless you have enough wherewithal to *retain* the risk. Many lenders will require insurance on other forms of property investments.

Avoid Risk	**Reduce Risk**
▪ **Avoid activities that incur risk** ▪ Use where probability and cost are high, where risks aren't necessary to take, or where they cannot be transferred ▪ *Example–dont' go rock climbing*	▪ **Reduce severity of associated hazards** ▪ Use where possible to reduce probability and cost ▪ *Example–double-check every knot*
Retain Risk	**Transfer Risk**
▪ **Acknowledge risk and take it on anyway** ▪ Use where probability and especially cost are low ▪ *Example–don't buy service agreement for earphone radio used while climbing*	▪ **Buy insruance or other contract to transfer risk to others** ▪ Use where cost is high and probability is low ▪ *Example–buy life and disability insurance to maintain family income if you fail*

FIGURE 8.1. Risk Management Tools

Develop and Implement a Plan

This is the action stage. Now you'll probably want to sit down (if you haven't already) with an insurance or risk management professional to review your exposures and discuss what you want to do about them. This may take several meetings. There are many options, especially with an insurance agent who offers products from different companies. Together you should decide on a strategy. Then complete this step by implementing your strategy. This is most important, of course, but often neglected. Entrepreneurs tend to procrastinate on this one, not buying insurance or not paying for it. We've also seen entrepreneurs leave good money on the table by procrastinating—they get rid of a piece of equipment but fail to cancel the policy. "Just do it" is important in this phase. That leads us to the final step.

Review Your Plan

Things change. Business—and life—are dynamic. As a result, the risk management process must be ongoing. It is a good idea to review risks and risk management tools in place at least annually. Do your general risk management approaches and specific coverages still make sense? In your business? In your personal life? It's a good idea to tabulate and review coverages and expiration dates (easier if most or all policies have the same dates) for all of your policies. Then, in most years, the annual review will take only a few minutes.

The exact nature of your risk management approach will vary according to the size and type of your business, the presence of employees, and, of course, the specific needs of your family. Risk management is not something you'll probably get "perfect" the first time through; it will take some time to evolve. Risk management approaches and insurance products also change and evolve over time. The most time will be spent upfront, but as your business moves forward, it makes sense to do an occasional thorough review, in addition to the annual checkup.

From here we'll move into the mechanics of the insurance mechanism for transferring risk.

INSURANCE

We have already identified insurance as a subset of an organized process of risk management: it is a tool for transferring risk. In this section we will discuss some of the fundamental concepts that underlie insurance and how to use each type of policy. The goal is to help you decide what you need and how much and to avoid paying for coverage you don't need.

LET THE INSURANCE BUYER BEWARE

As you identify insurance needs and start the process of purchasing insurance, keep in mind that insurance is a product that is more often *sold* than *bought*. The legacy agency and commission structure, combined with the complexity of insurance products, cause the marketing of insurance to be heavy on sales. Insurance products are often so complex that ordinary people—even businesspeople—can't understand them or take the time to do so; as a result, they're more likely to rely on a sales pitch. We're not saying all agents are irresponsible; in fact, most not only are responsible but will also help you in many key areas of your business. But, as the saying goes, let the buyer beware—and also be aware that many insurance Web portals—such as InsWeb.com and eHealthInsurance.com—are making strides to level the playing field, inform buyers, and offer choices.

The Insurance "Product"

Insurance is a contractual arrangement to transfer risk. We contract with an insurance company to take on certain risks, subject to limitations and stipulations of the agreement laid out in the "fine print" of the contract.

Insurance companies are in the business of calculating risks and the costs of those risks. Premiums— prices—are set to be paid by whoever would like to contract for the insurance company to take the risk according to the terms of the contract. The insurance company then pools the risks with others having similar risks. A loss that would be catastrophic for the insured is affordable to the large pool. Premiums don't cover just a share of losses; they must also cover basic business marketing cost, research, overhead, and profit.

We as entrepreneurs pay someone else to take risk that we cannot afford to take in exchange for a premium that we can afford to pay. The insurance company spreads the risk over all the policyholders and makes a profit. Like Peter Bernstein said in the quote earlier in the chapter, this concept for all intents and purposes made modern commerce possible. That's something to remember the next time you begin to begrudge paying an insurance premium that you hope you never collect on!

INSURANCE CONCEPTS

This next section lays out some of the more important technical concepts in the insurance product. Unless you are an insurance professional or want to "go deep" on this topic, some of what follows in this section may not interest you. You can skip ahead a page or two to "Types of Insurance Policies." If you keep reading, the following discussion will help you better understand the insurance product, from both sides. Here we further define the types of risks that can be insured and some behaviors of the insurance clients that affect the insurance product.

Objective (Measurable) Risks

Insurance professionals define an *objective* risk as one that can be measured or quantified—as opposed to a subjective risk that may be perceived "in the eyes of the beholder." A fire or accident loss is measurable, as is the probability of death or disability in a given year. When a risk is objective, the actuaries are able to measure the probability of loss in the long run. A concept known as the *law of large numbers* holds that the chance of a probable outcome will equal the actual outcome when the number of observations is large. The expected aggregate losses of the claims are shared by those in the pool. Therefore, the bigger the pool through which the losses are spread, the greater the certainty in pricing the insurance contract and the greater the potential for lower costs to the insured and/or profit for the insurer.

Perils and Hazards

Risk, the chance of loss, is often confused with the *cause* of losses. Here is where human behavior enters the picture. First, insurance professionals define a *peril* as the cause of a loss, whereas a *hazard* is the condition that creates the loss. As an example, specific perils include fire, theft, flood, and collision, while a hazard is a condition on your property or in your life that may have allowed the peril to cause the loss—faulty wiring, a slippery step, etc.

Insurance policies can be written to include only *named* perils or to cover *open* perils. An *open perils policy* covers any causes of loss, whereas a *named perils* policy covers only those perils specifically mentioned. Understanding the breadth of perils

covered is important to understanding and purchasing any insurance policy.

Causes and Conditions of Loss

Losses are usually the result of a combination of presence of a peril and a hazard specific to your situation that allowed it to occur. But human behavior, being what it is, can often have interesting influences on the hazards leading to a loss.

Risk managers recognize three primary types of conditions that create losses: *moral hazards, morale hazards,* and *physical hazards.* A *moral* hazard is a character flaw that increases the potential for loss, like dishonesty. Moral hazards are in play when someone deliberately sets fire to a building or reports a loss that didn't really happen. A *morale* hazard (not the same thing) is also personal, but it's about indifference. "I don't care about locking the door—everything is covered anyway" is a line that might be heard from a person creating a morale hazard. Morale hazards emanate from carelessness, complacency, and apathy—and often a desire to "get back" at an insurance company. A *physical* hazard is a condition that increases the probability of a peril or increases the potential for greater loss from a peril. This is the honest—and fortunately most widely occurring—form of hazard, examples of which might include untrimmed tree branches or bald tires.

Adverse Selection

Adverse selection is another two-bit industry professional phrase. It's a natural phenomenon occurring when those who have a greater potential for loss are more likely than others to buy insurance—or more insurance. If you decide to buy dental insurance because you've had a lot of tooth problems, insurance companies would consider that adverse selection. There's nothing immoral or illegal about it; it's a fact of life that raises the costs of all those in an insurance pool—and thus your cost of insurance.

USE OF INSURANCE

When is insurance appropriate? It is appropriate when a potential loss may be severe and yet occur infrequently. That is because you could not afford the loss if it were to occur, but the low probability makes the cost of insuring against the potential loss affordable. It may seem counterintuitive that insurance should be used when a loss incurs infrequently. If the loss were severe and likely to occur frequently, the insurance would be unaffordable and, really, you shouldn't be doing whatever you're doing.

TYPES OF INSURANCE POLICIES

This section, before going into more detail, gives an overview of the types of insurance policies available for both business and personal needs. There are three basic types of insurance: property and liability (often called "property and casualty"); life, health, and disability; and social insurance. Within these categories, the variations and combinations of these three types are almost endless. We'll focus mainly on property/liability and life/health/disability forms, for these are the areas in which you, as business owner and family protector, will have the most decisions to make.

Property and liability insurance covers the potential loss of property and liability to others that may occur from the ownership and/or use of a piece of property. "Property" is, of course, not just real estate but any form of physical property or asset. Examples of property and liability insurance include standard homeowner's and commercial property coverage, auto insurance, and coverage enhancements like the "umbrella" liability coverage. *Life, health, and disability* includes life insurance, disability income, health insurance, and long-term care coverage. *Social insurance* comes mainly from governments or government legislation; it includes workers' compensation, unemployment insurance, and government entitlement programs like Social Security, Medicare, and Medicaid.

PROPERTY AND LIABILITY INSURANCE

This general category of insurance is also referred to as *property and casualty*. A casualty is typically a human loss from an accident, as exemplified by bodily injury, causing a tort or liability. Property and liability insurance protects assets and covers the liabilities that might arise because of them.

Business Insurance

Business insurance typically includes commercial property and commercial liability, along with several other features or riders covering certain perils of the business experience.

Commercial property insurance is important whether you own or rent your business space. It provides protection from losses from damage or loss of property and much more. In addition to traditional perils like fire, theft, and some natural disasters, policies often are written to include such business losses as business interruption and employee dishonesty.

Commercial liability insurance covers general liability and employer's liability in the form of workers' compensation. General liability insurance covers the liability of the business for claims from customers and others who are injured on the employer's property and for claims from losses from the use of products or services produced by the business. (Liability to employees is covered by workers' compensation insurance.)

Property coverage includes several items beyond the typical fixed structures in a business, including business personal property, personal property of others, money and securities, income and extra expense, equipment breakdown, and other property specified. *Liability* coverage includes medical expenses and personal injury as well as damages to the property of others or property rented to you. Each of the coverages has limits and deductibles. Many policies will have *stretch* coverage, often identified with specifically worded and priced *riders* or *endorsements* or a packaged *schedule* covering a wide variety of extras, like extended business income, property off premises, accounts receivable, fine art, outdoor signs, and so on. Your risk management point person and/or agent can explain these extras, costs, and relevance.

AUTO AND OTHER VEHICLE INSURANCE

Because this is the most common of all forms of property and liability insurance, it's probably the best place to start to understand how to manage risk emanating from owning and using an asset. We know that driving is a risky activity. Even owning a car is risky, because a tree can fall it on or someone may steal it and injure someone else when driving it.

Do you remember the four risk management tools outlined above? You could *avoid* risk altogether by making a choice to not own an auto. Not practical, right? You can *reduce* risk by driving more safely, wearing your seat belt, owning a safer car, not driving as much, or choosing to not let your teenagers drive until they are more mature or have completed additional driving school. But that falls far short of completely mitigating this potentially very expensive risk. You *retain* risk—at least some of it, anyway—by choosing higher deductibles. But for the remainder, you *transfer* it by buying insurance.

The Standard Auto Policy

Most states require the ISO (Insurance Service Office) standard policy, commonly called the *personal automobile policy* (PAP). There are six parts of this standard policy:

- **Part A–liability coverage.** Part A provides for protection for your liability for bodily injuries and property damages. It covers you and your family for driving your vehicle or one that you've borrowed or rented. It also covers someone else driving your vehicle. An organization such as an employer or a charitable organiza-

tion may be covered if the organization is responsible for the conduct of someone driving your vehicle. However, the policy typically spells out a lot of exclusions—one common one being the use of a vehicle for business if limited as an individual policy. Coverage limits are identified separately for per-person bodily injury, per-occurrence bodily injury, and per-occurrence property damage.

- **Part B–medical payments.** Medical payments reimburse you for injuries for someone who is in your vehicle. This part provides no-fault first-party insurance to pay for bodily injuries from an auto accident. The person injured must collect from his or her own insurance company; the person causing the accident does not have to pay.
- **Part C–uninsured motorists.** Uninsured motorist coverage pays for losses covered by those who do not take financial responsibility: they are not insured, they are underinsured, or they flee the scene of the accident.
- **Part D–damage to insured's auto.** Property damage to your car consists of two types. *Collision* covers your loss from a collision with another vehicle or another thing, like a tree, a rock, a building, or a body of water. *Comprehensive* covers the other damages, like when a rock damages your windshield while you are driving or an identified driver smashes your fender in a parking lot.
- **Part E–duties after an accident.** The standard PAP identifies your duties if a loss occurs. You must notify the insurer and you must provide proof of the loss and cooperation with an investigation.
- **Part F–general provisions.** There are a number of general provisions, like geographic coverage. For instance, the PAP provides coverage only in the United States, its territories and possessions, the Commonwealth of Puerto Rico, and Canada. Driving in Mexico (where

an auto accident is a crime) is not covered without special arrangements.

HOMEOWNER'S AND RENTAL INSURANCE

For most individuals, a home is usually the largest personal asset. Even if we don't own the home, it is essential to protect it and the rest of our assets from liabilities that could arise from the home. Fortunately, homeowner's or rental insurance is designed to protect more than the property or structure.

Types of Homeowner's Policies

Like the standard auto policy, there are several standard forms for homeowner's policies developed by ISO. Since insurance is regulated at the state level, you will see some minor variations in these standard forms. Unlike with auto insurance, these "HO" forms don't reference specific inclusions but instead describe different types of policies.

- **HO-1 Basic Form** is a limited policy for items specifically identified in the policy—*named* perils instead of *open* perils. As a limited policy, this is generally not attractive to most people.
- **HO-2 Broad Form** adds some additional perils, but is still limited.
- **HO-3 Special Form** is the most common type of homeowner's policy. It is an open perils policy, covering all perils not specifically excluded. Although these packages cover almost everything, it is still smart to complete an inventory of personal property to make sure.
- **HO-4 Contents Broad Form** is basically a renter's policy, covering all personal liability and contents of the dwelling without covering the structure.
- **HO-5 Comprehensive Form** is similar to the common HO-3 form but has even broader coverage for losses. For instance, it might cover

a college student under age 24 living away from home.

- **HO-6 Condo Unit Form** is specifically for owners of condominiums. It includes coverage for the part of the building owned by the condominium owner, personal property, and personal liability.
- **HO-7 Mobile Home Form** is specifically designed for mobile homes.
- **HO-8 Older Home Form** is for the owner of an older home that is more expensive to repair and construct and thus has higher functional replacement cost coverage.

Types of Property Coverage

Now we get to the list of items covered, similar to the auto policy. Coverage types are fairly self-explanatory:

- **A**—The dwelling and attached buildings, such as a garage.
- **B**—Outbuildings, i.e., structures not attached to the dwelling.
- **C**—Personal property
- **D**—Expenses for loss of use
- **E**—Personal liability, including the cost of litigation
- **F**—Medical payments

Amount of Coverage

The valuation of home and real property assets is done on either an actual cash-value basis or a replacement-cost basis. The actual cash value basis is the current replacement cost depreciated by the amount of use or percentage of useful life elapsed, whereas the replacement-cost basis is the amount necessary to replace the property at the time of the loss. Policies define what percentage of replacement cost you must be insured for in order to receive full value. It is usually 80 percent. So, in order to receive full replacement cost, you need to pay for coverage

LAND–NEITHER CREATED NOR DESTROYED

Most policies do not cover the value of the land component of a property. Land is typically not considered by insurance companies as damageable by peril. So most homeowner policies cover structure, contents, etc., but not land. Coverage, as a result, might seem low compared with market value. Some coverage may be provided for trees and other landscape features, which are generally not considered part of the land. It's good to review your coverage limits in terms of market and replacement value with your insurance professional, leaving land out of the equation.

of at least 80 percent of full replacement cost. This give you a cushion in times of rising construction costs, but you must keep tabs on replacement costs to make sure you do not become underinsured. Also, some coverages within your policy, like outbuildings or personal property, may not have a provision for automatic replacement cost. It is important to understand your policy, which may mean asking your agent a lot of questions. (That's why you have an agent!)

Earthquake and flood are not covered by homeowner's insurance. Typically you need separate policies for these perils, some of which may be packaged and sold by the government. Also, to cover valuable personal property such as art, jewelry, collections, and antiques usually requires specific riders.

Business Endorsements for Homeowner's Policies

Now, for the entrepreneur, we get into an important set of considerations and endorsements to the basic homeowner's policy. These endorsements apply specifically to situations where business is conducted at home, as either a primary or a secondary place of business.

Business Pursuits Endorsement. This endorsement covers activities of an employee doing business on behalf of someone else. Here are three major versions of this endorsement:

- The *Permitted Incidental Occupancies* endorsement covers a business not primarily located at home but where some home business activities—like a home office or studio—may occur.
- The *Home Business Coverage* endorsement (HOBIZ™) covers a wide assortment of typical home business risks, like the risk of stolen equipment or the fall of a delivery person, as mentioned earlier.
- The *Home Day Care Coverage* endorsement is for a specific type of business, the perils and hazards of which are obvious. Other special business coverages are usually available.

Umbrella Liability

This is one of the least expensive insurances and can have potentially the most value when you need it. It can cover your entire net worth in a catastrophic liability claim. An umbrella policy is a comprehensive personal liability policy written in conjunction with your auto and homeowner's policies. Sometimes called *excess liability*, it covers your personal liability in a very broad way. The primary feature—and why it is generally inexpensive—is that it generally does not pay until the limits of your auto and homeowner's policies have been reached.

Unlike homeowner's and auto policies, these policies are not standardized. Coverage usually extends beyond the underlying homeowner's and auto covering bodily injury, slander, and defamation of character: the details vary policy by policy. They do not typically cover business activities and usually exclude rental property you own.

The usual minimum for an umbrella policy is $1 million and policies are written in $1 million dollar increments. How much should you get? Financial advisors recommend buying enough to cover your current net worth plus the present value of 25 percent of your expected future earnings. The reason for 25 percent: if you were subject to collection on a judgment, 25 percent of your income is all that can usually be attached (taken by legal authority). Coverage is usually inexpensive enough to be a bargain up to about $10 million; then it gets more expensive per million. If your net worth is beyond that amount, you might want to retain some of your personal liability risk.

Other Personal Liability Considerations

If you own property in more than one state, aircraft, watercraft, horses, art, or collectibles, coordinating your personal risk management becomes more complex and you need to pay particular attention to your exposure. There are still a few more liability considerations:

Directors' and Officers' Errors and Omissions Liability. Directors' and officers' errors and omissions insurance (E&O) is a unique form of coverage to protect corporate offices and directors from lawsuits that may be brought by shareholders or by others outside the firm. There is no standard form for this type of policy.

Employer Liability. Willingly or otherwise, as an employer you expose your employees to risk. Depending on the business, this risk may be moderate or severe. As a form of social insurance mandated—but usually not sold—by state government, you must carry some form of workers' compensation (workers' comp). It is business insurance and thus listed here: it protects workers from occupational hazards and work-related accidents. State laws differ and the costs of workers' comp vary extremely depending on your type of business and your state.

LIFE AND HEALTH

This broad category contains, in addition to "pure" life and health insurance, disability and long-term care insurance. We will address the topic primarily from a perspective of personal finances. However, since there are some uses of these forms as employee benefits, we'll cover the business aspects, too.

HEALTH INSURANCE

In recent years, the costs of health care have been rising at about twice the rate of inflation as measured by the Consumer Price Index (CPI). Remarkably, the cost of health insurance has risen about twice as fast as the cost of health care, in part explained by the greater use of health care resources by the insured. Many small businesses and larger corporations have been scaling back or even dropping health insurance benefits. The health insurance woes of major corporations like General Motors are well publicized, but be sure that health insurance is a huge issue for smaller businesses, too. In this section we'll discuss traditional health insurance arrangements and new developments that have potential to help resolve the problem of skyrocketing premiums.

Basic health insurance provides direct payment or reimbursement for medical expenses, either through managed care or through physicians and resources chosen by the insured. Policies can be written as *individual* or *group* policies, that is, purchased as individual policies or as part of a larger group of employees or business associates purchasing policies together. Because of administrative costs and the pooling of risk across larger numbers, group policies are much more cost-efficient than individual policies.

In the last 20 or 30 years, the structure of the health care industry has changed dramatically. Major corporations that have been funding most of the health care costs have been working hard to drive cost reductions. One solution is adopting managed care and group practices, which tend to be more cost-effective than paying for employees to use individual medical practices because of greater cost control, economies of scale, and lower administrative costs. As a result the number of individual medical practices has declined, while group practices, health maintenance organizations (HMOs), and other types of systems of managed care have emerged rapidly.

Types of Health Care Providers

The *health maintenance organization* (HMO) concept was pioneered by aluminum and steel maker Kaiser Permanente in the 1940s and has grown rapidly in recent years. HMOs, in concept, provide prepaid health care. The HMO gets a fixed monthly fee upfront and takes responsibility and risk for providing a broad range of services to its members, including preventive checkups.

Preferred provider organizations (PPOs) are similar to HMOs in that there is a contractual relationship with the insured, the insurer, and the providers. There are, however, two main differences. Members are allowed to use providers outside the PPO, although they pay more for that privilege through higher deductibles and co-payments. The other difference is mostly internal: in PPOs, health care professionals provide their services to the organization for a fee, not as employees of the organization, as is the case in HMOs. They have some latitude to set fees and they must handle their own administration, which tends to make costs somewhat higher than with HMOs.

Point of service systems (POS) are quite similar to PPOs but do not offer the patient as much choice in care providers. A patient needs approval from the *primary care physician* to go to a specialist. However, as some POS providers are now offering direct access to specialists, the differences between POSs and PPOs are eroding.

Health Savings Accounts

The features of health insurance plans are extensive and complex; it would not serve well to try to cover them all here. We want to use this space—and your time—for presenting a new tool, currently being heavily promoted by the federal government, to reduce costs to employers and employees alike. The tool, health savings accounts (HSAs), uses tax breaks and personal savings to mitigate health costs on a tax-preferred basis, driving down health insurance costs and shifting some burden—and financial opportunity—to employees. This section describes how the HSAs work.

HSAs are used in combination with a specially constructed health insurance policy known as a *high-deductible health plan* (HDHP), which nominally shifts or "shares" costs with you for the first several thousand dollars of coverage. The HSA is similar to an Individual Retirement Arrangement (IRA) (covered in Chapter 10). Technically, it is a tax-exempt trust created to pay for medical expenses on a tax-advantaged basis. Contributions are tax-deductible "above the line," that is, for calculating adjusted gross income (AGI). Funds in an HSA grow tax-deferred and can be used anytime for medical expenses or penalty-free after age 59½ for retirement. So, the insured has the incentive to keep healthy and keep medical costs low.

High-Deductible Health Plans. With the high-deductible HSA-compatible health plan (which is much less expensive than traditional health plans), the participant must pay high amounts before the health insurance takes over paying. That deductible amount may then filled in with funds from the HSA, which can also be used to pay for other out-of-pocket costs like *co-payments* (co-pays) (the $10, $20, or similar fee the participant pays at the time of the visit), simple prescriptions, and even over-the-

HSAs–GOOD OR BAD? THE DEBATE RAGES ON

One of the big challenges to health care and health insurance costs is the lack of transparency of medical costs by providers and the lack of accountability by the patient. In fact, currently your employees and family members probably have no idea of the true cost of a doctor's visit or why it's so expensive. Ask a typical employee how much a typical office visit costs and the answer will likely be only the cost of the co-pay. Unlike with most goods and services, which come with price tags and disclosures and estimates of cost of service, not even the staff in a physician's office can tell you how much a visit will cost. How can anyone hold down costs and keep within budgeted expenses in a system like that? Little wonder costs are expanding so quickly.

To be fair, there are other drivers of health care and health insurance costs. First, there is a factor known as *cost shifting*. In trying to reduce costs, Medicare and Medicaid are paying less and less to providers. What the government doesn't pay tends to get shifted back to the private sector. Medical inflation is being driven by the costs of expanding new medical knowledge and technology. Research is constantly developing more procedures costing more and more. Higher use of these new advances is a factor. Catastrophic health care costs are soaring. As health insurance gets more expensive, more individuals and employers are dropping coverage, so more people are uninsured. Medical malpractice defense costs are a major problem for all of us, with some providers paying annual premiums in the six figures. There is no single solution for such a complex problem.

We feel the health savings account (HSA) approach will help–if only by making costs more visible and borne by those who receive the benefit. However, we recognize they may also exacerbate the cost-shifting problem, as those who are healthier may use HSAs and thereby reduce the size of the insurance premium pool by buying only HDHPs, leaving fewer people to absorb the cost burden of providing for the unhealthy (sort of adverse selection in reverse). Still, we think HSAs will produce more good than bad, particularly for small business owners who might not otherwise be able to afford health coverage at all–and obviously their employees as well.

counter medications. The typical HSA HDHP provides for preventive annual checkups and physicals and "well-baby" visits before the deductible is applied.

A typical plan would have a deductible of $2,400 (single) or $4,800 (family), with a maximum annual out-of-pocket of $3,600 (single) and $5,500 (family). The plan participant would have to pay those costs before the catastrophic coverage would kick in. HSA funds can also be used to pay the *co-insurance*—the amount, often 20 percent, individuals must pay beyond the deductible limit.

HSA Contributions. For 2006, the maximum HSA deduction is $2,700 for an individual and $5,450 for a family. An additional deduction of $700 is allowed for an individual 55 or older (See www.irs.gov for latest limitations.)

HSA Logic. The employer or employee may contribute into an HSA an amount equal to 100 percent of the annual HDHP deductible. Contributions may be made in installments or a lump sum before April 15 of the year following. The logic of HSAs for employees is that healthy employees who do not use much health care would rather build up money in an HSA, which is their money, than have the money go to an insurance company and be lost. The logic of HSAs for employers is that they can attract and keep healthy employees and, because the HDHP insurance is less expensive, it puts a lid on rising health insurance premiums. It remains to be seen how the increasing incentive to keep health care costs down will affect rising health care costs and rising medical premiums.

What's New—and Better—About HSAs. HSAs can be funded by either individuals or the employer. Before HSAs there were Medical Savings Accounts (MSAs), similar but with much tighter rules and lower contribution limits. MSAs were handled by only a handful of administrators, while HSAs have become much more universal and are handled by many "money-center" banks. We expect that trend to continue.

Flexible spending accounts (FSAs), which are part of Section 125 "cafeteria" plans, are offered by many employers and liked by many employees for their flexibility. However, they have tough IRS rules and qualifications under the Employee Retirement Income Security Act (ERISA) (see Chapter 10) and therefore require an expert. Worst of all, they are a "use-or-lose-it" proposition—employees must spend all the dollars they've contributed each year or lose them. Few can accurately even come close to predicting their annual health care expenditures.

You Own Your HSA. The HSA account belongs to the employee (or you, the entrepreneur—you're eligible for these plans too), who can take the account when he or she changes jobs or retires.

Administration. The account is administered by a third party, usually a health insurer, bank, or specialized third-party administrator. The administrator takes the employer out of the administrative loop and relieves the employer from worrying about how plan contributions are managed or used. Expense eligibility for reimbursement is mainly an issue between the employee and the IRS; employees may be required to demonstrate the validity of expenses. Employer contributions are reported as pre-tax W-2 income at year's end. If the employer has a Section 125 cafeteria plan, the HSA can be a part of it.

Most HSA plan administrators have made these plans easy for participants to use. Typically, HSA owners receive debit cards to use at the time of service to pay for the medical expenses. Plan maintenance fees are modest and often go away altogether when a minimum balance threshold is achieved.

HSA accounts can be funded by either individual or employer. If an employer makes a contribution, there are fairness rules stipulating that the employer must contribute to all eligible employees. (Contact a tax professional or a professional benefits administrator about specifics.) Contributions can be based on either a dollar amount or a percentage. In order to be eligible for an HSA, an individual or family must be covered by a qualified high-deductible health insurance plan, a specific set of products now offered by most insurance companies.

Health Insurance Checklist

As we stated above, each health plan and strategy has features and choices to examine. In many cases these choices may be evaluated by employers and employees together, often with a third-party benefits specialist helping out. The goal is to select a plan that will meet the objectives of the employer (you) and the consumers (you and your employees).

Here are some features distinguishing policies, which you'll probably want to discuss with a specialist or a provider:

- Exclusions, such as for pre-existing conditions
- Co-payment, deductible, and coinsurance
- Coverage for prescription drugs
- Availability of advice without going to doctor, e.g., from a nurse practitioner, by phone, online, etc.
- Process for pre-approval for procedures

- Total lifetime limits of coverage
- Ease of administration for reimbursements, customer service wait times, etc.

We have not talked about many issues of health insurance. We'll conclude with some issues that are big.

DISABILITY

We are conditioned, seemingly from birth, to think that everyone needs life insurance. If you die early, you leave your family and maybe your business in the lurch. However, the risk of incapacity is a matter of life as well as death: incapacity can result in various ways during life. Bottom line: the focus on life insurance often causes people to overlook disability income insurance.

Disability insurance provides income to replace wages in the event you can no longer earn because of illness or injury. It is many more times likely that a healthy entrepreneur will become disabled than die during his or her most productive working years.

In a death, aside from a funeral, the deceased incurs no further expenses. However, if you become *disabled*, the cost of living continues and there are potentially significant medical costs. Also, you may have to pay for others to do things that you did while healthy, such as mow your lawn, shop for food, prepare meals, and so on. One study showed that 80 percent of families have life insurance, but only 15 percent of people are covered with group long-term disability policies and 7 percent with private policies. As with health insurance, group disability is more affordable than individual policies—bad news for individual entrepreneurs or small employers.

Following are key provisions of disability policies to help you decide whether to buy coverage and, if so, what kind and how much.

Definition of Disability

In order for a disability policy to pay, you must meet the definition of disability in the contract. We usually see policies defining disability as when the insured is either unable to perform *any occupation* or unable to perform his or her *own occupation*. The latter provides coverage—payments—if you cannot continue in your profession. The former provides coverage only if you cannot provide income in any reasonable way. "Own occupation" coverage is more expensive, for you are more likely to suffer a disability that keeps you from doing one specific occupation than to become disabled altogether. For example, a cabinet maker who becomes blind can't keep building cabinets, but can do other jobs, say with computer audio devices, even with less compensation. "Own occupation" would cover the cabinet worker, but "any occupation" might not cover if the cabinet maker can work in another occupation requiring substantially the same education and experience. As "any occupation" coverage is broader and allows for the possibility that you might not make as much income, the insurance is more affordable. Further, a *split definition* policy has an "own occupation" period during which the insured could receive some additional training and then converts to "any occupation." It is a good alternative policy.

Here are some other disability coverage features:

- **Benefit period.** Policies are typically divided between short-term and long-term. A short-term policy covers up to two years. Long-term disability provides for a specific length of time or until a specific age, typically 65, although some policies provide coverage beyond that age.
- **Elimination period** is the time before benefits begin, so insurance companies can reduce claims from pre-existing conditions. It is analogous to a deductible.
- **Partial disability** has a requirement to perform some duties or work a shorter week; this policy will cost less.
- **Waiver of premium** is a rider that pays the pre-

mium and keeps the policy in force during a period of disability.

- **Cost-of-living riders** can adjust benefits each year, based either on an index like the Consumer Price Index (CPI) or on a certain percentage named in the contract.
- **Benefit restrictions.** Most benefits are capped at 60 or 70 percent of current income to avoid malingering or feigning a disability.
- **Taxation of benefits.** Effectively, benefits are taxed once. If premiums are paid by pretax dollars as a company benefit, then they are taxable to the insured if he or she receives any benefits. However, if paid with after-tax dollars, then the benefits are tax-free.
- **Integration of benefits.** Some policies may have benefits integrated with Social Security disability income (or another private policy); if so, the private benefits would be reduced if the government benefits are paid.

As an entrepreneur, you have a responsibility both to your business and to your family to examine disability coverage. Disability can arrive in many forms and a business can die even if the entrepreneur is only disabled.

LONG-TERM CARE INSURANCE

Long-term care (LTC) insurance pays to take care of us if we are unable to take care of ourselves. As we live longer, the possibility that we'll need assistance as we age grows. Costs, meanwhile, have skyrocketed to the point that assisted living may costs upwards of $100,000 per year for an individual. Thus, many more individuals are looking at purchasing insurance to take care of these costs.

There are two schools of thought on long-term care. One is self-insurance—accumulate assets through life and use them for long-term care needs *if necessary*. The other strives to protect those assets as part of a family legacy; there's no way you want to

jeopardize an inheritance, let alone a business, to pay for such care. Further, if you end up with few assets by the time you reach that age, social programs like Medicaid kick in. So many advisors see LTC insurance as something to consider for those with moderate wealth—$100,000 to $2,000,000 in net worth. Those with more can afford their own long-term care, while those below can rely on other sources.

These policies are somewhat like disability insurance in features of waiting period, benefit period, and cost of living adjustments. To receive benefits, we must be chronically ill, as defined by needing substantial assistance with at least two of the six *activities of daily living* (ADLs) for at least 90 days. ADLs are eating, bathing, dressing, being able to get in and out of bed, using the toilet, and continence—not a pretty picture! But those who have gone through this with parents and/or grandparents know it happens to the best of us.

The best policies provide benefits for skilled care (nursing home), at-home care, adult day care, assisted living (apartment style), and hospice. It pays to buy young—LTC insurance, for obvious reasons, becomes more expensive to buy as we get older. A policy bought in your 50s will be most cost-effective—the premiums are lower but your funds aren't tied up for too long.

LIFE INSURANCE

There are a variety of purposes of life insurance. When we introduced the uses of insurance, we said that when a potential loss may be severe and yet occurs infrequently, insurance is appropriate. In terms of severity, mortality risk is one of the most serious risks a household may face. Life insurance ensures that some economic benefit will be paid to beneficiaries if the insured dies. The world of life insurance is complex, with many forms and provisions available; we'll cover some of the key features and considerations here.

Determining Amount of Life Insurance Needed

In determining the need for life insurance and the amount needed, the first important step is to determine what the insurance is designed to do. Here are some of the possibilities.

1. Replace the income the deceased was earning.
2. Pay for the household labor the deceased was performing.
3. Pay debts.
4. Provide a bereavement, settlement, and training period.
5. Replace a key person's skill or leadership contribution in a business.
6. Replace a key person's financial stake in a business.
7. Provide for estate liquidity (funds) to pay for estate taxes.

Determining the dollars of coverage needed is the next step. It comes down to the question: "What would I do if my spouse or business partner suddenly died?" In response to that question, if you want to replace the earned income of the deceased permanently, the amount of insurance needed is typically 20 to 25 times annual living expenses. It depends on the ability of the survivors to contribute—if a spouse is able to go to work, you may only need a year or two of expenses. Naturally, it takes a lot of "what-if" thinking and analysis.

Key Person Insurance

A small business is very dependent upon its key personnel. Careful consideration should be given to the effect on the firm if a key person were to meet an untimely death. The firm has an insurable interest in its key people, whether in sales, operations, finance, or management. What would happen if you lost one of your crucial people? How would you replace them? The valuation of the person for insurance purposes would be an educated guess, but wouldn't it be smart to consider it?

Buy-Sell Agreements. Life insurance is often used in business to fund a *buy-sell agreement.* The insurance is often called *business continuation* insurance. If you have more than one owner, there are two ways to approach this. In a *cross-purchase* plan, each primary owner carries enough life insurance on the lives of the others to be able to buy their interest in the business from their estate. Under an *entity* plan, the firm owns the policy and is the beneficiary. Upon death of an owner, the firm purchases ownership from the estate of the deceased. Your risk management or insurance professional will be able to walk you and your partners through the various options.

Parts of a Life Insurance Policy

In order to begin to answer the question of which type of life insurance will meet the needs of a particular situation, it is first important to understand the driving features and costs of a life insurance contract. These parts consist of *mortality expense*, *investment return*, and *overhead expense* and *marketing* costs.

Mortality Expense. Mortality risk is the probability of dying. Insurance companies are very good at estimating this across history and with large groups of applicants. Armed with historical records, the applicant's medical history, and results from a current examination, trained actuaries can estimate this expense accurately.

Investment Return. Regardless of the type of policy, insurance companies collect money (your premiums) and invest it. The types of investments and their success determine their profitability, of course, and ultimately affect your rates. Investment options for some policies are tightly regulated: the funds must be invested in safe, fixed-income securities. *Variable* policies pass on investment returns and risks to you. If the investments do well, the policy might pay for your premiums. If they do badly, you'll write a premium check—and maybe a bigger one the next time you need a new policy.

Overhead and Marketing Expenses. Overhead expenses include normal costs of running the insurance company, costs to service the policy, and company profits. Marketing costs are the most variable component of overhead expense from company to company and among policy types. They include agent commissions as well as the traditional advertising and promotion costs. Frankly, we wish they were more transparent. Commission costs can be substantial, which says something about the marketing process you will probably experience and the types of products you will be sold.

TYPES OF LIFE INSURANCE

Life insurance comes in a variety of highly differentiated forms. You may have experience with simple *term* insurance or you may have purchased or seen a presentation on more complex, esoteric *whole life* or *permanent* forms. Before going to a professional, it helps to have at least a working knowledge of the various forms.

Term Life

Term insurance is life coverage purchased and granted for a given length of time, a fixed *term*. It is the least expensive type of life insurance, particularly when the insured is young and healthy. Why? Because the insurance company effectively eliminates exposure to the greater risks of old age.

Term insurance may be renewable annually, meaning premiums—and eligibility—can change. Annually renewable insurance is cheapest, particularly if the insurer can require you to prove insurability each year.

Level-term insurance has a premium structure that is leveled, constant, for a number of years, say 5, 10, 15, 20, or even 30. With level term, you overpay for the mortality costs for your given age during the earlier years and underpay during the later years. You don't have to prove your insurability each year and you're protected from rising premiums in later years. If you know how long you will need the insurance and can afford the level premium in the early years, it works well.

Whole Life Insurance

Whole life insurance provides a fixed amount of insurance coverage for life. The higher premiums you pay in the early years are invested by the insurance company and subsidize the higher mortality expenses in the later years. *If* you need the same amount of insurance your entire life and *if* you can afford the premiums in the early years, the advantage is guaranteed insurability for life. Those are big ifs. Most individuals don't need much if any coverage when in their 80s: they aren't providing income for anyone else, have exited their businesses, and don't need the insurance for other reasons. Whole life insurance usually carries some *cash value*—the difference between what you've paid in and what is required to cover mortality costs (less profit, overhead, marketing costs, etc.). But cash values can pale by comparison with what you could accumulate through sound investing elsewhere. Most financial advisors recommend buying cheaper term insurance (level term, usually) while you need it and investing the difference in cost between term and whole life some other way.

Universal Life

Universal life is a more flexible type of cash value insurance. You can pay more in premiums in some years and less in other years. You take more of the investment risk. Interest rates vary: when interest rates are high, you get greater earnings, it builds up

▼ WATCH INSURABILITY–AND RENEWABILITY–CAREFULLY

Insurance companies are *not* required by law or any other consideration to insure everyone. They can pick and choose their risks. People in high-risk groups will find it more expensive to get insurance than others–if they can get it at all. Most customers must show that they are insurable, usually through a physical exam. (One advantage to *group* insurance is that it often waives this requirement.) Further, as in the case of term life, health, or many disability policies, insurance companies can require a review of eligibility to renew or continue the policy. Riders can be sold that guarantee renewability. For most people, it makes sense to buy insurance with guaranteed renewability and it often makes sense to buy insurance before you need it to avoid possible problems with insurability. Buy a life policy in your 20s and perhaps you're just insuring the fact that you'll be able to buy insurance later.

your cash value, and you pay less in premiums if you like or get a greater build-up of value.

Variable universal life (VUL) is a more complex and still more flexible form. Also a cash value policy, a VUL has still more variable investment returns. As policyholder, you assume risks and enjoy returns provided by not only income but also capital gains through the investment choices of your insurance company. You have some choices in the investment options and can build a diversified portfolio with stocks, bonds, and cash investments. These returns accumulate tax-deferred. You have the potential for greater returns than with whole life. The best of these policies have a great deal of transparency and you can determine the mortality costs and investment expenses. But be careful: like many insurance products, VULs are heavily marketed and usually have substantial commissions and marketing costs.

SOCIAL INSURANCE

"Social insurance"—including Social Security, Medicare, workers' compensation, and unemployment insurance—usually doesn't make the business owner's list of favorites. For most entrepreneurs, these forms of insurance represent an omnipresent expense, a taking that supports giving to employees or others outside the business. However, social insurance provides some societal value and, with today's legal and liability climate, probably shields business owners from some obligations that would probably come their way anyway. We won't go into the details here; many are beyond scope or aren't controllable or, like workers' compensation, vary greatly from state to state.

▼ BORROWING FROM YOUR LIFE (INSURANCE)

Most cash value life insurance forms have some form of borrowing provision. Sales pitches claim that you can borrow accumulated cash value, usually at low rates. It seems especially attractive for variable and variable universal life forms, where you can accumulate some investment returns tax-free, then borrow for retirement or, say, to start a business. But be careful—if you borrow so much that too little cash value is left to pay for mortality expenses, all the tax-deferred earnings will become suddenly taxable. Ouch!

GETTING HELP

It's a safe bet that as an entrepreneur you'll need tax help from time to time, for the complexity and sheer amount of work to keep up with taxes and provide proper forms and documentation will overwhelm you.

The same goes for insurance and risk management planning, *especially* if you have employees. While it's unlikely you'll have insurance questions as often as tax issues, when you do need help, you'll really need help. The choices and the complexity of those choices is staggering, and the cost differential among risk management strategies can be equally significant. When employees enter the picture, you'll be buried with health insurance questions in particular you'll wish you never had to answer.

The first stop on the risk management tour is usually with an insurance agent, although some business owners, especially with larger or riskier businesses, may want to get help from a professional *risk management consultant* first. These consultants have experience dealing with esoteric or complex forms of risk and are not (usually) selling any product, so their advice may be more balanced.

Insurance agents come in two forms generally: captive and multiple lines. *Captive agents*, like State Farm or Farmers or Allstate, handle only products of their home company. This can be good, because they can offer a consistent fit-together set of products, often with discounts for buying multiple policies at once, but it can be bad, for they may not offer some products you need (like health insurance) or may not have the most competitive products in some areas. *Multiple-lines* agents, as the name implies, offer products from different carriers or companies. Multiple-lines agents specializing in commercial or business lines can be especially helpful, for they shop the alternatives before you even walk in the door. Like any retail salespeople, they can be motivated by whoever is offering the best commission or incentive at a given time.

Finally, for those of you with employees, full-line *benefits specialists* can be more than handy. These firms, usually evolved from garden variety insurance agencies, specialize in health, life, and disability lines for businesses and their employees and they offer retirement plan administration as well. They can help you select the best benefit-and-insurance "bundle" and they often provide administrative and "help desk" functions for your employees, enabling you to get out of those energy-gobbling, time-consuming loops.

CHAPTER 9

Grow It: Investing for Entrepreneurs

SO FAR, WE'VE DEALT WITH HOW TO CREATE AND protect *income* from your business. Assuming you have a sound business idea and are able to execute it, sooner or later you'll move forward through the investment and early growth phases of the business. You'll first reach a point where the business becomes profitable on paper. At the same time or shortly thereafter, your business will throw off surplus cash, even after allocating funds to capital expenses and "rainy day" reserves. At this point, you are creating personal *wealth* through the business. How much of that wealth you choose to move into your personal finances depends on the needs of the business and its investors. But the detail isn't important—you're creating wealth.

Now comes the next challenge—what to *do* with that wealth. Why, of course—create more wealth with it! Yes, it is said, often sarcastically, that "money breeds more money." Those who don't have money or wealth look on jealously as those who do simply add to their piles. Is there anything wrong with this situation? As an entrepreneur, you probably have few objections. Capital should produce a return: you knew that when you paid out precious resources to obtain capital to fund your business in the first place. Now you're on the receiving end—*you* have cap-

ital to dole out to others seeking to emulate your success. There's nothing wrong with that.

Financially speaking, you're moving into territory where you're creating—not consuming—wealth. We called it the *accumulation phase* in Chapter 2. At this relatively happy transition in your entrepreneurial experience, your personal financial objective changes over—at the risk of oversimplifying—from staying out of debt to accumulating wealth. You save. You lock funds away toward achieving financial and lifestyle goals: retirement, college for the kids, an improved home, a new boat, and so on.

THE ENTREPRENEURIAL WEALTH BUILDING LIFECYCLE

When you make the transition into the accumulation phase, and even more so as you reach the *preservation* phase, a funny thing happens. You poured your soul into your business. You worked so hard for your money as you started the business, nursed it through its baby steps, and got it onto its feet and walking, now *climbing*. Almost without notice, you start to create excess cash, save, and build wealth. You *invest* that wealth. Ever so gradually, this wealth produces more wealth. At first, investment returns arrive in a trickle—a few dollars in a dividend here, a small capital gain there, some interest on a bank deposit or CD, rental income going positive on a real estate investment. But as these returns compound and as you put more earned cash into the till, slowly but surely these investment returns add up. The cycle continues, ever so gradually. You start to delegate more direct business involvement to others in the business—employees, hired managers, partners, and so forth. Pretty soon, your investments, including your direct stake in the business, are making as much or more as you were making through your efforts. Eventually, you may withdraw completely and let your investments take over.

If you were to put this cycle of events into a picture, it might look something like Figure 9.1.

Figure 9.1 shows an idealized model of this discussion—a gradual transition toward having your wealth work for you, instead of you having to work for *it*. Yes, it sounds idealistic: get so rich that your investments take over and you never have to work a day more in your life. And it sounds simple, like another of those elusive dreams you lie awake at night thinking about.

But don't put the book down just yet. This is a *model* for financial independence. It is a model not only for what you'd *like to* become, but also for what you *should* become. Why? For one thing, you can't

work forever. For another, you probably don't want to. And your spouse and family don't want you to, either.

We'll admit that usually people do not follow this model exactly as shown. Practically speaking, Microsoft founder Bill Gates went to 100 percent right out of the gate, so to speak. More likely, most real-world entrepreneurs experience a more curvilinear trip to the top, starting at first very slowly, but picking up speed over time, and maybe never getting 100 percent there, maybe always taking a percentage of their income directly from their work. It's OK. What's important is the idea; every entrepreneur should have a vision of this model somewhere in the back of his or her mind.

THE INVESTING IMPERATIVE

This may seem a roundabout way to get into a topic that seems straightforward, so much so that an amazing number of books have been written about it. Yes, we're talking about investing. Put simply, *investing* is the deliberate deployment of personal assets with the idea of achieving a return with a *goal* of building personal wealth. If you don't invest your assets, the accumulation of wealth will take longer—if you even get off the bottom floor of our entrepreneurial wealth-building lifecycle model at all.

Investing is clearly a good thing to do, yet so many entrepreneurs are so focused on their business and producing the investing "seed corn" (not to mention paying the bills and keeping the business going) that they tend to undermanage the investment part of their financial picture. How many entrepreneurs keep their stash virtually "in a mattress," earning little to no return? How many entrepreneurs simply don't have the time to focus on their investments, or are happy with investments that underperform, or are too risk-adverse to dip their toes into the investing pool. (Imagine that, after dip-

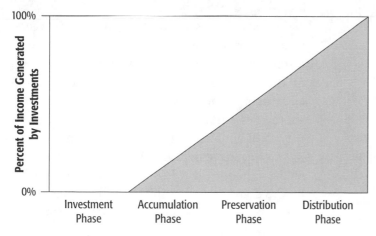

FIGURE 9.1. The Entrepreneurial Wealth-Building Life Cycle

ping toes into the entrepreneurial pool!) We see many examples of entrepreneurs who give far less attention and less care to their investments than to their own businesses.

A Strategic Overview

We want to get one thing straight: the *Ultimate Guide to Personal Finance for Entrepreneurs* is not an investing book. There are lots of those out there and they're easy to find. Compared with other personal finance concepts, the basics of investing are easy to learn and we assume you know some of them already anyway—what a stock is, what a bond is, etc. This one-chapter treatment is more of a strategic overview, how to think of investing from an entrepreneurial viewpoint. We give a pep talk on what to accomplish—and an entrepreneur-centric thought process for accomplishing it. We deal with how you as an entrepreneur should approach investing and how you as an entrepreneur already possess some of the key traits necessary to become a successful investor. Just like other aspects of entrepreneurship, it's OK to hire others—investment advisors and so forth—to manage the details, so long as you are in charge and these others don't cost more than they're worth.

BOOKS THAT SPEAK VOLUMES ABOUT INVESTING

There is more to learn about the tactics and mechanics of investing, as well as specific investing styles, than can be successfully presented here. We recommend a few books, including two of our own:

Standard & Poor's Guide to Money and Investing (McGraw-Hill/Lightbulb Press, 2005), by Virginia B. Morris and Kenneth M. Morris

Investing for Dummies (John Wiley & Sons, 4th edition, 2006), by Eric Tyson, summarizes general investing

Value Investing for Dummies (John Wiley & Sons, 2002), by this book's author Peter J. Sander and Janet Haley, digs into the value investing approach, most highly recommended for entrepreneurs

Active Investing—Take Charge of Your Portfolio in Today's Unpredictable Markets (Adams Media, 2005), also by Peter Sander, offers many investing basics and a strategic approach to investing for busy people

THROUGH THE EYES OF AN ENTREPRENEUR

Entrepreneurs are nothing if not creative, inquisitive, and independent-thinking. It's worth saying a few words about how that approach to life intersects with the investing world. Many traditional "book approaches" for individual investors may not always work for the typical entrepreneur. Examples include the largely risk-avoiding and risk-spreading approaches of asset allocation and mutual fund investing. Asset allocation models build portfolios according to prescribed percentages of *asset classes* consisting of stocks, bonds, cash, and real estate, and many subclasses, such as large, medium, and small companies. They don't look at specific investments on their own merits. The asset allocation approach and many common mutual fund investing approaches emphasize avoiding risk and particularly the risk of not knowing what you're doing.

Don't get us wrong: it's a good thing for entrepreneurs to recognize when they don't know what they're doing. Such humility comes in quite handy when it comes to judging business matters; in an area away from an entrepreneur's expertise or energy like investing, it may be even better. Our point is more that entrepreneurs can apply their innate skills and instincts to investing, thus achieving something better than the average individual investor.

The Entrepreneurial Advantage

When you step back and "catalog" the advantages the typical entrepreneur possesses that can be applied to investing, an interesting list emerges.

Business Knowledge. Granted, there are all kinds of entrepreneurs out there, but our experience tells us that most have a good understanding of business and business concepts. They understand markets, costs, return on investment, inventory, the importance and use of capital, and the management and control of daily business activity. They've experienced it all. They can sense when a business is being run well and also when it isn't. They can put themselves in the place of the CEO of another company and imagine what they would or wouldn't do in that situation. Such entrepreneurial and business instinct can be applied to investing in companies.

In fact—as we'll cover shortly—investing in stocks, real estate, and, to a lesser extent, bonds and other fixed-income vehicles should be viewed like buying the business itself. If you as an entrepreneur are evaluating buying 100 shares of Ford or Johnson & Johnson, for example, the operative question is, would you want to own Ford or J&J yourself? Are these "good" and well-run businesses likely to generate adequate returns on your investment to compensate for the risk and capital tied up? It's just like evaluating the risk of buying the corner coffee cart, except that, fortunately, you don't have to factor a lot of your own personal work and time into your decision. Aside from some real estate investments, most personal investments don't take much direct time off your busy schedule.

The "buy a business" approach is key to investing and you, as entrepreneur, are uniquely qualified to make that kind of decision.

Industry Knowledge. Not only do you understand business and how it works, but you, as an entrepreneur, are working in an industry and have some unique knowledge and experience with that industry. If you run a coffee cart, you know something about the restaurant business and the coffee business. If you are a concrete contractor, you know something about construction and the cement business. You know the ropes—the rules, both written and unwritten—about how the business really works. It's like having "insider" knowledge, which in this case of course is perfectly legal.

Entrepreneurs should not put all their eggs into one basket; that is, the coffee cart owner probably shouldn't invest everything in Starbucks or Peet's Coffee & Tea. Why? Because if America's caffeine binge ever dissipates, they would lose twice: once in their business and again in their investments. But running a coffee cart probably provides enough insight into the coffee business to identify the industry players that seem to be getting it right.

The Millionaire Mentality. Entrepreneurs have a unique perspective on money. It's real. They know what it takes to make it and that every dollar wasted or poorly invested is hard work and entrepreneurial return on investment thrown out the window. Money is a precious resource, not just a self-regenerating commodity that shows up in paycheck after paycheck. As a result, entrepreneurs typically develop prudent spending and investment habits. If there's any doubt, consider the research of Thomas J. Stanley and William D. Danko in one of our favorite financial books, *The Millionaire Next Door* (Longstreet, 1996) who found that fully *two-thirds* of the millionaires they surveyed who were still earning an income were self-employed. No statistic could more strongly support that entrepreneurs have something—the instinct, the care, the habits, the due diligence—that helps them create and grow their wealth. The entrepreneur-investor should take advantage of this unique mentality.

Intelligent Risk. Among the traits most supporting the entrepreneur's success in business and, in fact, the desire to get into business is the ability to take *intelligent risks*. What are "intelligent risks"? They are risks not avoided but taken using a rational, experience-driven judgment of upside and downside potential. Upsides and downsides are judged and compared with the next alternative. An entrepreneur-investor might take a little more risk on one investment because he or she has taken less on another, developing a portfolio of different risks designed to achieve larger and smaller, longer- and shorter-term returns. These are the sorts of decision made daily—and often subconsciously—in most businesses. Most entrepreneurs are trained by experience to take intelligent risks. It's a matter of instinct. Most entrepreneurs are able to apply a good mix of business knowledge, industry knowledge, due diligence, and intelligent risk appraisal and they will more often than not exceed expectations when investing.

The Entrepreneurial Challenge

So far we've created the impression that entrepreneurs are "perfect" investors. If they were, they'd *all* be millionaires and could sell their businesses and simply live by investing. Don't get too cocky—it isn't so easy. There are some important inhibitors that get in the way:

Time. Entrepreneurs are first and foremost dedicated to running their business. Successful investing takes a lot of time, to analyze companies, keep up with the news, and keep up with the markets. Most entrepreneurs simply don't have the time or energy to fully engage in investing. And just as with the business itself, a half-hearted effort will produce insufficient results—or worse. Some entrepreneurs will want to put money into long-term investments that don't need to be actively managed. Others will

want to be more "active" in their approach to investing, but most will prefer an investing style requiring minimal daily activity—perhaps a daily market check and a weekly to monthly session to evaluate investments.

Enough to Go Around? It's hard enough for most individuals to come up with enough extra cash to invest; it can be even harder for entrepreneurs. Businesses require cash, not only upfront but later on for capital asset replacement, expansion, and so forth. It's hard for the entrepreneur to set aside—and *keep* aside—enough to really get going with investments. Typically, it starts out with cash set aside for retirement, an investment that, as we'll explore in the next chapter, is necessary and often in significant quantities. Unfortunately, cash set aside for retirement isn't readily available to meet short-term needs. The entrepreneur's reluctance to lock away investable cash is understandable, but gets in the way of achieving the financial independence laid out earlier in the chapter.

Safety Nets. Until the business and personal finances reach really sound financial footing, entrepreneurs are confronted with uncertain cash requirements during any given period of time. Sure, everyone would like to invest long term, locking away money in steady and high-return investments. But unexpected (or even seasonal but expected) business requirements can force a cash need upon the entrepreneur. If the investments aren't performing right at the time, these needs can force an untimely sale at an unfavorable price. More than ordinary individuals, entrepreneurs must look over their shoulders to make sure no short-term shortfalls eat up their investments—and keep enough liquid reserves on hand to handle these issues. Unfortunately, such needs get in the way of achieving the highest possible returns on investments.

A FEW WORDS ABOUT "THE NUMBER"

Much has been made recently in the financial press and bookshelf about "the number"—the amount of wealth really required to ensure financial independence, especially in retirement. This focus understandably arises from the insecurity and inadequacy of our Social Security system and the rising burdens of health care. Also, we *expect more* from retirement—a lifestyle at least as good as during our working years and probably better. But, especially with health-care costs, it costs more. And finally, maybe the biggest "burden" of all—we live longer, so it all has to last 30 or 35 years, not just the 20 or 25 years for which our parents and grandparents planned. The analysis of retirement needs is covered in the next chapter.

The Role of Investing

It is often said that if you don't know where you're going, surely you won't get there. OK, we'll subscribe to that notion—but only to a point. Most people know that they want to have more wealth, more money, to do the things they want. That can be taken as a given. And the unspecific objective of investing to grow wealth can be further taken as a given.

But what if you have a specific objective in mind? A global number for yourself and your family or perhaps a number for a specific goal, such as a college education? How do you figure out what you need and how do you develop a plan to achieve it?

The answer originates back in Chapter 2, where we introduced the idea of accumulation and distribution annuities. Refer to the discussion of annuities and the accumulation and distribution annuity factor tables (Figures 2.8 and 2.10). The discussion first shows how to come up with a number expressed in terms of a desired payout during non-earning years, using the distribution annuity concept and the table, and then shows how to accumulate savings and investment returns to achieve that number using the accumulation annuity concept and the table. If

you're saving a fixed sum for something such as a college education or a boat, simply plug the sum and the number of years or months you wish to save into the table to figure out what you need to save every year or every month.

Now, what about the rate of return? That's where investing enters the picture. As we saw back in Chapter 2, higher rates of return mean more savings power on the accumulation side and more lasting power on the distribution side. Good investing is the key to achieving higher rates.

How Much Wealth Should You Have?

OK, the formulas are nice and particularly handy if there is a specific financial goal in mind. But first things first: what should that financial goal be?

Only you can decide, based on what you want, what you need, and the lifestyle you desire.

It is truly difficult to give a formulaic answer to the question "How much wealth should you have?" But sometimes the best answers to any "where should you be?" question come from benchmarking where you are relative to everyone or everything else. If you're ahead of the pack, that's a good thing.

In that spirit, we once again refer to *The Millionaire Next Door* findings and model. Market researchers by profession, Stanley and Danko set out to examine personal wealth and what it takes to achieve the favorite "number" of most—millionaire status.

As mentioned earlier, they found a high preponderance of entrepreneurs in their "millionaire" research. Work ethic, spending habits, and general view of the importance and role of money all played a part. What they also found is a relatively predictable benchmark for the range of average American wealth based largely on age and income levels. They found, for instance, that average wealth could be predicted by taking a person's age, multiplying annual income, and dividing the result by 10:

Average Wealth = (Age x Annual Income) / 10

So a 40-year-old earning $50,000 per year should have, on average, a net worth (total assets less total liabilities) of about $200,000, including home, investments, business equity, and all other forms of financial worth. Similarly, a two-earner family with annual income of $80,000 and a 50-year old head of household would have $400,000. Note that all *inherited* wealth and related trust income, etc. are excluded.

So if you want a number, this is a good one to start with. Notably, the number is quite sensitive to the estimation of annual income and we know well that most entrepreneurs have incomes that are far from steady (and often from multiple sources). So as you use this formula, it's a good idea to realistically estimate your long-term income base.

Stanley and Danko, most interestingly, go on to identify the tops and bottoms of the wealth curve—the overachievers and underachievers. They found that about 25 percent of the population have accumulated more than twice the amount suggested by the wealth formula. People in that group get the tag of Prodigious Accumulators of Wealth (PAWs), while people in the bottom quartile achieved less than half that amount, making them Underaccumulators of Wealth (UAWs). The terminology isn't so important, but as an entrepreneur, to set your sights on a number congruent with a "PAW" level of net worth—mathematically, (Age / 5) * Annual Income—seems like a good idea, regardless of your specifically identified needs.

THE (IMMENSE) POWER OF COMPOUNDING

In Chapter 2 we also touched on the power of compounding. In this chapter we'll do it again—to reinforce its importance and make an additional point, which we'll do in a moment.

Compounding is indeed powerful. Why else would have Einstein considered it one of the most awesome forces in this world? Put some money aside and it steadily earns a return—and the *returns* earn returns. Leave the goose and its exponentially accumulating golden eggs intact and soon you'll have a tidy sum. Leave it all intact a little longer and earn a good return on it. If you're like most people, you'll be amazed at the result. If you're still not sure, consider the numbers shown in Figure 9.2.

Do you want to make a million bucks? Simply deposit $1,000 at 19 percent and leave it in place for 40 years. OK, that isn't realistic, but how about $100,000 at 8 percent for 30 years?

The best way to save, of course, is through regular contributions, not just "one-time" infusions; that's where the accumulation annuity enters the picture. But it isn't hard to see that 8 percent is much better than 6 percent—almost twice better if it is left at work for 30 years.

OVER AND UNDERPERFORMANCE

Now here's the point we really wanted to make, and you probably saw it coming. Your savings, whether in a bank account or in some more active form of investment, will earn a return. Generally speaking, the more actively you manage and the more risk you're willing to take, the better the returns you can achieve.

If you leave your funds in a bank account, you'll get a return, but it's likely to be pretty stingy—perhaps 1 or 2 percent at best. Sure, there's no risk and the funds are readily available, but this isn't much, especially if you consider that with an inflation rate around 3 to 4 percent the purchasing power of your savings is actually declining.

So what return should you try to get? Arguably, your funds should grow at least at the rate of inflation and, more to the point, at the rate of growth of the U.S. economy. Otherwise, you're simply being left behind. That means you should strive to achieve about a 4 percent return. You can do that rather easily with money market funds or even U.S. Treasury securities.

If it's so easy to get "market" returns, why are we

Wealth accumulation, $1,000 invested at X percent over Y number of years

Rate of Return	Number of Years							
	1	2	5	10	15	20	30	40
4.0%	$1,040	$1,082	$1,217	$1,480	$1,801	$2,191	$3,243	$4,801
5.0%	$1,050	$1,103	$1,276	$1,629	$2,079	$2,653	$4,322	$7,040
6.0%	$1,060	$1,124	$1,338	$1,791	$2,397	$3,207	$5,743	$10,286
7.0%	$1,070	$1,145	$1,403	$1,967	$2,759	$3,870	$7,612	$14,974
8.0%	$1,080	$1,166	$1,469	$2,159	$3,172	$4,661	$10,063	$21,725
9.0%	$1,090	$1,188	$1,539	$2,367	$3,642	$5,604	$13,268	$31,409
10.0%	$1,100	$1,210	$1,611	$2,594	$4,177	$6,727	$17,449	$45,259
11.0%	$1,110	$1,232	$1,685	$2,839	$4,785	$8,062	$22,892	$65,001
12.0%	$1,120	$1,254	$1,762	$3,106	$5,474	$9,646	$29,960	$93,051
13.0%	$1,130	$1,277	$1,842	$3,395	$6,254	$11,523	$39,116	$132,782
14.0%	$1,140	$1,300	$1,925	$3,707	$7,138	$13,743	$50,950	$188,884
15.0%	$1,150	$1,323	$2,011	$4,046	$8,137	$16,367	$66,212	$267,864
16.0%	$1,160	$1,346	$2,100	$4,411	$9,266	$19,461	$85,850	$378,721
17.0%	$1,170	$1,369	$2,192	$4,807	$10,539	$23,106	$111,065	$533,869
18.0%	$1,180	$1,392	$2,288	$5,234	$11,974	$27,393	$143,371	$750,378
19.0%	$1,190	$1,416	$2,386	$5,695	$13,590	$32,429	$184,675	$1,051,668
20.0%	$1,200	$1,440	$2,488	$6,192	$15,407	$38,338	$237,376	$1,469,772
21.0%	$1,210	$1,464	$2,594	$6,727	$17,449	$45,259	$304,482	$2,048,400
22.0%	$1,220	$1,488	$2,703	$7,305	$19,742	$53,358	$389,758	$2,847,038
23.0%	$1,230	$1,513	$2,815	$7,926	$22,314	$62,821	$497,913	$3,946,430
24.0%	$1,240	$1,538	$2,932	$8,594	$25,196	$73,864	$634,820	$5,455,913
25.0%	$1,250	$1,563	$3,052	$9,313	$28,422	$86,736	$807,794	$7,523,164

FIGURE 9.2. The Power of Compounding

so concerned about investing? Shouldn't you just lock your funds away and stay focused on your business instead?

Well, yes and no. Your business is number one. But consider what happens when you improve your returns, even a little bit. Or the flip side when you mismanage your investments and underperform this "base" return rate.

Outperforming the Market

If you invest your funds at 4 percent, you'll achieve a decent return, and that return grows, nicely if not to stellar proportions, if it's left alone for a while. Invest $1,000 at 4 percent and it becomes $2,191 in

20 years (see Figure 9.3, top line).

Now, suppose you boost this 4 percent just a bit. What happens? Figure 9.3 shows that if you beat the market by just 2 percent, achieving a 6 percent annual return on average, your $2,191 becomes $3,207—a 50-percent increase! If you can beat that 4 percent by another 4 percent (an 8 percent rate of return), you'll wind up with $4,661—220 percent better than at 4 percent. The story gets even better the longer the funds are left in place.

Now, is it easy to achieve 8-percent returns consistently for 20 or 30 years? No, especially with the occasional downturns that roil the markets from time to time. But consider that stocks, on average,

Additional long-term returns gained by beating the market by X percent, $1000 invested

Nominal Rate	Number of Years							
	1	2	5	10	15	20	30	40
4.0%	$1,040	$1,082	$1,217	$1,480	$1,801	$2,191	$3,243	$4,801
Beat the Market by								
2.0%	$1,060	$1,124	$1,338	$1,791	$2,397	$3,207	$5,743	$10,286
4.0%	$1,080	$1,166	$1,469	$2,159	$3,172	$4,661	$10,063	$21,725
6.0%	$1,100	$1,210	$1,611	$2,594	$4,177	$6,727	$17,449	$45,259
8.0%	$1,120	$1,254	$1,762	$3,106	$5,474	$9,646	$29,960	$93,051
10.0%	$1,140	$1,300	$1,925	$3,707	$7,138	$13,743	$50,950	$188,884

FIGURE 9.3. Comparative Returns: Beating the Market

including dividends, have achieved historic long-term returns around 10 or 11 percent since the 1920s, as the economy has grown and corporate entities have taken an increasingly large share of economic output. Consider also that Warren Buffett has achieved returns, on average, exceeding 25 percent for more than 30 years (which is why he's the second-richest person in the world). We don't expect you to go this far; in fact, an all-stock portfolio may be too risky and time-consuming for you. (Buffett is a full-time investor.) But 6, 7, 8 percent? It's within the realm of possibilities. The message here: don't get greedy, but investing your way to a little better return is clearly worthwhile.

Underperforming the Market

Now we must take a look at the flip side. We dangled the carrot of *over*performance just now. But what if you blow it with your investments or get just a little too conservative? What happens? Consider Figure 9.4.

The table shows, quite clearly, the cost of underperformance. Starting with the 4 percent benchmark, if you underperform the "market" by 2 percent, earning only 2 percent on your money, instead of earning $2,191 earned in 20 years, you earn fully 34 percent less, $1,455. Of course, the result at 0 percent return

THE RULE OF 72

Time out to review a little mathematical shorthand first introduced in Chapter 2. Tired of looking at tables to figure out investing returns and the effects of compound growth? Consider the Rule of 72, one of the best mental shortcuts ever invented (and incidentally, one of the favorite tools of Mr. Buffett, who reputedly uses it constantly).

is obvious. And if you underperform by 6 percent, dropping you to a negative 2-percent return, your nest egg shrinks by two-thirds. You get the idea.

AN ACTIVE APPROACH TO INVESTING

From what we've just seen, it's clear that even *small* improvements in investment performance can have big effects on your long-term wealth. It pays to invest—and it pays to invest *carefully*, avoiding the wealth-stifling effects of underperformance. The best advice we can give entrepreneurs: don't ignore your investments! It's impossible to get it perfect; even the best investors (Buffett aside) don't do that.

Nominal Rate	Number of Years							
	1	2	5	10	15	20	30	40
4.0%	$1,040	$1,082	$1,217	$1,480	$1,801	$2,191	$3,243	$4,801
Beat the Market by								
2.0%	$1,020	$1,040	$1,104	$1,219	$1,346	$1,486	$1,811	$2,208
4.0%	$1,000	$1,000	$1,000	$1,000	$1,000	$1,000	$1,000	$1,000
6.0%	$980	$960	$904	$817	$739	$668	$545	$446
8.0%	$960	$922	$815	$665	$542	$442	$294	$195
10.0%	$940	$884	$734	$539	$395	$290	$156	$84

Long-term returns lost by underperforming the market by X percent, $1,000 invested

FIGURE 9.4. Corporate Returns: Underperforming the Market

But it's clearly worthwhile to strive for a little more, perhaps market plus a percent or two. As we've seen, that means a lot and will get you a lot further up the wealth-building life cycle introduced at the outset of this chapter. That, in a nutshell, is what we think your *investment* goals should be: a base market return—plus a percent or two.

But how do you get the extra return? It requires a little more than just socking your funds away in a government bond. It means taking charge of your investments, *actively* managing them. Does that mean sitting by your screen, watching every quiver or pulse of the market and your investments? Not at all. But you (and your advisors, if you choose to use any) should *work* your investments to squeeze out this extra bit of return with as little risk as possible.

A QUESTION OF STYLE

We call this investing approach an *active* investing style. Not trading—and certainly not *day* trading. With active investing, you stay in charge, do the research when you can, and manage your investments with a light touch. The goal is to achieve the *modest* extra return and stay ahead of potential bumps in the road.

This sounds pretty basic, not as simple as "buy low, sell high," but what's so different about "achieve returns, avoid bumps in the road"? There is a clear mandate for modesty: don't "shoot the moon" or "try to hit home runs," but rather stay within yourself and manage your investments carefully—as you would your business—to achieve modest returns. For many entrepreneurs, the first adage is "Get going, don't be so conservative, invest to better your returns and get your money to work for you." For many others, it's "don't be greedy." The *active* approach sits in between these two.

A Do-It-Yourself Approach

A big part of the active investing framework embodies the spirit of the do-it-yourselfer, which is a good fit for the entrepreneur. Homeowners who are do-it-yourselfers do it themselves to save money and to be fully involved in the result. It's much the same with investing. If you throw your investments completely over the wall to an investment advisor or even a mutual fund, you'll pay fees for the service, typically 1 percent, sometimes much more. Now as we saw, even this modest percentage will dramatically eat into long-term returns over time.

Moreover, throw it over the wall and you may not like the result. Financial advisors do it their way, not yours. Sure, they'd like to make money for you, but they have other objectives, too, not the least of which is to make money for themselves and their firm. As a sobering thought, some 70 percent of stock mutual funds don't even achieve the average returns of the major U.S. stock market sectors they invest in. So, like a home-building project, you're likely to like the result more if you do it. Even if you employ a contractor, you will be more satisfied with the result more if you're involved in the decisions and, perhaps, some of the heavy lifting.

We feel that do-it-yourself investing reduces costs and gives you better control and perspective on your investments. We don't recommend this approach for everyone, but it seems a best fit for the entrepreneur and entrepreneurial style.

A Tiered Approach

Active investing, as the name suggests, means managing your investments actively. Not unlike your business, you collect information and make decisions based on that information. Some decisions are short-term adjustments and course corrections; others are larger-scale decisions on major purchases or sales or even the approach you use to do business.

Beyond the direct commitment of hands-on management, the active approach, as we bring it to your situation, involves a strategic approach to investing. The word "strategic" means a lot of things in business. One meaning—and a most useful concept for all business owners—is the division of a business into segments following the so-called "Pareto principle," known more widely as the "80-20 rule," according to which, for instance, the most attention is paid to the 20 percent of your business that generates 80 percent of your profits. Most things in business life and life at large can be divvied up this way—20 percent of your customers generate 80 percent of your revenues, 20 percent of your products account for 80 percent of your production costs, 20 percent of your employees do 80 percent of

your work, etc.

Applying this principle to investing gives a similar, if not quite identical, result: 20 percent of your investments require 80 percent of your attention, while 80 percent of your investments can be left alone. It may be that 20 percent of your investments account for 80 percent of your returns, too, but that is not an intended consequence of this approach. It's the attention factor—and the activity—that we focus on. Simply, a small portion of your portfolio should get the most attention, while the rest is left to perform with the market. In this manner, we achieve the 1 or 2 percent extra return beyond market returns, we keep investing from becoming a full-time activity, and, in some cases, we reduce investing costs.

We find that, even without a business to run, people who try to actively manage all portions of their portfolio at once tend to not do as well. Their efforts are diffuse. Moreover, in investing, like in business, there's no one-size-fits-all model. In our investing model, different parts of a portfolio should be set up to achieve different objectives; for example, part should be set up "slow and steady" to generate income, while another part might be set up to benefit from the business growth inherent in up-and-coming businesses. Obviously, the techniques and time involved in managing one part of this portfolio differ from those required to manage the other.

THE ACTIVE PORTFOLIO(S)

Our strategic investing approach divides your portfolio and investment efforts into two major components: a *foundation* or cornerstone portfolio and an *opportunistic* or venture portfolio. The foundation portfolio represents the slow, steady, solid, safe, and relatively less time-consuming portion of your investments. The opportunistic portfolio, in contrast, is actively managed as your own personal private venture capital—that is, to capture investing

WHAT ABOUT DIVERSIFICATION?

Read any investing book or tune into any investing program on the radio or TV and you'll hear a lot about *diversification*. Diversification is all about *not* putting all eggs into one basket, about minimizing risk and exposure to the fortunes of a single company or a single investment. The concept makes sense. Don't buy stock in only one company and don't put all your eggs into the stock market. Brokers go on about how much of your portfolio should be in stocks, bonds, and cash, as if a 5 or 10 percent adjustment in these categories is the secret to investing success. We also hear a lot about large-cap, mid-cap, and small-cap investments. ("Cap"—capitalization—is the market value of a company expressed in terms of outstanding shares times the market price.)

Active investing recognizes the value of diversification but adds a layer with the management of different portfolios. What active investing seeks to avoid is *over*diversification or diversification for diversification's sake. Repeatedly we see portfolios constructed of five or six general stock mutual funds. These funds probably all own the same stocks or at least overlap significantly! If you overdiversify, you'll most likely underperform the market, for it's hard to achieve greater-than-market returns on a very broad portfolio, and then management fees will wipe out those gains and likely take you negative. This is a primary reason why 70 percent of stock mutual funds underperform the market.

We feel the diversification needs to be more strategic, that is, segmented by risk-return ratios and the amount of time and effort required to search for higher returns. Such is the foundation for our active approach—diversify where you

want to achieve average returns and reduce risk, and focus where you want to beat the market. With actively managed investments, like those found in the opportunistic portfolio, we subscribe to the Buffetonian notion that diversification is a safeguard for those who don't know what they're doing.

opportunities as they present themselves.

Further, the foundation portfolio, for most investors, will be the "80 percent" chunk requiring 20 percent of your management time, while the opportunistic portfolio may take 80 percent of your time, comprise perhaps 20 percent of your total investments, and generate most of your returns beyond the steady-state 4 or 5 percent, largely risk-free market rate of return. For typical investors, these percentages will vary; it isn't important to divvy things up exactly 80-20. It's the thought process that counts.

Some investors may also manage a separate portfolio lying somewhere in between "cornerstone" and "venture." In the more complete active investing treatment outlined in *Active Investing—Take Charge of Your Portfolio in Today's Unpredictable Markets* (Adams Media, 2005), we define a *rotational* portfolio. The rotational segment is managed more actively than the foundation segment, typically capturing business or industry cycles through sector or sector-fund investments. Rotate some capital to whichever sectors are hot—health care, energy, and so on. The rotational portfolio captures movements in the business cycle without undue risk or excessive time consumed with picking individual investments.

Foundation Investing

The goal of the foundation portfolio is to achieve a relatively risk-free base market return with relatively little investing effort or cost. Currently (2006) the risk-free return ranges from 4 to 5 percent, with liquid short-term money market funds at about 5 percent. Funds placed in these investments are safe and require little in the way of active management. Large portions of foundation investments typically consist of *fixed-income* investments, that is, investments bought for the purpose of producing a defined income stream, i.e., interest or dividend payments.

It's usually a good idea to diversify somewhat within the fixed-income portion of a foundation portfolio. Fixed-income investments are not without risk. First, the income stream may stop, as in a suspended dividend or a defaulted interest payment. With quality investments, this occurrence is relatively rare. More pertinent are *interest rate* and *inflation risk*—the risk that the fundamental value of your investment may decline if interest rates or inflation rise, making your investment relatively less attractive. Securities with long-term maturities, primarily bonds, carry this risk. If you buy a ten-year bond for $1,000 paying 5 percent and the market interest rate climbs to 10 percent, the value of that bond drops in sympathy—toward a level half what it was (because the 5 percent "coupon" yield, without a price adjustment, is half the market rate). Now, the price in reality doesn't usually drop by that much, for if you hold the bond for the entire 10-year period, you'll get 100 percent of your money back. But the value may drop substantially in the short term. Notably, bank and credit union CDs do not experience this price depreciation, because they are most often held to maturity.

Laddering. Foundation investors learn to diversify their fixed-income investments to have different types of investments with different maturities. Some may be invested in short-term or liquid investments like money market funds, some in intermediate-term, and some in longer-term securities, which usually pay a little more. Such *laddering* is a popular approach for investors with significant foundation investments—where maturities are staggered so that some come due and are replaced each year, effectively hedging against major interest rate changes.

IS YOUR HOME PART OF YOUR FOUNDATION?

The active investing approach is as much a philosophical construct as a specific formula for managing your investments. Whether your foundation portfolio really is 80 percent of your investments and whether it is exclusively committed to steady, conservative investments is of course entirely up to you. You may want to take more risk to generate higher returns and set up your opportunistic portfolio at 30 or 40 percent of your assets. You may construct these portfolios to include non-security investments. For many, a home is part of a foundation portfolio (although in recent years, many real estate investments have behaved more like venture investments!). Same goes for the investments in your business. If you're looking at your personal finances as a whole, it probably makes sense to incorporate your home (equity portion only) in your foundation portfolio. But from the perspective of managing investments, we're really talking about cash and security investments.

Index Funds. A slightly more active approach is to mix some broadly diversified market-performing investments into this portfolio. This can be accomplished by buying investments driven by market indexes, like *index funds*. Index funds are portfolios collected and sold by fund companies to mirror the performance of major stock indexes, like the S&P 500. If you buy the popular Standard & Poor Depository Receipts (SPDR) fund, your performance will almost exactly match the performance of this highly diversified fund.

As we'll explore further in a moment, management and other fees are a big part of investing and especially fund investing. If you buy a fund that generates a 5-percent return but has a 1.5-percent management fee—guess what!—you've underperformed the market. Happily, most index funds, especially *exchange-traded funds* (ETFs) (an SPDR is an ETF), have very low management fees, as low as 0.1–0.2 percent. Buying a SPDR is almost a no-brainer investment, allowing you to do as well as the market with little cost or effort. More on ETFs in a moment.

Opportunistic Investing

Opportunistic, or venture, investing seeks to find "overachieving" investments with the premise of expanding your total portfolio return, again without taking undue risks in the entire portfolio. As an opportunistic investor, you're essentially functioning as a venture capitalist, seeking above-average business opportunities in which to invest.

Opportunistic investments usually consist of individually picked equities (stocks). These investments are picked using a *value* approach (described more fully below) for short-, intermediate-, or even longer-term capital appreciation. Value investors look for quality individual companies at attractive prices.

We don't necessarily subscribe to the notion of *trading*—the short-term buying and selling of securities to capture minor fluctuations in value—for

entrepreneurs. But there are some situations where a trade, especially a "swing" trade entered over a few days, makes some sense. This type of trade is really a value investment too—an investment cheap enough in the short run to merit a short-term play.

A STOCK INVESTING PRIMER

As we said at the outset, we can't cover all features, techniques, and vehicles found in the investing world. There are simply too many and the descriptions fill volumes. We refer you to other resources, a few of which were noted earlier. What we can do is share some thought processes and strategies, which will, hopefully, guide you toward getting started or toward improving your personal investing approach.

Why You Should Invest in (Some) Stocks

Earlier we noted some reasons to invest in stocks, that is, equities in U.S. or even international corporations. Over time, these are the investments that participate in economic growth. Notably, fixed-income investments do not normally participate in such growth and may even be hurt by it, as growth leads to inflation. Inflation reduces the value of fixed investments, for they are paid back (or cash returns paid) with less valuable dollars later.

Although stock prices can be hurt in the short term by inflation—by rising interest costs and raw material and labor costs in the business—they generally keep up with inflation in the long term. Future revenues and costs will all be measured in future dollars and thus so will the stock price. Perhaps for this reason and because corporate America is grabbing an ever-larger share of the business world (Wal-Mart is but one example), stock prices in general have exhibited the strongest long-term returns. Aside from commodity investments or most real estate, there is no surer way to keep up with inflation.

▼
… AND WHAT ABOUT YOUR RETIREMENT PLAN?

For most, retirement plans are part of the foundation—the steady-growing, long-term base of your investing portfolio. But some self-directed individual retirement accounts (mostly IRAs and SEP accounts, see next chapter) may present a unique opportunity for venture investing. Why? Because gains aren't currently taxed. So make a hundred here and there with a few swing trades and the entire gain stays on the table without a tax bite.

Finally, as discussed earlier, we think that entrepreneurs have a unique innate ability to ferret out good businesses, good business practices, and thus good investments.

The Value Investing Approach

Value investing is couched in two fundamental principles:

- **Buying a stock is really buying a business.** Of course, we're talking about buying a *share* of the business, but the same principles apply. Any business worth buying must be a "good" business capable of producing returns worth the capital risked. Good businesses produce steady, predictable, and preferably growing returns in the form of cash flow and tangible business value. You want your own business to be a "good" business; here we simply apply to other investments the principles that make your business good or bad. Good markets, strong customer acceptance, and unique value propositions lead to high profit margins and return on capital investment and, of course, cash to the owners.

- **You want to buy cheap.** Buying cheap increases the chances of being right by taking at least some downside risk out of play. If you acquired your business, you certainly looked for the best deal for the price and you probably worked with the previous owner to lower the price to reduce your capital requirements—and your risk. Value investors operate much the same way, looking for "stocks on sale"—that is, stocks beaten down by the market. The *market* is really a group of appraisers who may or may not be right about a business's value in the short term. If you see things differently than they do—and it happens all the time—you can capitalize on the opportunity.

EVALUATING A STOCK

OK, fine. Find good businesses and buy cheap. But how? If it were so easy, wouldn't everyone be doing it?

First of all, not everyone is a value investor. Some investors (traders, really) play the markets for their short-term price fluctuations. For many, the stock becomes a slot machine, a ticker symbol—and these "investors" buy and sell without having any idea what the company is or does. This trading serves a purpose, for it makes for a more perfect, efficient market, which is the natural result of having more players involved. But it's not really investing in the sense that we as entrepreneurs think of it.

Many more investors simply don't know how to evaluate a good business or they buy on the name alone or they buy on the recommendation of brokers or advisors or they buy simply because the stock represents a part of some group they wish to invest in. These all can be good reasons to invest, but they stop short of value investing—the way we see it.

There is no "cookbook" formula for evaluating a stock that works every time. Again, if there were, we probably wouldn't be writing this book, for we wouldn't need the money to achieve our financial goals! The value approach appraises a business according to many factors, room for all of which we don't have here. But there is room for a summary—a "business brief," if you will—on finding good businesses.

Financials

As we all learned in the late '90s tech boom, neither a good idea nor a fancy business plan, by itself, will make money. You know that, too, from your own business. No matter how much your customers love you, no matter how good or innovative your idea sounds, it must deliver profits sooner or later or else you don't have a viable business.

Not being accountants ourselves, we don't expect you to focus on every number on every income statement, balance sheet, or statement of cash flow. Nonetheless, financials are important. As diligent investors, we focus on a few key things. We call those things *strategic financials*—financial numbers or indicators that tell us the most about the success and health of the business.

Is the Business Profitable? It sounds rather obvious to shine a flashlight on business profitability. Does the business make money? That's a good first question. Revenues less costs should yield a positive number.

It's important—and relatively easy—to drill down just a bit into profitability. We like to learn more about the growth and consistency of profits. We also like to look at profit margins—*gross margin* (sales less costs of goods sold) and *net profit margin* (sales less all costs). Are margins healthy? Compared with the margins of competitors? Are margins increasing? Are some parts of the profitability, like gross margin, increasing but other factors, like operating expenses, wiping out that gain? Does the business appear to be growing sales at the expense of margins, that is, discounting to gain more, but less profitable market share? This is all part of the analysis.

Cash flow is also important. Earnings, or profits, don't always match cash flow. Why? Because of the accounting treatment of depreciation and the timing of revenues and expenses. Diligent investors

look beyond earnings, using the statement of cash flows, to see where money is really coming from and going.

Any business (including *your* business) is worth the sum of all cash flows produced, now or later. It's worth the cash generated now and in the future, with an appropriate discount factor applied for the time value of money, plus the amount generated by the business—again discounted—when it is sold. This is known in the professional world as *discounted cash flow analysis*. Any value for the business other than this value is, by definition, an over- or underappraisal of the business. The problem, of course, is that it is impossible to estimate these future cash flows precisely. That's where the market and your judgment come into play.

Does the Business Produce Capital—or Consume It? You remember when most of your time was spent arranging for funds to invest in your business. You wondered whether the business would ever produce capital that you could put to other use. Think of that in investing. Some businesses *consume* capital; others *produce* it. Better businesses produce capital and do it consistently.

How do you tell? Look at the statement of cash flows. Does cash inflow—measured as "Cash Flow from Operations"—consistently exceed capital and financing outflows—measured by "Cash Provided by (Used for) Investments" and "Cash Flow Provided by (Used for) Financing," respectively? If so, you're looking at a "good" business from a financial standpoint. Investment pros use the term *excess free cash flow* to describe companies that are earning more than enough cash to meet all requirements, including capital expenditures.

Growth. Talk with any investor and soon the topic shifts to *growth stocks*. Instead of growth *stocks*, we are looking for growth *businesses*. Why is growth important? Because business growth, ultimately, pays its owners a growing return, which makes an equity investment more attractive than a fixed-income

GOING TO SCHOOL—BY INVESTING

As you read through the list of investment and business appraisal techniques, do you find yourself in a better position to appraise—and even run—*your own* business? If you think being a good investor makes you a better business person—and vice versa—you're onto one of the best-kept secrets of entrepreneurial personal finance.

investment. Growing companies can pay more dividends and produce higher net worth for their owners, both in small businesses and in large corporations.

Asset Quality and Productivity. Just as a banker would evaluate your business, you should examine the kinds of assets on a company's balance sheet and how much debt it has incurred. Some assets are better than others—cash and current receivables are better than old buildings, most inventory, and dated receivables. Especially in recent years, asset valuation problems have surfaced at some companies. If you remember an old value investing adage—"Debt is real, while asset values may not always be"—you'll do fine.

It's also smart to look at asset productivity. How much inventory, receivables, or floor space is necessary to produce a dollar of sales or profits? A business that generates sales or profits more efficiently has an edge on one that can't. It's more profitable and it's more *flexible* to meet ever more rapidly changing marketplace needs.

Intangibles

Value investors realize that financials are only *part* of the business picture. The rest of the story is contained mainly in a group of factors we'll describe as *intangibles*—immeasurable or only partly measurable characteristics that drive the business and, *as a result,* the financials. Good businesses have good numbers, but something must be right in how the business positions itself, produces and markets its products and services, and manages the whole thing to make the numbers come out right. It's probably obvious to you as an entrepreneur that business success starts before the numbers are recorded, but it's amazing how it escapes the analysis of many investors and investment professionals.

Market Position. A company's position in a market and the products it produces for that market will drive success. Value investors look at a company's

> ### ◤ IS IT REALLY GROWTH *VS.* VALUE?
>
> You'll hear investment professionals talk about "growth" and "value" as though they were mutually exclusive. To them, value companies produce steady returns and have undervalued assets and relatively low stock prices that reflect their underlying asset values, while growth companies are priced higher because of their future growth. To us, value and growth are not mutually exclusive. Assets that produce growing returns are more valuable than assets that produce steady-state returns, assuming similar risk profiles. To us, companies with solid business fundamentals and strong growth prospects are the best value candidates. For example, we think Starbucks is a "value" stock because of the fundamental strength of the business and its growth prospects.

competitive profile—that is, how well it stacks up against competitors.

Position is important. Is it the price leader? The innovator? The one-stop shop? Whatever it is, it better be clear and the company must execute well on it. In past years, think of Dell (direct sales, low cost, Intel-based platforms) vs. Hewlett-Packard (everything for everybody). Which is clearer and more focused? Which has a clearer brand and *brand promise* to its customers? Which is more highly regarded in the media and in public opinion?

Value investors appraise market position, market share, share growth, brand strength, and brand perception. From this, they assess *pricing power*. Can the company control its destiny on the store shelf? Can it *differentiate* itself? Can the company generate more profit from sales without significant threat of being undercut by rivals? (Such undercutting eventually caught up with Dell, but it was a nice ride while it lasted.) Similarly, the appraisal looks at supply chain and costs. Can the company control its costs? Does it manage the supply chain effectively to get the lowest price and to avoid supply disruptions?

Airlines are a classic case of a bad business in a value investor's mind. No control over costs (fuel, labor) or price (competition, undifferentiated product). Only Southwest really succeeds, because it has simplified its operations. Not unlike Dell, Southwest has cut out intermediaries and other costs of complexity, like servicing different kinds of aircraft, for example. It has created a solid brand and executed every promise, including on-time performance, perfectly. But Southwest remains just one or two missteps from the morass of failed airline businesses that have lost control of their key business intangibles.

Management. You manage a business and have developed your own unique style for doing so. So have the managers—the executives, the officers, the customer service managers—of the firm you want to invest in. Do they do a good job? Are they clear and forthright with their investors, as you are with yours? Do investors come first or do the executive managers always seem to do what's right for themselves before they do what's right for you or their customers? It's hard to tell for sure: there are many layers of professional PR people and spin doctors between you as a shareholder and what the execs are thinking and doing. But there are ways to pick up clues. Look at what they say and what they do. Do they make good decisions? Do they produce consistent and improving business performance? Do they do things to enhance shareholder value, like pay dividends and buy back shares? If they buy back shares, do the buybacks exceed the amounts gifted to themselves and employees in the form of option grants? Are they transparent and clear with financial and marketing messages? If they make a mistake, are they willing to admit it?

There is no surefire way to determine any of this, except perhaps the options if you're willing to dig deep enough. But your business appraisal should take these factors into account, even though it's mainly a gut feeling.

Price. Once you determine that a business is a good business to invest in, the next issue is price. If you buy shares in a good business that everyone else has recognized as such, it's easy to pay too much, even if the business is good. Value investors look for good businesses *on sale*—that is, selling at a discount to their true value. Now, since it's impossible to know that value exactly, even with the best discounted cash-flow guess/analysis, it becomes a judgment call.

Investment analysts depend on price ratios— price-to-earnings (P/E), price-to-sales (P/S), and price-to-book-value (P/B), at least for starters. There are some variations on these, like price-to-cash-flow and enterprise value/EBITDA, which we won't get into here. We like price-to-cash flow, because it sidesteps some of the accounting "games" and one-time write-offs that can affect P/E, but you must be careful to take capital expenditures into account, so "free" cash flow is better.

A SHORT FUND-INVESTING PRIMER

Funds are really shares of investment companies— companies set up under federal law to invest and pass proceeds on to their investors without paying corporate taxes. Legal definitions aside, funds are really *managed investments*. You need to decide, as an entrepreneur investor, whether you want to leave the driving to someone else. There are compelling reasons to do so—time, expertise, diversification— and there may well be a role for funds in your portfolio, especially its foundation portions. Here are a few thoughts about investing in funds.

Mutual Funds—Why and Why Not

There are some 9,000 active mutual funds in the U.S. Most are part of fund families, with such household names as Vanguard, Fidelity, and Franklin Templeton. *Open-ended* funds pool

ABOUT *SELLING* STOCKS

So far, we've discussed some factors to consider when buying a stock, but what about selling? When do you sell? Some of the best stock pickers fail by not knowing when to sell. It's one of the hardest things for an investor, particularly a long-term value investor, to do. Such investors tend to "marry" their stocks and wait out bad times perhaps more than they should.

Much has been written about selling, but it comes down to this: sell when the fundamentals have changed and/or when there's something else better to buy. If a business loses its way—with declining competitive advantage, profits, or management credibility—that's a good sign to sell. Of course, no alarm goes off on your PC telling you when this has happened, but if you follow the papers and follow your gut, the signs will be there. And if there's something better to buy, whether it's another company or a safer money market return, and you feel it in your gut, that's a good time, too. Many unsure investors resort to the tactic of half-selling—selling half a position to lock in a profit (or a more moderate loss) while still leaving some of the investment on the table.

And about that 10-percent rule you've heard about from brokers—sell when something declines 10 percent—if you did your homework before buying and the business is a good business, the 10-percent drop might instead be a signal to buy more. Always try to understand the reasons for the 10-percent drop.

investor dollars and invest them in the markets according to the guiding principles of the fund and its professional research. Each investor owns a share of the fund's *net asset value* (NAV) corresponding to the number of fund shares he or she has bought. The NAV is recalculated at the end of every market trading day.

Obviously, with 9,000 choices there are many styles and investing focuses to choose from. Value, growth, small-cap, large-cap, industry specialty, bond, and more specialized funds are available. Most funds allow free switching among funds within a family.

Mutual funds are businesses and they charge for their services. Most assess management fees ranging from 0.5 to over 2 percent and 12b-1 fees (marketing fees) to pay for attracting new customers. These fees are deducted from the returns produced by the fund before determining NAV or paying out dividends or capital gains. Yes, you read this right: you pay the costs of attracting new customers. And funds also collect sales charges—effectively commissions—either upfront ("load" funds) or in some manner when you cash out. These charges can run 5 percent or higher.

Funds have received a lot of criticism recently for high fees and some shenanigans with allowing certain investors to trade in and out in advance of NAV recalculations. Some big names have paid large fines and many have announced reduced management fees. Fees are the bugaboo with even the best-managed funds; if the fund earns 8 percent and charges 2.5 percent for management and marketing, you're left with only 5.5 percent even in a favorable market—and we saw earlier how much that really costs.

Mutual funds can still be the right answer, particularly if you have little interest or time for individual investing. The trick is to find a fund with a good manager with a proven track record that charges fees reasonable for its performance. The lower the fees the better, in general, but sometimes it's worth paying a little more to get a good fund manager.

There is a lot of educational and investment material available on mutual funds. If you want to invest in mutual funds, we recommend Morningstar, a consumer-friendly portal loaded with mutual fund information (*www.morningstar.com*).

Exchange-Traded Funds

In an environment of growing frustration with mutual funds, another type of managed investment has exploded in popularity, *exchange-traded funds* (ETFs). Exchange-traded funds are portfolios of stocks (mostly) intended to track a popular market index—either the broader market indexes like S&P 500 or NASDAQ 100 or some more specific segment of the market, like energy or retail companies. Stocks are accumulated into an ETF based on which stocks or sectors are represented in the target index, so little active management is required. The resulting fund is then traded on a major exchange, like the New York Stock Exchange, the American Stock Exchange, and NASDAQ.

The value, of course, is that you get diversification and market performance (at least in line with some sector of the market) without paying high fees and with easy entry and exit. There are now some 200 ETFs and the number is expanding almost daily to bring in commodities and some "lightly" managed portfolios.

ETFs are mainly targeted to do-it-yourselfers who like to buy diversified portfolios without building them themselves and without the transaction costs of accumulating small bits of dozens of companies. ETFs are a particularly good way to bring in some international exposure, for it's difficult to pick international companies individually. ETFs are good for a foundation portfolio and for a rotational portfolio. More information on ETFs is available at Morningstar and an assortment of ETF provider sites, like iShares (*www.ishares.com*).

WHAT ABOUT REAL ESTATE?

"They're not making any more of it." So goes the buy-side adage about real estate. Many entrepreneurs have eschewed stocks and bonds in favor of real estate over time, for they understand this supply-demand proposition. Frankly, in a world of financial shenanigans and less-than-transparent corporate management, what's not to believe in a piece of prime property?

We don't have room here to divert into the mechanics of real estate investing. But we offer a few high-level strategies and principles for you to consider.

Real estate comes in various forms: land, residential, commercial. You may buy it for your own use or invest in it to rent out as a business. You may buy individual pieces of property or shares in real estate portfolios, usually through *real estate investment trusts* (REITs).

The long-term performance of real estate has been strong, although, somewhat surprisingly, not as strong as the stock market. But recent decades have brought marked real estate booms, especially in desirable coastal and city markets. As more people seek high-paying jobs in attractive places like the San Francisco Bay Area or around Boston or New York, demand has clearly outstripped supply. Add highly educated immigrants into the mix and many of these markets have risen to dizzying heights. "Second destination" markets, like Sacramento, Phoenix, Charlotte, Las Vegas, and Atlanta have, on a percentage basis, boomed even more.

Residential Real Estate

Does it make sense to buy a home? Whether you're an entrepreneur or not, the economic and tax systems have been set up decidedly in favor of owning. Here are a few of the benefits.

- **Mortgage interest deduction.** You can deduct mortgage interest if you itemize deductions, which is nice (although 35 cents saved on a dollar spent still leaves you down 65 cents!).
- **Capital gain exclusion.** The capital gain exclusion is extremely important in long-term

wealth-building. If you have lived in your home for two years or, if you've rented it out, two of the past five years, you may exclude $250,000 (single) or $500,000 (married filing jointly) from capital gains taxes. In the personal finance world, this is the best tax shelter you'll find; no other shelter even comes close. Of course, you must have a capital gain in order to exclude it—meaning you must pay a reasonable price upfront and stay in the property for a while.

- **Leverage.** Most residential real estate can be bought with 20, 10, and sometimes even zero percent upfront equity. So if the property appreciates 5 percent in a year and you have 20 percent down, you actually earn 25 percent on your invested capital. Modest long-term appreciation rates can still produce substantial returns on investment. Of course, this leverage works the other way in a down market. No matter what you buy or where you are, prudence is important. Nothing is automatic—even in real estate.

What's the "Right" Price? As with any investment, if you invest in real estate you should use a value investing approach. Is it a "good" piece of property? Does the potential return substantially exceed the risk? Is the price right?

It's hard to give definitive guidelines for the first two questions; it depends on the market, the quality of the property, and what's around it. But we do have a benchmark for what you should pay for a property: 4.86 times your annual income.

How did we arrive at *that* number? No, it's not some obscure principle of physics or Ph.D.-level mathematics. If you buy a home, put 20 percent down on it, borrow the 80 percent at 6 percent, and use an industry-standard mortgage-debt-to-income ratio of 28 percent, working backward through the numbers you'll arrive at the 4.86 figure. So if you buy a home five times your annual

income, you're probably OK. If you move to California, where average homes approach nine times average annual income levels, you might be in for trouble. If you move to Texas or Kansas or many places in the Midwest, South, or intermountain regions, you'll find ratios in the 2.5–3.5 range—quite comfortable for you and your finances.

A Few Words About Financing. You (hopefully) financed your business successfully and wisely; it should be no different with your home. Extremely leveraged and exposed financing techniques, like zero-down adjustable loans, should be avoided. You already have enough risk in your business. What if interest rates rise, simultaneously hurting your business and raising your mortgage payment?

We think that entrepreneurs, above all, should prefer steady, predictable mortgage payments. A 30-year fixed loan is OK; for real wealth-building potential, consider a 15-or ten-year fixed loan. The more rapid equity building not only increases your net worth but also gives you a potential pool of capital to be tapped should you need it in the business. It may be wise for entrepreneurs, particularly with unpredictable incomes, to get the 30-year loan with lower required payments and then to make extra payments when business is good. The goal for most people should be to pay off their homes before retir-

FOR MORE ABOUT LOCATION ...

Co-author Peter Sander also produces popular reference geography books comparing real estate prices and affordability (and many other factors) for major U.S. and Canada locales. See *Cities Ranked and Rated—More than 400 Metropolitan Areas Evaluated in the U.S. and Canada* (John Wiley & Sons, 2nd edition May 2007) and *Best Places to Raise Your Family* (John Wiley & Sons, 2006).

ing, for retirement planning is more stressful when a mortgage payment must be included. Although you may run into financial advisors who advise against it, it's a good feeling to pay off a home. Equity in a home is equivalent to a taxable bond investment paying the going mortgage rate—this is what you are saving in mortgage interest. Are these advisors sore because they don't get to manage the money you could put at their disposal if you still owed on your home?

Commercial Real Estate

Buying commercial real estate is like any other investment—price, quality, return on investment. The special case: buying commercial real estate to house your own business.

Generally, we like the idea of buying your building. If you're having trouble saving other funds for retirement, at least your building will be around long term. It will give you something tangible to sell when you sell the business. In most markets, you can assume a modest growth in value. It fixes your building costs—no increases in rent or lease payments. And if you play the tax game right, it may produce some tax savings. As introduced in Chapter 7, the model is to buy the building personally, then lease it to the business. If you own a corporation, the building is protected from creditors and capital gains will generally be taxed at lower personal rates.

CAVEAT INVESTOR

This chapter is an overview of investing philosophy and strategy. We end it with a warning: do not invest until you take the time to study up a bit on investing and markets. Nothing is more frustrating than to finally get over the hump with your business, only to pour your hard-earned funds down the drain in bad investments. Start slowly, practice on paper, and get advice where you need it—but never forget that you are in charge.

CHAPTER 10

Plan It: College Expenses and Retirement Income

N O MATTER HOW FOCUSED YOU ARE ON your business, you probably pick up the newspaper, catch the evening TV news, or listen to drive-time news reports on your commute. Weekly if not more often you hear news stories about the escalating costs of college, health care, and retirement. Again and again you hear about how Social Security and Medicare are bound to fail in the long term if "we don't do something." Over and over you hear about pension funds collapsing, bankruptcies resulting from health costs, high schoolers fighting for every last spot in prestigious universities. And even if they get in, they face an average cost of $12,000 for public institutions and as much as $29,000 for private, a cost rising between 5 and 10 percent per year. It's enough to scare anyone, particularly anyone who has a family, plans to start one, has health problems, or hasn't saved enough for retirement.

A CALL TO ACTION

These issues can be particularly scary for the entrepreneur. As an entrepreneur, you don't have many of the safety nets provided to the corporate employee, like health insurance and (at least for most) some form of retirement plan. We all envy those "legacy" employees with committed and funded pension plans—a check every month for life with guaranteed inflation protection. Few of us have such a comprehensive safety net available. OK, there's Social Security, but it's getting a bit wobbly and for most of us it will provide something less than half the income we need or expect in retirement. And most entrepreneurs, at least the ones who once had a day job, have some other form of retirement savings—an IRA or a 401(k) or a 403(b) or some other arrangement. But unless you're very fortunate, these won't make it either, especially if you used any of these funds to start your business.

Less for More

The harsh reality is that the big things in life— retirement, college, peace of mind in the form of health and life security, not to mention your home—have all become more expensive, both in absolute terms and *relative* to other things we need and purchase. At the same time, the social and economic structures that used to provide for some of these needs have declined or become more shaky. Social Security, pensions, Medicare, state subsidies for universities, employment-for-life promises from big companies, and even the home mortgage interest deduction have declined or are at risk.

A Do-It-Yourself Proposition

What this means, of course, is that you as entrepreneur need to take more responsibility for setting aside the fruits of your labor to meet these needs. While setting aside anything can be particularly challenging in the formative years of a business, particularly during the investment phase, entrepreneurs should quickly learn their options and gain the discipline to do what's needed. As an entrepreneur, you're a natural do-it-yourselfer and, for better or for worse, retirement, college, and similar obligations have become a do-it-yourself enterprise.

Not *All* Bad News

In this chapter we'll explain how to plan for two large obligations (specifically, college and retirement) and how to save for them. As you'll see, entrepreneurs have a broader and potentially much more powerful assortment of retirement savings plans available. It is possible, as a business owner, to set aside large chunks of income, creating a tax deduction for the amount set aside and, subsequently, getting tax-free compounded growth on the savings. If you're fortunate to earn enough in your business to set aside a healthy amount, there's hardly a surer way to become a millionaire than to use some of the retirement savings tools available for business owners. So the news isn't all bad, is it?

SAVING TOWARD GOALS

We've touched on the practice and mechanics of saving in a few places—in budgeting (Chapter 5) and in calculating required savings amounts using accumulation annuity tables (Chapter 2). The principles of compounding and self-generated "organic" growth in savings were described in the last chapter. Here, we'll apply some of these concepts to a more complete picture of the financial planning process as applied to college and retirement planning.

BY DEFINITION: PLANS AND PLANNING

Retirement *planning* is the art and science of mapping out what you need in retirement and how you will get there—generally a combination of externally provided entitlements and internally generated savings. *Retirement plans* are specific savings instruments, created by federal tax law, to help you save on a tax-preferenced basis. Thus, retirement planning would tell you that you need a million dollars at retirement age to achieve your desired retirement lifestyle, while retirement plans such as IRAs, SEPs, 401(k)s, and a host of others are the tax-preferenced vehicles designed to help you get there.

Needs Planning

Whether for college, retirement, or some other major life event, the needs-planning process has two basic steps: determine the total cost, that is, the total funds needed, and then subtract entitlements, like Social Security or earned pensions for retirement or scholarships or grants for college, to arrive at the amount you need to save to make up the difference. Once the amount is determined, savings strategies and vehicles are applied, taking into account tax breaks and the effects of compounding.

Scenario Planning

The best plans have some *scenario* planning. That is, different scenarios are constructed for total needs, entitlements, and savings assumptions. A good retirement plan will explore several lifestyle scenarios: for instance, whether you plan to live in a cheap place or an expensive place, to travel a lot, or to pay off your home, and how long you plan to live. Savings assumption scenarios would incorporate different investment rates of return and possibly different tax and inflation rates. Entitlement scenarios may also vary, particularly if you have a long time left in the working world.

DETERMINING THE "NUMBER"–AN EXAMPLE

Retirement needs are generally determined by deciding what percentage of your pre-retirement income you can live on, given your chosen lifestyle, and modeling a distribution annuity to provide that income.

Suppose your current lifestyle requires $4,000 in income per month, after taxes, to pay bills, meet unexpected expenses, and accumulate a little for travel, property tax bills, and the like. You should have a pretty good handle on this number from your current budgeting, as examined in Chapter 3. We'll call this monthly figure the "little number," in contrast with the "Big Number"—the nest egg—you'll need to achieve to provide this little number in income each month.

Many financial planners model the little number by taking a percentage of pre-retirement income. For most retirees, 70 to 80 percent of monthly pre-retirement income is considered sufficient, for in retirement, many slow down, don't commute, and don't eat restaurant lunches during the workday— of course (we hope) the kids are gone. Your individual goals, lifestyle, location, health, etc. will all play a part. Whether you've paid off your house is a big swing factor in determining this little number.

Let's say that $4,000 after taxes is your "little number." Let's also suppose that, in retirement, you need to produce $5,000 monthly before taxes to achieve this figure. The exact number requires careful calculation because only a portion of Social Security is taxable and you must consider state income taxes. A good tax advisor experienced in retirement tax planning can be helpful while you're planning.

Once you calculate $5,000 as the gross of the "little number," now what? Enter here the *distribution annuity* calculation, in which we work backwards to figure out what sum of money will produce an ongoing revenue stream of $5,000 per month. For

Size of sum required to receive $1 paid out each year for n years

Rate of Return	Number of Years							
	1	2	5	10	15	20	30	40
1.0%	$0.99	$1.97	$4.85	$9.47	$13.87	$18.05	$25.81	$32.83
2.0%	$0.98	$1.94	$4.71	$8.98	$12.85	$16.35	$22.40	$27.36
3.0%	$0.97	$1.91	$4.58	$8.53	$11.94	$14.88	$19.60	$23.11
4.0%	$0.96	$1.89	$4.45	$8.11	$11.12	$13.59	$17.29	$19.79
5.0%	$0.95	$1.86	$4.33	$7.72	$10.38	$12.46	$15.37	$17.16
6.0%	$0.94	$1.83	$4.21	$7.36	$9.71	$11.47	$13.76	$15.05
7.0%	$0.93	$1.81	$4.10	$7.02	$9.11	$10.59	$12.41	$13.33
8.0%	$0.93	$1.78	$3.99	$6.71	$8.56	$9.82	$11.26	$11.92
10.0%	$0.91	$1.74	$3.79	$6.14	$7.61	$8.51	$9.43	$9.78
12.0%	$0.89	$1.69	$3.60	$5.65	$6.81	$7.47	$8.06	$8.24
15.0%	$0.87	$1.63	$3.35	$5.02	$5.85	$6.26	$6.57	$6.64
20.0%	$0.83	$1.53	$2.99	$4.19	$4.68	$4.87	$4.98	$5.00

FIGURE 10.1. Distribution Annuity Factor Table

convenience, we'll reintroduce a version of Figure 2.10 from Chapter 2, showing factors to calculate distribution annuities.

Just as in Chapter 2, the first step is to decide on a rate of return and a number of years. Herein lies the first critical question: when do you expect to retire? More people are working longer or working part time during retirement for extra income and to stay mentally and physically sharp. Of course, you may well aspire to retire early! So when the retirement clock starts is key to arriving at the Big Number.

Now the next critical question is how long do you expect to live? The answer probably isn't in your PDA; you're going to have to pick a reasonable number and plan scenarios around it.

Most people today are planning their finances as though they will live a maximum 30 years after retirement, while some choose 20 and some 35 or longer. Let's use 30. Then let's suppose that your investments, over the long haul, can be invested to bring in consistent 6-percent returns. (Remember: Treasury bonds in 2006 produced 5 percent.) Look up the factor for 30 years, 6 percent: it's 13.76. Now, if you're striving to achieve $5,000 before taxes each month, multiply that figure by 12 to annualize it ($60,000) and then multiply that figure by 13.76. You get $825,600, which would be your Big Number—the nominal amount you need on Retirement Day 1 to produce the $5,000 gross income per month to fund your retirement.

But Wait …

OK, so we oversimplified this a bit.

First and foremost, we haven't applied your entitlements yet. You're going to get Social Security (assuming you've been paying self-employment tax and FICA all these years). Applying entitlements, of course, reduces the "little number," which in turn reduces the "Big Number." Some retirement planners exclude Social Security, using it instead to make house payments or meet some other fixed

---

RECAPPING: THE BIG NUMBER

The Big Number depends on at least four factors:

- *when* you plan to retire
- *what kind of lifestyle* you expect to have (including health needs) and how much that costs
- *how* long you expect to live in retirement
- *what returns* you expect to earn in retirement, considering inflation

We cannot know the future and we cannot be certain what numbers to plug into this calculation, so good scenario planning is *extremely* important.

---

obligation, but most planning scenarios factor in Social Security. We'll show how in a moment.

Second, what about inflation? In 30 years, that $5,000/month isn't going to buy as much as it does now, even if inflation continues a modest 3-percent inflation rate as experienced recently. In fact, if you compound 3 percent for 30 years, you'll find that $5,000 will likely have an equivalent purchasing power of just $2,060 $[([\$5,000/(1.03^{30})]$ for you math geeks). The mathematics of increasing each month's nominal dollars to arrive at $5,000 "real" dollars using this formula is daunting; a more useful approach is to subtract inflation from the investment return rate. Since we've been using a return rate of 6 percent in our example, we now have 3 percent. If we want more protection against inflation, we might deduct 4 percent from your investment return of 6 percent, leaving you now with 2 percent. Now, you'll notice we added a couple of rows to this version of the distribution annuity table, giving factors for 1, 2, and 3 percent. This is to allow you to plug in an after-inflation rate of return. Using the 2 percent factor from the table (22.40), the new Big Number is $1,344,000, significantly higher than the $825,600 we calculated earlier. You can see how sensitive this calculation is to investment return and inflation rates.

The Entitlement Factor

Now, this may seem grim—you have to save $1.3 million by retirement just to achieve $5,000 in equivalent gross income per month, $60,000 per year. While $60K will provide a reasonably comfortable lifestyle—in today's terms, anyway—it's hardly the sail-around-the-world retirement you thought you deserved for all your hard work as an entrepreneur. So, what do you need? Two million? Three?

Before getting too emotional over the thought of being on an endless saving treadmill, let's factor in entitlements. For now at least, if you'll have 40 quarters of active deposits in the Social Security system through payroll or self-employment taxes, you'll get a Social Security check some day. How much you as a household will get depends on how much you earned during your highest 35 years of income, when you decide to start collecting, and whether or not you're married and, if so, the income-producing status of your spouse.

Estimating Social Security

A precise calculation of Social Security benefits is an elusive and complex goal, best left to a visit with your local Social Security Administration (SSA) office. Here are some guiding principles to rough out what you'll get.

First, through a complex formula, the Social Security Administration determines your primary insurance amount (PIA), which is largely based on the average indexed monthly earnings (AIME), which is a direct reflection of your actual earnings indexed for inflation during your working years.

Without getting into too much detail, once the PIA and AIME are known, benefits for retiring at 65 are calculated using the following set of "break points" and the AIME amount:

- 90 percent of the first $656 of the AIME, plus
- 32 percent of the AIME over $656 and through $3,955, plus
- 15 percent of the AIME over $3,955.

So if your AIME is $5,000, roughly corresponding to $60,000 per year in earnings, and if you retire at 65 your Social Security benefit would be:

- $656 * 90 percent, or $590.40, plus
- $3,955-$656, or $3,299 * 32%, or $1,055.68
- ($5,000-$3,955), or $1,045 * 15%, or $156.75

So you would receive a monthly Social Security benefit of $1,802.83.

Spousal and Maximum Benefits. For most individuals and households, estimating total Social Security entitlements doesn't stop here. If you're married, your spouse is entitled to Social Security benefits, which are the larger of the amount calculated based on his or her income or one half of your Social Security benefit if you've been married at least ten years. For simplicity, let's say the latter is the case: your spouse would receive $901.42 and so your total household Social Security benefit would be $2,704.25.

Now the SSA puts a cap on maximum benefits so as not to enrich high-earners in retirement too much at the expense of others. For 2006, the maximum *individual* retirement benefit is $1,961, based on an AIME of $6,058, and the 2006 maximum *household* benefit is $3,626, based on a formula we'd rather not get into here.

Does It Make a Difference When I Start? Unless disabled or otherwise a special case, nobody can collect Social Security benefits before age 62. Beyond that, when to start is an important factor in determining your entitlement. Social Security doesn't pay a larger total entitlement if you wait until age 70 or beyond or a smaller one if you retire early. It simply spreads out your entitlement over a smaller or larger number of years based on actuarial calculations. The results are still significant, as Figure 10.2 below shows.

Retirement Age	Average Indexed Monthly Earnings (AIME)	Monthly Benefit	Difference from Age 65 Benefit
62	$6,515	$1,530	22% less
65	$6,058	$1,961	–
70	$5,072	$2,420	23% more

FIGURE 10.2. Effect of Retirement Age on Social Security Income

If you wait until age 70, your Social Security entitlement is fully 58 percent higher than if you retire eight years earlier, at 62. You can see how this decision affects your retirement planning.

Recalculating the Big Number

Unless you decide to set aside your Social Security income to meet a special need, like a mortgage payment, the next step is to work backwards to figure out the *net* monthly income you'll need to finance in retirement *through savings*:

- Total gross income required: $5,000
- Less Social Security household entitlement: $2,704
- *Net need* to be financed through savings: $2,296

And now, we calculate a new number, using the distribution annuity table, using a more conservative, inflation-based rate of return, for 30 years:

- $2,296 per month
- Factor at 2% for 30 years: 22.40
- Result: $514,304 as the savings goal

This number, as you can see, is more realistic for most to achieve, but still may not be high enough—if inflation is understated, if Social Security benefits are cut back, if you can't produce the 4-percent return after inflation, if your lifestyle (or health care requirements) exceed your monthly $5,000 income. So while this is a good "stake in the ground" for planning your retirement, it's wise to do some careful scenario planning—and include some kind of buffer in case you're wrong.

What About My Pension?

If you're one of the lucky few who have accumulated a defined-benefit pension during employment prior to becoming an entrepreneur, simply enter this monthly amount alongside your Social Security entitlement and deduct it from the gross monthly income required from savings.

▼ A PENSION YOU CAN *BUY*

OK, so maybe you didn't work for the telephone company or your state government before becoming an entrepreneur. You have no pension. There are still ways to achieve this kind of guaranteed-for-life income—essentially by *buying* it. Sure, it will take some savings to buy this pension, but you get the advantage of predictability. Moreover, you get the protection of knowing that it's paid for life, like Social Security, and will never run out. Preventing such *superannuation*—the financial planner's term for outliving your money—is possible by buying an *immediate annuity*.

An *immediate annuity* is essentially a fixed-income investment, part of a larger and complex set of financial instruments usually sold by insurance companies and specialized securities dealers. Most annuities are "sold" financial instruments too complex to discuss in this book and bringing high commission rates and provisions not particularly friendly to the individual investor. An immediate annuity is effectively a purchased pension—buy a contract for a fixed upfront sum and you get paid a fixed amount for life. Different flavors allow for *period-certain* payments, thus giving your heirs some residual if you die early. There are *joint-and-survivor* versions available for married couples.

Period-certain and joint-and-survivor versions, for obvious reasons, pay a little less each month.

The downside of annuities is that the money you pay to purchase them is committed and you can't pass it on to heirs; when it's gone it's gone. And some careful and disciplined investors may be able to do better by keeping their money invested and paying themselves a monthly stipend. But figure, for planning purposes today, that an immediate annuity will pay somewhere around $600 a month, for life, for a $100,000 contract. Many retirees use these instruments to guarantee at least part of their income. For more about immediate annuities and a handy calculator, the portal *www.immediateannuities.com* is a great place to learn about and shop for annuities.

SAVING THE REST

So now we have the Big Number adjusted for entitlement. We know where you want to go with your retirement savings. The next step is to figure out how you're going to get there.

The Next Number: Monthly Savings

Now we put the accumulation annuity table to use. Accumulation annuities tell you how much you have to save each month to accumulate a sum. So, for convenience, we reprint Figure 2.8 below as Figure 10.3.

Earlier, you had to decide how much return your investments would produce during retirement. Now you have to pick a return rate for the years between now and retirement. This return rate may be different from your return rate in retirement—and more aggressive. However, to achieve the full return rate you have in mind, your savings should be in tax-deferred retirement savings plans so as to not lose some return and compounding power to taxes. If you want to be extra careful, you may factor in inflation; however, recall that we have already factored in some inflation in determining your original Big Number.

Suppose you want to plan using a 7-percent return for your investments and you're planning to retire in 20 years. You need to accumulate a sum of $514,304 for Day 1 of retirement, as calculated above:

- The factor for 20 years at 7 percent is 41.00.
- Divide $514,304 by 41, for $12,544 per year.

Sum accumulated with $1 deposited end of each year for n years

Rate of Return	Number of Years							
	1	2	5	10	15	20	30	40
4.0%	$1.00	$2.04	$5.42	$12.01	$20.02	$29.78	$56.08	$95.03
5.0%	$1.00	$2.05	$5.53	$12.58	$21.58	$3307	$66.44	$120.80
6.0%	$1.00	$2.06	$5.64	$13.18	$23.28	$36.79	$79.06	$154.76
7.0%	$1.00	$2.07	$5.75	$13.82	$25.13	$41.00	$94.46	$199.64
8.0%	$1.00	$2.08	$5.87	$14.49	$27.15	$45.76	$113.28	$259.06
10.0%	$1.00	$2.10	$6.11	$15.94	$31.77	$57.27	$164.49	$442.59
12.0%	$1.00	$2.12	$6.35	$17.55	$37.28	$72.05	$241.33	$767.09
15.0%	$1.00	$2.15	$6.74	$20.30	$47.58	$102.44	$434.75	$1,779.09
20.0%	$1.00	$2.20	$7.44	$25.96	$72.04	$186.69	$1,181.88	$7.373.86

Divide target sum by table figure to get annual savings required

FIGURE 10.3. Accumulate Annuity Factor Table

- Divide $12,544 by 12 to get monthly savings: $1,045. (This is approximate; if your investments compound monthly or daily, your required savings will be slightly less.)

So that's your goal—$1,045. If you have more than 20 years to save, obviously you can save less. If you're fortunate enough to invest for a higher return, all the better, but financial advisors and good common sense dictate reducing risk as you get older, for you'll have less time to make up for the unforeseen.

SAVING FOR COLLEGE

We want to touch on saving for college, too. College planning is similar to retirement planning in that you must determine an amount to save to achieve a goal. There are a few minor differences and one *big* difference between college planning for your kids and retirement planning. The big difference: you can *borrow* to meet college needs, typically at favorable rates, while you can't borrow for retirement at all. In fact, one of the resulting maxims of financial planning is quite clear: if you can't save enough for *both* college *and* retirement, save for *retirement*. You can borrow for college needs and funds saved for retirement typically will not be counted in calculating eligibility for financial aid.

Determining the Big Number

Determining your "Big Number" for college is simpler than for retirement, for you don't have to make as many assumptions about how long you'll live, when you'll retire, and how much you'll earn on funds during retirement. You know exactly when college will start, and (at least more or less) how long it will last.

You don't know the exact costs, for that depends on which college is chosen and how much tuition and living costs will rise between now and then.

Most college planners today are assuming a 5- to 6-percent annual rise in average college costs, driven in part by the decline in state subsidies for state-supported schools.

To get an approximate number for a kid currently ten years old, the best is to take today's costs for a private school and a state-supported school and project them forward, say, 10 years. The 2006 average cost for the state school is about $12,500. So take $12,500 and multiply by 1.06^{10}—6-percent inflation over 10 years—for 1.79. Multiply $12,500 by 1.79 and you'll get $22,375. That's for one year of education. Multiply that by four (an optimistic figure) and you'll have an approximate Big Number of $89,500.

Some advisors will determine this Number more precisely, by projecting forward eight years for freshman year, nine for sophomore, and so on. They will do the same for savings: a portion of it, in fact, has 14 years to grow. While this approach is more precise, it doesn't seem necessary, at least to start your planning. Suffice it to say, you'll need 90 thousand bucks and you might as well plan to have it on College Day 1. By the way, the Number for private school for the same ten-year-old, using 2006 average costs, is about $213,000.

Your total college needs are driven not only by the choice of schools, but also, of course, by the

> ## COLLEGE PLANNING MEETS BUSINESS PLANNING
>
> There is more assistance—aid, loans, scholarships, and so forth—for people with more modest incomes. As a business owner, you have knobs and levers to pull in terms of reporting income and passing it on to yourself, especially if you own a corporation. Buy new equipment, put more into retirement plans, etc. Use these knobs and levers—and get what they give you.

number of kids and their ages. You may create more than one savings goal, perhaps one for each kid.

Meeting the Need: A Three-Pronged Approach

Retirement planning may have trickier assumptions, but there are fewer sources of funds to take into account than with college planning. There are fund sources and tools, many of which are government-sponsored, to take the heat off college costs for you and your family, particularly if you fall into more "challenged" income status.

Developing your college savings strategy requires a careful look at the many tools available. First, there are various forms of *tax relief*, including more lucrative tax credits. Many advisors then suggest examining various sources of *financial aid*, including scholarships, grants, and finally student loans. Then, they say, save the rest (as we did for retirement).

We advocate a different approach: save what you can *and only then* depend on grants, scholarships, and loans to make up the rest. We see too many families rely too much on financial aid, only to be disappointed by what they're eligible for when the time comes or, more to the point, burdening themselves and/or their kids with a huge pile of debt. We think that's the wrong approach.

If you save for college and then don't use those funds for college, you can typically use them for something else. In tax-advantaged college plans, you may pay as much as a 10-percent penalty if the funds aren't used for education, but the penalty is a small price to pay for the tax-free compounding and the disciplined saving. And the definition of "education" is becoming broad enough that many purposes would qualify, even if you don't use them for your kids as planned. You can transfer savings to grandkids or other family members or you can take that course in welding or quilting you've always wanted to take.

Here—briefly—are the tools available to help fund college.

Tax Relief

Congress wants to see more citizens, particularly those economically disadvantaged, realize the benefits and experience of a college education. They also want to look like the "good guys" politically in an environment where they are otherwise perceived to be in the way of a family's best savings intentions with taxes and tax policy. Therefore, in their usual way, over time, they have created a "crazy quilt" of tax relief and incentives to help finance college for your dependents and, in many cases, for yourself. While these tax benefits all together help, they won't even come close to paying for a normal four-year education. It's ironic, in a way, that you need a college education to figure out those benefits!

In addition to tax-advantaged savings plans, which we'll cover momentarily, there are four tax breaks—two credits and two deductions—for most families. There are income maximums: for married filing jointly, $107,000 in AGI (with a phaseout starting at $87,000) for credits, $130,000 for deducting interest, and $160,000 for deducting tuition.

- **Hope credit.** The Hope credit reduces taxes up to $1,500 for qualified education expenses for each of the first two years of higher learning. One Hope credit can be taken for each eligible student in your household. The student must be pursuing a degree.
- **Lifetime Learning Credit.** The Lifetime Learning Credit covers all postsecondary education, including job skill enhancement and training, and provides up to $2,000 per family (not per student) each year. The student does not have to be pursuing a degree.
- **Tuition deduction.** Taxpayers can deduct up to $4,000 per year in qualified tuition and related expenses for AGI (that is, you don't have to itemize deductions on Schedule A).
- **Student Loan Interest Deduction.** You can deduct up to $2500 each year in qualified student loan interest.

The rules are more complex than this and worth investigating with a tax professional. For instance, the definition of "qualified education expenses" is important, generally including tuition and other "direct" education expenses but not fees, books, housing, or living expenses. Most savings plans, described below, have a more liberal and inclusive definition. There are rules against taking more than one credit simultaneously and taking credits and deductions simultaneously. Fortunately, tax benefits and savings plans can both be used simultaneously, so long as the two aren't covering the same expenses. Determining the most effective tax strategy is complicated; it depends on the costs, the number of dependents attending college at one time, the year level(s), your income, and your tax situation in general.

Savings Plans

College savings plans are similar to retirement accounts in that they provide tax-advantaged long-term savings, allowing you to take advantage of the power of compounding. Savings plans do not allow you to deduct the contributions, but they offer the distinct advantage of being tax-free, not just tax-deferred—earnings on your savings balances are not taxed if withdrawn for qualified education purposes. For savings plans, the definition of "educational expenses" is wider than for direct tax benefits: it includes room and board and other necessities of college life.

Savings plans come in two primary flavors: the Coverdell Education Savings Accounts (ESAs) that work like Roth IRAs and the section 529 college savings trusts administered by each state (named for the IRS Code section). There are also education-preferenced forms of U.S. government bonds and state prepaid tuition programs, which are less flexible, less lucrative, and less popular; we won't examine those here.

Education Savings Accounts. Up to $2,000 can be pledged to an ESA, for households with an AGI up to $220,000. ESAs are *self-directed* accounts (meaning that you determine and manage the investments) and all income earned from interest, dividends, and gains is tax-free.

529 Plans. Known more generically as *qualified tuition plans*, these are state-directed trusts set up for college funds, again tax-free. You can deposit funds in any state's 529 plan; it does not mean your kid has to go to a school in that state. Each plan is administered by a major investment company (usually

---

▼ ARE YOU NEEDY?

Whether you are "eligible" for needs-based financial aid—whether loans, scholarships, or grants—depends on how you score on the Expected Family Contribution (EFC) test administered by the U.S. Department of Education. The EFC test examines assets, income, number of family members, and the number of family members in college simultaneously. Income figures will typically add back in amounts contributed to retirement plans, but exclude the retirement plan assets. The family home is excluded, but business or farm assets are generally included. Depending on details, the EFC might be $4,500 per year for a family of four with $50,000 in eligible assets and $50,000 in annual income, and it might be $25,000 when income rises to $100,000 and assets rise to $150,000. Aid can be used to acquire the rest. There are a number of Web sites and online calculators to help you approximate EFC and estimate financial needs in general. The Department of Education (*www.ed.gov*), the College Board (SAT test administrator among other functions, *www.collegeboard.com*), and a financial aid portal, FinAid (*www.finaid.org*), are good places to start. Quite soon you will see how it helps to drive recognized business income downward, if you can.

TIAA-CREF, Vanguard, or Fidelity) and the money is invested in a narrow selection of funds offered by that company. Choosing a state plan involves examining management companies, fee structures, and investment choices. Many depositors invest in their own state plan to get state income tax exemptions. The biggest advantages of 529s: there are no income or annual contribution limits. (Most states have a per-beneficiary total cap of $200–$250,000.) The student is the beneficiary, but you, as the donor, own and control the funds. They excel as estate planning tools, for they are eligible for accelerated gifting up to $60,000 upfront without incurring gift taxes, while retaining control of the funds all the while. In short, 529s are a top choice for those wanting to save large amounts for their college-bound beneficiaries.

Financial Aid

Financial aid, effectively, comes in two forms: money that you pay back and money you do not pay back. Naturally, grants and scholarships, the forms requiring no repayment, are financially best for you but also least predictable. As such, you probably should not include them in your college planning but instead treat them as a special bonus (maybe to get Junior into a better school or to buy that boat you've wanted with the savings no longer needed for college). Loans, on the other hand, should be used to fill savings gaps (or *needs* gaps, in case your daughter decides she must attend Harvard Medical School to realize her dreams) but should not be part of your college plan.

Most grant and loan programs are available from either the federal government or the educational institutions.

Grants and Scholarships. There are too many kinds of grants and scholarships to elaborate on here. Basically there are two categories: needs-based and all others. "Needs" for needs-based programs are determined by a complex eligibility formula. The other scholarships—the ones you hear about more often—are for academic or athletic overachievers.

Student Loans. At a high level, student loans come in two types, based on eligibility. *Subsidized* loans don't accrue interest or require payments until after six months after graduation and the interest rates may be lower. *Unsubsidized* loans may accrue interest costs right away, although in some cases these costs can be added to the loan balance.

There are several loan programs, most administered and/or backed by the federal government. The loan programs have different requirements, limits, and payment plans. Most are originated through your local bank according to government guidelines and with a government guarantee. Interest rates are usually below market, although you must watch the fees associated with these loans, which may be as high as 4 percent.

- **Stafford loans** are made to the student. The repayment terms are up to ten years and the interest rates are up to 8.25 percent. Stafford loans come in subsidized and unsubsidized forms.
- **PLUS loans** (Parent Loans for Undergraduate Students) are, as the name implies, made to the parents. Parent credit ratings are considered. These loans are usually available only if other financial aid forms have been exhausted. The interest rate is capped at 9 percent.

A SPECIALIST FOR EVERYTHING

Yes, indeed, there are financial specialists specializing in college planning. Professional Certified College Planning Specialists (CCPSs) can be summoned to help you navigate the complex waters. They offer the advantage of being current on college planning tools, available aid (scholarships, grants, and loan packages), and "needs management" strategies. See the National Institute of Certified College Planners (NICCP) Web site, *www.niccp.com*.

- **Sallie Mae loans** are granted by the quasi-government Student Loan Marketing Association (*www.salliemae.com*), which offers a variety of products similar to a home mortgage lender.

We've covered some of the principal college planning tools, but certainly not all of them and not in the depth that you should before starting your savings program and especially before sending kids off to college. Initially, if you can, it makes sense to set up a savings program—a 529 if you have the resources. As college approaches, it's wise to sit down with a financial professional well-versed in college programs to figure out what makes the most sense for you, especially with your business involved.

RETIREMENT PLANS

Among all financial opportunities for the prospective or experienced entrepreneur, few match the raw wealth accumulation power offered by the assorted retirement savings plans and tools currently available. It is as if Congress, to make amends for the tax burdens and administrative complications inflicted on business owners, decided to throw a lifeline in the form of generous retirement plans. Indeed, a successful business owner can easily salt away hundreds of thousands in these plans and build wealth quite rapidly.

Of course, with most plans, income taxes will have to be paid when funds are withdrawn, ostensibly when we are in lower tax brackets. Cynics like to point out that what Congress *really* wants is to encourage us to accumulate massive amounts of wealth and then to tax us on these larger amounts. We're not sure, but doubt that Congress was really thinking that far ahead.

The 401(k) Millionaire

As an employee, you probably had a 401(k) salary-deferral plan, where you could defer up to $11,000 (for many years) or $14,000 (in 2005) of your salary, get a company match (with some employers), and

let it ride. Invest well and stay employed long enough and you could turn this into a million bucks with a little patience.

We'll share a little secret with you. Suppose you were making $60,000 in salary a year and had set aside $11,000 of it in your 401(k) plan. Your employer matched 3 percent of your salary, so the total annual deferral was $12,800 ($11,000 + ($60,000 * .03)). You did this for 30 years and invested modestly well, achieving a 6-percent return, with, of course, no tax bite. The accumulation annuity factor table (Figure 10.3) gives a factor of 79.06 for 30 years at 6 percent. Multiply this factor by $12,800 and get $1,011,97. You would save a million bucks on a moderate salary. With the new limit of $14,000, the power is even greater: it would take only 27 years to become a 401(k) millionaire.

For Entrepreneurs: More, Better, Faster

Becoming a 401(k) millionaire as a moderately paid corporate employee is nice and the example serves well to illustrate the power of tax-free compounding and disciplined saving. But it's somewhat beside the point. After all, you're not someone else's employee any more.

Here's the point: as an entrepreneur, there are many more retirement savings vehicles available to you. And you can set aside much, much more. If $11,000 or $14,000 annual contributions created a lot of wealth, what do you think would happen if each year you set aside $20,000? $30,000? $42,000? $170,000? All while deducting those amounts from your taxable income (state and federal but *not* employment taxes)? The wealth accumulation potential is staggering. It's not surprising that figuring out ways to pull more money out of a business and into personal retirement arrangements is a priority for most successful entrepreneurs. (Of course, you have to accumulate these amounts to set aside.)

Plans vary: some are designed for employees (and requiring contributions for them, too) and some not. Some are administratively complex; some are relatively simple. In the rest of this chapter, we provide summary facts on some of the more popular retirement plans oriented toward the self-employed and small businesses.

RETIREMENT PLANS—PRINCIPLES AND FEATURES

The essential purpose of retirement plans is to provide individuals, both as business owners and employees, the opportunity—and incentive—to save money for retirement. There are two primary incentives: first, the ability to deduct contributions from taxable income in the year they're made, and second, the ability to grow funds tax-deferred or even tax-free. Most but not all plans feature deductible upfront contributions, but all have some tax preference favoring the growth of savings.

The assortment of retirement plans has evolved over time and numerous Congressional "tweaks." Taken together, like most tax law, the convoluted assortment of plans is like the idea that "a camel is a horse designed by a committee." There are dozens of retirement plans available—some designed for individuals, some more suited than others for small businesses, and some clearly designed for large employers. Each plan offers advantages and disadvantages in the amounts that can be set aside, compliance and employee "fairness" rules, the amounts that can be deducted, whether it's your money or the employee's, and administrative cost. Before diving into retirement plan choices, we'll first identify the key features and attributes to look for.

Tax Preference

All retirement plans have some degree of tax preference, else they would be little more than ordinary savings accounts. We covered the principle (and power) of compounded growth in the last chapter. With *tax-free compounded growth*, returns are

greatly improved: a sum is allowed to grow without losing a chunk every year for taxes. If you're still not sure about this, take another look at the accumulation annuity table (Figure 10.3). If you made 8 percent for 30 years on an investment of $1,000 per year, you'd end up with $113,260 (factor 113.26 * $1,000). Suppose your marginal federal and state capital gains tax rates total 28 percent. That would reduce your effective rate of return to 5.76 percent (72 percent of 8 percent). The factor for 5.76 percent (not shown on the table) is 75.80. So if the plan were taxed, the amount accumulated would come to only $75,800. Put another way, you'd have to save $1,494 a month—almost 50 percent more—to achieve the same $113,260 savings as you'd accumulate with $1,000 tax-free.

Tax-Deferred vs. Tax-Free. Most retirement plans are set up on a *tax-deferred* basis; that is, they allow you to set aside funds to compound tax-free, but when you withdraw funds in retirement, those withdrawals are taxable. The conventional wisdom holds that, with your income lower in retirement, your tax rate will be lower. You may also then be living in a state without a state income tax, like Florida. This is probably true and certainly worth considering in your retirement planning, but with increasing federal deficits and a greater chance of working into your "retirement" years, who knows if your tax rate will really be lower? However, even if it's not lower, it makes more sense to pay taxes 30 years from now than now.

Front-End Deductibility. Most retirement plans are also *tax-deductible* upfront or allow you to set aside pretax earnings. The current tax deduction is very handy, especially if you're having a good year in your business. A few plans, like the Roth IRA, are funded with after-tax dollars, that is, you get no front-end tax deduction. But—and it's a big "but"—growth is tax-free—that is, you never owe taxes on qualified withdrawals. What you put in is after taxes and the earnings grow tax-free.

Defined Contribution vs. Defined Benefit

Of all the retirement plan attributes we'll discuss, this is the one most likely to be familiar to most readers. Why? Because it's the central theme of pension debates going on mostly around larger, older corporations. *Defined-benefit* plans call for a fixed or predefined *benefit* to be paid in retirement and put all the responsibility—and risk—on the employer to make sure that happens. Defined benefits, which guaranteed pension for life, are of course very attractive to employees and originated largely as an incentive to attract and retain employees. But the responsibility to provide that benefit has become increasingly costly to corporations, particularly those not doing well in the business cycle. Those firms must continue to contribute even in bad times, when their profits are lower and when the returns on their pension fund investments—a big part of the funding picture—are also lower. This "double whammy" has led to many of the storied pension fund defaults in the steel, airline, and auto industries and will likely lead to more. As a result, companies large and small with employees are now eschewing defined-benefit plans.

Replacing defined-benefit plans and growing ever more popular—with employers anyway—are *defined-contribution* plans, for which the plan arrangement defines the amount paid in, not the amount paid out. Whether it is a percent of profits or a minimum or maximum annual amount or an employee salary deferral, what goes in is defined. What comes out is strictly a matter of savings and investment performance: there are no guarantees. Upshot: the risk is transferred to the employee.

Individual and Employer Plans

Some plans are engineered for large organizations with employees, others are designed for individuals only (and their families), and a few are designed for small businesses, usually with 25 or fewer employees, but can be used (quite advantageously) by self-employed individuals.

Do You Have Employees? Whether or not you have employees will affect your choice of retirement plan. The decision to offer retirement benefits to employees is pretty much up to you, subject to the nature of the work and the labor market you operate in. Retirement benefits are often offered in lieu of salary or as an added incentive to attract employees, especially key employees, to come work for you.

Employer Contributions vs. Salary Deferral. When employees are involved, the source of funding for retirement plans becomes important. Some plans call for the employer to make all plan contributions; others, like the popular 401(k), are based on salary deferral, that is, they're largely funded by pretax dollars paid in by employees from their salaries. (That, of course, is one reason why they're so popular—they cost employers relatively less in direct contributions!) Many plans allow for employer match; that is, employers can stimulate employee contributions by making small matching contributions.

Qualified and Non-Qualified Employer Plans. The term "qualified" applies to most employer plans. "Qualified" means they meet the specifications of the Employee Retirement Income Security Act (ERISA) passed in 1974 to regulate retirement plans and level the playing field for employees. ERISA arose in part in response to the move away from traditional pension plans; although pension plans are included under ERISA, much of the new content of the law applied to the various defined-contribution plans. ERISA rules call for a fair distribution of retirement contributions among employees and compliance testing and reporting to make sure this is so.

If a plan is so *qualified* (and most are), employer contributions and administrative costs are tax-deductible. If it is *non-qualified*, upfront deductions are lost. Most entrepreneurs will be concerned with individual and qualified plans, but non-qualified plans can be used by larger business owners to pull still more money out of the business and achieve tax-deferred growth. Such non-qualified plans are beyond our scope.

Mandatory Contributions. Most employer plans have mandatory contributions set forth either by law or by the plan agreement. The reason, of course, is to prevent employers from shortchanging employees and to make sure employees get their fair share of the pie. Mandatory contributions can be defined as a fixed amount, a percentage of profits, or a percentage of what is being set aside for the owners.

Employee Eligibility and Vesting. Maybe you're not sure that the 18-year-old you hired to sweep the floors part time should get a slice of the retirement pie? You may not have to share. Most plans specify which employees can be and must be included. Frequently, employees under 21 and/or part-time employees are excluded from eligibility. Vesting—the eligibility of an enrolled employee to *keep* employer contributions—is specified by each plan. Vesting rules are complex, but were made simpler by the Economic Growth and Tax Relief Reconciliation Act of 2001. Plans choose between *cliff vesting* (all at once) after three years or *gradual vesting*, requiring 20 percent vesting after two years, rising to 100 percent after six years.

Contribution Limits

Each plan type sets a maximum limit for contributions per year. Most limit you to a percentage of earned income or a fixed amount, whichever is smaller. As we saw in the opener to the section, these limits vary widely, from $4,000 annually for IRAs to $170,000 per year for defined-benefit pension plans for individuals age 52 and older. This range is huge; if your business is profitable, it behooves you to select plans carefully. We'll detail these limits in the discussion of each plan.

Income Caps

Eligibility for some forms of individual retirement plans, notably IRAs, may be governed by the amount of total income you or your household

▼ PLAYING CATCH-UP

As public policy makers increasingly recognize the need for individuals to fend for themselves to an ever larger degree in retirement, "catch-up" contributions are making their way into more plans. Originally, pension plans allowed or required employers to make larger contributions for older workers in order to fully fund their benefits with fewer remaining years of work. Naturally these extended contribution provisions have been used by business owners and especially professionals like doctors and dentists to beef up their retirement nest eggs. Now, catch-up provisions are showing up in defined-contribution and individual retirement plans. Individual Retirement Accounts (IRAs) now allow additional contributions of $1,000 for employees 50 or over, and employer-oriented 401(k)s and SIMPLEs (Savings Incentive Match Plans for Employees) allow up to $4,000 additional to be contributed by each employee.

earns. Your ability to deduct IRA contributions may also be dictated by such limits.

Investment Choices

Most plans set some restriction on the kinds of investments allowed. You can't put your home, for instance, in your IRA. Nor is it easy to invest in real estate, for plans don't allow you to borrow inside the plan to finance investments. Plans are usually self-directed, meaning investment choices are limited only by what you can buy and sell through a bank or stockbroker, or are limited to a few choices, mostly fund investments, designed into the plan and offered by the plan administrator.

Deposit Requirements

Most retirement plans require funds to be deposited during the tax year in which they are deducted. A few, notably individual and SEP-IRAs, allow contributions up to the tax filing date. This can come in quite handy for business owners because it is difficult to precisely forecast total yearly income and tax liability while the books are still open. You can use the flexibility of the later date for contributions to manage your personal taxable income after you know more about the year's tax situation.

Administration and Paperwork

Particularly with ERISA compliance rules, the administration and paperwork for retirement plans, especially where employees are involved, can be a daunting task best left to professionals. The good news: most of the individual and small business plans are simple enough that most broker or financial service firms—as much to lure your deposits as anything else—will handle the paperwork.

Of course, administrative costs rise with the amount and complexity of paperwork. The paperwork and annual administration for an IRA might be free, while a pension plan might cost thousands each year. Entrepreneurs need to decide whether the advantages of a complex plan outweigh the costs.

RETIREMENT PLANS—THE CHOICES

We haven't mentioned too many plans by name; that comes now as we outline, compare, and contrast the major features and benefits of each plan. We break plans down into individual/small business plans and qualified employer plans, which should cover most plans of interest to entrepreneurs. Those wanting the quickest take might refer to the summary table in Figure 10.4 at the end of this section.

AS THE WORLD TURNS—PLANS CHANGE

Once you've established a plan, you aren't locked into your choice for life. It's possible to change plans and, in many cases, add new plans to the mix to achieve your goals. As your business becomes more profitable and you grow older, for instance, you may want to set up a SEP-IRA or a defined-benefit pension plan. You may need to modify or evolve plans to accommodate the needs of employees. You may add an individual plan to a company-sponsored 401(k) plan or pension. With multiple plans it may not be possible to deduct all contributions upfront, but tax-free compounding still works. Regardless, it's not a one-shot deal; you should never consider yourself done with retirement planning or retirement plans.

INDIVIDUAL AND SMALL BUSINESS PLANS

Individual plans are set up for individuals either as primary vehicles or as supplements to another plan, usually an employer plan. *Individual Retirement Arrangements (IRAs)* are the most common form. *Simplified Employee Pension (SEP) IRAs* and *Savings Incentive Match Plans for Employees (SIMPLEs)* evolved from individual plans to cover employees. As we'll see, SEP-IRAs are powerful savings tools for self-employed individuals as well as employers.

Individual IRAs

Anyone with earned income can contribute to an IRA. (As a reminder, *earned income* includes wages or business income but not investment or rental income.) IRAs feature relatively modest contribution limits—$4,000 annually with a $1,000 catch-up bonus for people 50 and older. IRAs are self-directed, meaning that you as director invest the funds as you see fit and earnings grow tax-deferred or tax-free. IRAs may be combined with other retirement plans, but total annual contributions to individual IRAs cannot exceed $4,000 per individual. There are varying annual income limits governing IRA contributions and deductibility.

There are three primary types of individual IRAs:

Traditional IRAs. Contributions to traditional IRAs are deductible, but there are limitations. If you are also participating in an employer-sponsored plan, your deduction begins phasing out at $70,000 (joint) annual income and is phased out completely above $80,000. Contributions can be made until the tax filing date (April 15). Investments grow tax-deferred, that is, distributions are taxable. Withdrawals before age 59½ are penalized 10 percent, but there are some exceptions for hardship withdrawals, higher education expenses, and first-time home buyers. Distributions must be taken after age 70½. IRAs cannot be inherited except by a spouse; that is, only a spouse can treat an inherited IRA as his or her own. If the beneficiary of an IRA is not the spouse of the deceased, he or she has two options: transfer the inherited IRA to a beneficiary distribution account (which in 2006 became an income-tax free transfer), cash out the account and pay taxes on the proceeds, or disclaim the IRA, in which case it passes to the next beneficiary named, if any.

Roth IRAs. Contributions to Roth IRAs are *not* tax-deductible, but the earnings grow tax-*free*. Roth contribution limits are the same as for traditional IRAs. AGI must be less than $160,000 (joint) to contribute to a Roth IRA. Roth IRAs can be used alongside other retirement plans so long as income limits aren't exceeded. Since they are made with after-tax dollars, Roth *contributions* (but not the earnings) can be withdrawn prior to age 59½ with-out penalty. Like traditional IRAs, Roths can be funded up to the date for filing tax returns. There are no mandatory distributions for Roth IRAs and funds can be passed on to future generations, making Roths a favored estate-planning tool. Because they can be combined with other plans and because original funds can be withdrawn without penalty for needed cash, Roths are a favorite vehicle for entrepreneurs.

Spousal IRAs. Often overlooked are spousal IRAs, a relatively recent addition to the IRA scene. Although most IRAs specify that contributions must be made from earned income, Congress has offered an exception for stay-at-home spouses. Another $4,000 (or $5,000 if over 50) can go into a separate spousal IRA account, so long as the primary earner has enough earned income. Thus, a couple owning a business, with one spouse working, can set aside $8,000 per year with almost no administrative costs.

SIMPLE Plans

SIMPLEs (Savings Incentive Match Plans for Employees) are IRAs designed for small businesses with employees and they expand individual and owner contributions beyond ordinary IRA limits. Business owners and employees may contribute up to $10,000 to their SIMPLE accounts each year. Catch-up provisions for those over age 50 allow for contributing another $2,500. While employees must fund most of the contributions, employers must at minimum either *directly fund* 2 percent of employee wages or *match* up to 3 percent of their contributions. Employer contributions are not required for employees earning $5,000 or less. An employer match can go higher, up to another $10,000, which makes SIMPLEs attractive for very small or closely held companies with variable incomes and for businesses with low-wage or part-time employees. Employer contributions are tax-deductible for the employer and employee contributions are on a pretax basis. Funds grow tax-deferred, as in a traditional IRA.

SEP-IRAs

SEP-IRAs are a lot like traditional IRAs but with potentially much higher contribution limits and, if there are employees, employee contribution requirements. The SEP lives up to its name (Simplified Employee Pension) a bit better than the SIMPLE plan. SEP-IRAs are designed mainly for small business employers with fewer than 25 employees, but they work best to build wealth for successful self-employed solo entrepreneurs.

The power of SEPs comes from contribution limits, which are the lower of 25 percent of employee compensation or $42,000, and 20 percent of a business owner's net income. So if you earn $100,000 in your business, you can put away $20,000, five times the IRA limit. If you earn $200,000, you can put away $42,000. No other plan, except for defined-benefit pension plans, even comes close.

The attractiveness of SEPs diminishes when you have employees. Plan provisions call for employees to get contributions in the same proportion as you; i.e., if you take 25 percent of wages or 20 percent of profits, all employees get 25 percent of their wages, too. These contributions are funded by the employer, not the employee. They are tax-deductible and the savings are self-directed and tax-deferred. Employees are eligible if they are over 21, have worked at least one day in the last three of five years, and earn at least $450. As you can see, using a SEP with employees, especially highly paid ones, can be expensive. But if these employees are members of your family, it might be a different story.

QUALIFIED EMPLOYER PLANS

Qualified employer plans are generally for businesses with employees, especially corporations and those with more than 25 employees, but in some cases may work for small businesses or individuals. These plans get the most legal scrutiny with ERISA requirements and administrative work and are subject to various fairness tests. Many business owners create qualified plans to cover everyone, then use individual plans or a different kind of qualified plan to beef up their contributions. Most of these plans will require professional administration, which is complex enough to cost money.

Profit-Sharing Plans

Profit-sharing plans (PSPs) dictate annual contributions according to the profits generated by the business. That is, as a defined-contribution plan, the percentage of profits is defined but not the contribution itself. Contributions are made by the employer and, unlike with many plans, no contribution is required even if there are profits. But if a contribution is made, everyone must share in it. Employees over 21 or with the business at least one year must be covered. Like SEP-IRAs, owners may enjoy a relatively high contribution, up to the lesser of $42,000 or 25 percent of the aggregate contribution of all plan participants; that is, you get to put one fourth of *all* contributions into your own account. Additionally, you may contribute 100 percent of business income, after other contributions are made, up to $42,000, making PSPs attractive for business owners with other sources of income. PSPs are attractive for businesses with a lot of employees and for businesses with highly variable incomes, since employer contributions rise and fall with incomes. Lastly, the tie between profits and contributions in PSPs may serve to motivate good employee performance.

401(k) Plans

A 401(k) plan is chiefly a salary-deferral plan, in which employees can contribute up to $15,000 a year (2006) in pretax wages, with another $4,000 in catch-up provisions. Additional percentage-of-salary specifications may be added by employers; many will match at least the first few percentage points of salary contributed. Many businesses contribute a half percent for each percent contributed by the employee, up to 6 percent of the employee's salary. Why do employers contribute matching funds? In part, to help attract better employees. But also, in part, because the tax code specifies a minimum percentage of employee participation in the plan in order that business owners and key managers can take their maximum contribution. For a business owner with a lot of employees, the 401(k) works well, for most of the contribution burden is placed on employees. Business owners can pull some out through their 401(k) and then supplement it if they choose with other retirement plans.

Defined-Benefit Plans

While used chiefly in large organizations with many employees, often in a union environment, defined-benefit plans can make sense for individual business owners with few or, better, no employees.

As outlined above, a defined-benefit plan fixes the benefit, not the contribution. The benefit can usually be taken either as an annuitized payment for life or as a lump sum. Some plans target the lump-sum benefit specifically, while others target the annuity payout. For the most part, the math follows the distribution and accumulation annuity math we've already covered.

When a plan tries to target a fixed benefit, the contributions to that plan are determined by mathematics based on chosen assumptions for return rates, time before retirement, and lifetime after retirement. Who chooses the assumptions? You, in tandem with your financial planner or pension specialist. This authority, combined with high contribution limits (up to $170,000 per year for older employees), puts a lot of retirement savings power into your hands.

As we've seen with accumulation annuity math,

the lower the return, the more you have to contribute per month or per year to achieve a financial goal. And the shorter the time period to save, the more you have to contribute. So, while you hoped for higher returns when you were doing do-it-yourself savings, now it works in your favor to assume low rates of return. The shorter the time period and the lower the rate, the more you have to put in to achieve a given pension benefit. And it's all legal, subject to guidelines too complex to present here. Business owners, especially older ones, can drop huge amounts of money into a private defined-benefit plan.

When employees are involved, most of the advantage goes away, for law requires deposits to be made for them and, of course, you assume investment performance risk for them, too. So individual business owners—consultants, professionals, and the like—find these plans very attractive. You can see why they prefer to hire contractors for extra help when they need it, rather than adding employees. Making the defined-benefit choice requires professional advice and management and may cost a few thousands of dollars each year.

Setting up Your Retirement Plan

If you're a small, self-employed entrepreneur, a trip to your local brokerage firm—Charles Schwab, Fidelity, or similar—will probably be enough to learn what you need to know and to set up a plan. These firms work primarily with IRAs and SEPs. Banks and bank trust departments can handle some of the more complex individual and small business plans. Benefits specialists, many tied with insurance and risk management services for small businesses, can help you through the maze and set up and administer more complex plans. With frequent law changes, complex paperwork, payroll tie-ins, and employee education, using a benefit specialist is highly recommended for small businesses with employees. Finally, there are professional pension and retirement plan administrators, known as *quali-*

fied pension administrators (QPAs), who can guide you through the stickiest plans. Be sure to work with them not only to set up a plan, but also first to figure out which plan best suits your needs.

Plan	Target	Description	Contribution Limits	Income Limits?	Mandatory Contributions for Employees?	Primary Funding Source	Administration and Cost	Comments
Ira • Traditional • Roth • Spousal	Individual	Designed for individual use, self-directed investment accounts. Traditional and spousal are deductible and tax deferred, Roth is non-deductible and tax-free	$4,000 + $1,000 catch-up provision	Yes	N/A	Individual	Low	Easy to combine with other plans. Roth IRAs have no mandatory withdrawals and can be passed on. Funds deposited in a Roth IRA can be withdrawn without penalty or tax.
SIMPLE	Small Business	Employees can contribute up to $10K, 2% employer contribution or 2% employer or 3% match required.	$10,000 + $2,500. catch-up from employee, $10,000 additional employer match	No	Yes	Employees	Medium	Higher contribution limits than IRA, may work well for owner/employee, providing up to $20,000 in deduction not tied to business income.
SEP IRA	Small Business and Self-employed Individual	Self-directed investment account, like a large IRA except employee contributions are required.	Minimum of 25% of business income (20% for owner) or $42,000	No	Yes	Business Owner	Low/Medium	Very high contribution limits, works especially well for high-income individual business owners without employees
Profit-Sharing Plan	Larger Employers	Qualified plan, employees get a share of the profits.	$42,000, owners may contribute tup to 25% of all contributions	No	No	Employer	Medium/High	No employee contributions. All contributions are optional in a given year. Good for businesses with highly variable income, owners can get a large share.
401(k) Plan	Larger Employers	Salary deferral, employees contribute pretax with optional employer match determined by individual plan design.	$14,000 + $4,000 catch-up	No	Determined by plan, employee contributions affect owner contributions	Employees	Medium/High	Very common, employee funding makes them attractive for owners. Easy to combine with other plans, to increase owner savings.
Pension	Larger Employers	Defined benefit plan, contributions determined by actuarial calculation.	Up to $170,000 depending on age of employee	No	Yes	Employer	High	Designed for old-economy businesses but good way for individual business owners to set aside very large amounts.

FIGURE 10.4. Retirement Plan Summary Table

CHAPTER 11

Transition It: What to Do When It's Time to Move On

I'S AS CERTAIN AS DEATH, TAXES, OR RISING GAS prices. Sooner or later, because you must or, preferably, because you choose, you're going to have to pack it up and move on from your business. For some, this comes with great regret, as they must close down or hand over to others a lifetime of accomplishment and achievement—and really, their identity. For others, it's a time of satisfaction and joy, as they reap the harvest of years of hard labor and good ideas. Regardless, sooner or later, it's the *distribution phase* and the focus shifts from getting more out of your business as income to one of getting more out of its assets and preparing it for its next phase without you at the helm.

DISTRIBUTION: DECISIONS AND CHOICES

Getting out of a business can be as challenging as getting into one—maybe more so. There are many decisions to make. You've learned the business and guided it toward profitability; now you must figure out how to dispose of it or transition it to others who almost surely won't have the same experience, skills, or perhaps passion as you. They won't see the business the same way, they won't value it the same way, they won't do things the same way. The process, by virtue of factors you can or cannot control, may have to happen quickly or may be carried out over a long period.

Ultimately, you'll have to choose between one of two primary forms of distribution for your business: *sell* it or *transfer* it to chosen successors, inside or outside your family. Selling the business can happen all at once or over a period of time, disposing of parts of the business or even individual assets, like real estate, production equipment, or intangibles like patents or portions of a customer base. Transferring means passing business assets to chosen successors through the *estate planning* process.

Estate planning is arranging for the legal transfer of *assets* and *authority before, at,* and/or *after* the death of the owner and, in most cases, his or her spouse. All individuals should do some estate planning, whether it is for a simple will outlining financial bequests to heirs or charity, for custody of children, or for the transfer of a prize family antique. But it's more challenging and important for the wealthy. Why? Because of estate taxes, which kick in generally with estates over $2 million in net worth (2006) and can grab up to 45 percent of wealth beyond that amount.

For most business owners, equity in the business represents the lion's share of their personal wealth and thus the largest portion of their estates. Failure to plan properly for this transfer is one of the leading causes of business failure, immediately or eventually. Typically, one of two things occurs. First, estate taxes can force the sale of the business if it is not distributed properly prior to death or if cash assets are insufficient to pay the taxes at the time of transfer. Second, failure to properly choose and prepare successors and to prepare the rest of the family for succession leaves a business without proper management; the outcome is predictable.

Sale or Succession?

Many entrepreneurs find it easiest to sell their business and retire to some friendly enclave in the sun to live out their golden years. This is the vision that most of us have when we get started—and the sooner the better. But a good business can be a treasured family asset, not only from a financial perspective but also as a defining legacy for the family. It is simply hard to let go and, further, it makes business sense to keep it in the family and provide sustenance and wealth for family members for years to come. In fact, according to one study, more than 50 percent of business owners choose to plan a succession for their business rather than just sell it on the open market and some 84 percent of those owners choose a family successor.

But keeping a business in the family is not as easy it sounds. Family infighting, transfer taxes, the misallocation of control, and similar problems often plague the successful transition of the family business. Studies show that only 30 to 35 percent of all businesses survive into the second generation beyond the original owners and only 5 to 15 percent into the third. Speed bumps along the path are numerous and some quite high: family dynamics, family member interest, response of employees to new and often young family leaders, skills and talent, passion, the desire of family members to do something different—all above and beyond the financial planning issues of transfer, equitable distribution, and avoidance of estate taxes.

The Succession Plan

Successful succession requires a good succession plan and a good estate plan, which is usually part of the succession plan. As suggested above, the estate plan handles concrete matters of transfer of assets and authority. The succession plan goes further to handle the family and "people" issues, providing a complete framework to prepare for the transfer. Estate planning is a very delicate and often emotional task, requiring good leadership and a common sense of purpose, not to mention a lot of time. The succession plan requires still more emotional energy, for the family must be prepared not just for the transfer, but also to keep things going afterwards. One study found that some 75 percent of family business owners want to retire in next 15 years, but only a third of them have a succession plan in place.

Making the Choice

Naturally, there is no one-size-fits-all approach to deciding on distribution and building a succession and/or estate plan. Ultimately you will decide based on the financial and personal merits of a situation and what works best for you and your family. The choice can be guided by the state of the business now, the state of your own personal and family finances, and the qualifications and interests of potential successors. Many disposition decisions depend on whether the business is growing and in a growing industry or is "tired" and in need of fresh ideas or investments—and whether there are other businesses that might be in a good position to acquire it. Timing is a major factor in developing distribution plans.

Choosing how to dispose of a business involves a lot of nuances and unknowns. It involves a good crystal ball for current and future financial ramifications. It involves a good sense for the "people issues" with potential successors. The choice involves many of the same business and personal instincts that got you going, yet the nature of disposition and espe-

cially succession choices can be much different and much more emotionally charged. First, it requires coming to grips with mortality—you can't run the business forever. Second, it requires the ability to let go—often difficult for entrepreneurs.

We've now given a framework for what follows in this chapter—a discussion of some of the issues, strategies, and mechanics of selling a business, estate planning, and succession planning. As with many areas covered in this book, we highly recommend further reading and/or consulting with experts to get the details and apply them to your situation.

▼ A MORE COMPLETE PICTURE

There is no way we can do justice to all of the factors and appraisals required to sell a business. Financial advisors, business appraisers, and consultants specializing in business sales should be brought into the process, especially for large or complex businesses involving substantial financial assets, complex ownership structures, and employees. What's "large"? What's "complex"? That's a judgment call. But if you're more than a sole proprietorship working out of your home, your business probably qualifies. Many worthwhile books have been written on selling businesses, including the following:

- *Entrepreneur Magazine's Ultimate Guide to Buying or Selling a Business* by Ira Nottonson (Entrepreneur Press, 4th edition, 2004)

- *The Complete Guide to Selling a Business* by Fred S. Steingold (Nolo Press, 2nd edition, 2005)

- *What Every Business Owner Should Know About Valuing Their Business* by Stanley Feldman, Timothy Sullivan, and Roger Winsby (McGraw-Hill, 2002)

SELLING THE BUSINESS

The decision to sell a business isn't easy. Most entrepreneurs choose to sell when they think the business has run its course, when there are no obvious successors, and/or when the price it will fetch is right. The decision is part business, part personal, so it involves both business and personal finances.

The sale of a business usually involves a deliberate planning process, including a well-developed appraisal of the value of the business, an assessment of tax consequences, and a transition plan to administratively complete the sale. It is highly advisable to plan beyond the execution of the sale to determine the deployment of the proceeds and to map out your role in the business in the future—as an advisor, consultant, or even a minority partner or owner. Many entrepreneurs start this process years in advance of putting the business up for sale.

Valuation

When you sell a business, you're really selling a set of assets. You look at your business as a going concern, a product of your leadership and hard work linking customers, products, production, and supply to make a profit. A buyer, on the other hand, looks at your business as a set of assets. Those assets can be tangible or intangible. Tangible assets are physical or financial assets with a measurable market value, like cash, working capital, inventory, or physical plant assets. Intangible assets include patents or other intellectual property, market position including location and brand names, customer bases, employee talent, business processes, supplier agreements, and the general know-how to operate the business. Naturally, the cash flow and "free" cash flow beyond asset purchase requirements are important. As we outlined in Chapter 9, a business is worth what it will produce for its owners in positive cash flow over time, nothing less and nothing more. This is what a rational business buyer looks for and it's a good approach for you to start the valuation process.

Business buyers recognize that the whole can be worth more than the sum of the parts. You can count the assets, but how they fit together also counts. Good businesses have the right mix and interaction of tangible and intangible assets to efficiently deliver products or services to customers and cash to the firm. So the appraisal goes beyond just what's in the checking account and the market resale value of your cameras or laser punch press.

As part of your planning process, a business appraiser (often a CPA with experience with small businesses) can help put a price tag on your assets and the "glue" that holds them together. Like a good real estate appraiser, he or she will incorporate "comps"—similar businesses in similar markets—into the appraisal. This is important, because, like a stock investment, a business is really worth only what the market will support at a given time, which in turn depends on such factors as the state of the economy and the position of your business in your industry. Having an appraisal report adds credibility when you go to market with your business and, obviously, it helps with your personal financial planning downstream from the sale.

Tax Considerations

As you rough out a value for your business, pay special attention to the income tax consequences of the sale. Most physical assets of a business—or the shares of the business, if a C corporation—are considered capital items and are thus subject to capital gains taxes. As with stock and other personal investments, it is seldom advisable to let the tax consequences drive the decision to sell; other factors are normally more important and taxes will be paid sooner or later. But to understand the financial impact and net benefit to your personal finances when you sell your business, you need to put some effort into tax planning.

The gain is based on the difference between sale price and the cost basis for the assets sold. When assets are sold individually, the gain is relatively easy to compute. When a business is sold as a whole, it must be determined what is being paid for which assets, tangible and intangible. This can be tricky and usually requires professional help.

The IRS has specific guidelines for breaking down parts of a business during a sale. They divide all assets into seven *classes* and require the buyer and seller to agree on the dollar value of each class. These are the classes:

- Cash and cash deposits
- Cash-equivalent securities
- Receivables
- Inventory
- Property
- Non-goodwill intangibles, such as intellectual property, non-compete covenants, or other agreements
- Pure goodwill and going-concern value, the difference between the price paid and the value of the first six asset groups

For tangible assets, the seller may have to pay more than ordinary capital gains on the sale. Tax rates are higher for depreciation recapture, that is, the difference between sale price and book value of an asset. So the seller prefers a relatively low appraisal on property to avoid this recapture and a high appraisal of goodwill. Meanwhile, the buyer prefers a higher valuation for physical assets to help secure financing and to maximize future write-offs. You can see how this exercise gets interesting and is best handled by a third-party professional. More on the topic can be found in IRS Publication 544, *Sales and Other Dispositions of Assets.*

Installment Sales

An installment sale, with the buyer making a down payment and then paying the rest of the purchase price over a contractually agreed number of years, is one popular way to reduce the tax bite of a business sale. It also serves to generate some long-term income from the sale. Effectively, the installment sale works like income averaging, spreading the income over a number of years, delaying tax payment, and keeping you in a lower tax bracket in each year.

Executing the Sale

The full range of activities involved in preparing and executing a business sale is beyond our scope here. At minimum, business agreements must be clearly terminated or modified, customers must be notified, and the title must be transferred. It's important to clean up the books and bring them up to date and to make sure there are no tax surprises, liens, or overdue payments, especially to government authorities.

You Sold the Business—Now What?

Suddenly, you have a big chunk of cash—and nothing to do. You sleep late, that is, at least until 6 each morning. You go to lunch and hang out at Starbucks with your buddies. You finally have time to prune those fruit trees and rose bushes in your back yard. You go to your kids' afternoon soccer practices or take care of your grandchildren. You wonder what to do with your cash.

Hopefully, the sale of the business brought enough to pay off business debts. Depending on how much you set aside for retirement and how old you are, retirement should probably be your first priority. It would be good to invest your assets to produce some or all of the "golden eggs" that your business produced over the years. That way, you won't miss the income. If you built enough value into your business that your proceeds from the sale produce as much return as the business did, that's great. If not, you will have to depend on other resources—or keep working life—to finance what's next. Of course, you can invest your proceeds in another business if you find one of interest.

ESTATE PLANNING ESSENTIALS

Now we get into transferring wealth and authority to future generations and other designees—whether or not you sell the business. Estate planning is an important yet often neglected part of personal financial planning, whether you own a business or not. You've got to face the facts: sooner or later you'll have to transfer your assets and authority to someone, somehow.

Estate Planning Goals

Stated simply, the goal of the asset transfer process is to get your assets to go where you want them to go, quickly and painlessly at minimal cost and taxation. More specific goals include the following:

- **Provide for specific family needs.** Making sure the right heirs get the right assets—and income from those assets—is important, especially if a business is involved. Providing a map for your financial legacy is even more important if there are prior marriages, kids from prior marriages or other relationships, and so forth.
- **Avoid probate.** Probate takes time, costs money, and introduces uncertainty.
- **Provide liquidity.** Without a proper estate plan, assets and income can be tied up, while expenses go on, leaving family members with

a mess. This mess can be bigger if there's a business involved and if there are estate taxes to be paid.

- **Achieve charitable intentions.** You worked hard through life and now want to give something back. Charitable contributions at or before death can be the right thing to do and can also reduce estate taxes.

Assets and Authority

As mentioned earlier, estate planning is arranging for the legal transfer of *assets* and *authority*, *before*, *at*, and/or *after* death.

The assets are the financial and physical things you own, including your business, investments, real estate, personal possessions, and intellectual property. Asset transfer can be done as you please and when you please. The transfer of assets may be subject to estate and inheritance taxes and, of course, it may cause conflict among members of your family.

The transfer of authority—the authority to make decisions affecting your physical and financial well-being—typically occurs before or at death. Child custody is one major facet of personal authority; in fact, when you have children, you need at least some sort of estate plan even if you're still in the early or middle stages of your life. Later in life, especially if you own a business and are a key figure in the business decision process, you will need a plan to transfer your decision-making authority, particularly if you become incapacitated before death. The business decision-making authority can be transferred in several ways, often through the business agreement if there are partners involved. If necessary, authority to make medical decisions is transferred through *medical power of attorney* documents. Also, if necessary, all other decision-making authority can be transferred, through *general*, *limited*, or *durable* powers of attorney. You will also appoint an *executor*—someone to manage the estate and asset transfer after death. You may also outline a gradual

transfer of wealth and authority, even after death, typically through the use of trusts.

Common Misconceptions

There are many misconceptions about estate planning. First, most people think of it as a "death plan"; that is, nothing happens until you die. Not true. There are good reasons for most people to transfer assets and/or authority before death, when they have the most control, when the process can be done most smoothly, and in some cases they can avoid undue tax burdens. People tend to think an estate plan is something you need when you get older. But what about your children? What about those priceless antiques that your ancestors brought over on the Mayflower? Who should get those? What about your great-grandmother's wedding ring? Granted, the estate plan you might come up with in your 30s before you've achieved business success might consist of a simple one-page will, but it's still worth doing and thinking about, because the alternatives can be unpleasant.

Second, most people equate estate planning to avoiding estate taxes. True, estate taxes are a big part of estate planning if your total net worth qualifies you for the $2 million-plus club. At this level, estate

> ### WHAT IF YOU DIE WITHOUT A WILL?
>
> So why do you need a will, anyway? Well, without one, your assets will be transferred according to state law or, more precisely, according to how a probate judge interprets that law. If you die *intestate*, that is, without a will, the court will decide where your stuff goes. Your family will have little if any control outside of what's prescribed by the law, which lays out a map of next of kin the way the state sees it. It's a long and usually painful process.

planning becomes more involved and complex. But it's not the trigger point for estate planning. Even if your net worth is only $500,000, you still need to decide where *that's* going. If it's made up of complex or hard-to-value assets—like a business—a good plan is all the more important. Even if you're not worried about estate taxes, you still need to cover the transfer of authority. Finally, a good estate plan can *speed up* the transfer process, which can mean a lot to your heirs. A complex estate without proper estate planning elements (trusts, wills, contracts) can take over a year or more to transfer; meanwhile, life and its expenses go on.

Bottom line: the nature and size of your estate affect the complexity of your estate plan; they do not determine whether or not you need one. Now we'll examine some of the specific features of an estate plan.

ASSET TRANSFER MECHANISMS

If you have a large, complex estate and a lot of potential heirs, obviously asset transfer planning can be a major challenge. Yet the more challenging it is, the more it's necessary. In this section we'll explore some, but certainly not all, of the strategies and mechanics of asset transfer. The possible scenarios are endless; estate planning experts have thought of almost everything possible to smooth the process and especially to avoid excessive taxation. Your case—like everyone else's—will be unique.

At a high level, it is important to know that asset transfer can be achieved in three ways: by *ownership*, by *contract*, or by *will*. Each applies best to certain kinds of assets or transfer situations and each has advantages and disadvantages.

By Ownership

If you own property jointly with someone else, transfer will occur according to how that ownership is set up. In some cases, the ownership contract is designed

▼ **WHAT'S SO BAD ABOUT PROBATE, ANYWAY?**

Everything you read in the estate planning world discusses avoiding probate—almost as if it were the primary objective of estate planning. The probate process goes through the courts, taking time and, of course, costing money. Probate fees are set by state statute and are stiff—from 3 percent to as much as 7 percent of estate value, depending on the state, and much more if there is a contested will. It can take a long time—up to a year, maybe more. Finally, there is the risk of loss of control, as probate can become a battleground for a will contest. If there is a business in your estate, be aware: the tie-up and uncertainty of the probate process can kill the goose you wanted to protect—the business. Suppliers, banks, and others are loath to touch a business tied up in an ownership transfer fight.

to make transfer automatic. The most common form of joint ownership is known as JTWROS—*Joint Tenancy with Right of Survivorship.* You buy the property—e.g., real estate, financial assets, or a business—in equal shares with someone else and put on the title both names, JTWROS. At death, your share automatically and immediately reverts to the other owner with no probate or court involvement.

JTWROS is far and away the most common way to handle husband-wife ownership. It is also used for businesses and business property. But property transferred through JTWROS is subject to estate taxation at current valuation, which may not always be the wisest way to transfer. (This is not an issue with marital transfer since marital transfers are not taxed.)

Tenancy in common (TIC) ownership occurs more frequently in business. With TIC, ownership shares don't have to be equal. When a tenant in common dies, his or her part transfers to his or her designated heirs. How that transfer is accomplished depends on how the transfer is set up—by contract or by will, as noted below. Whereas JTWROS is automatic, TIC transfers typically go through probate.

Another form of ownership—*tenancy by the entirety*—is a special form of joint tenancy when the joint tenants are husband and wife. Ownership of the property is treated as if the husband and wife were a single legal person. Each tenant effectively owns the entire estate. Neither can sell the property without the consent of the other. This form is not recognized in all states.

States have different forms and different interpretations of the forms just outlined. Property ownership for larger estates or estates with a business should be reviewed with a qualified attorney.

By Contract

Transfer by contract is probably the most common form of asset transfer for larger estates in particular, especially for the larger assets within the estate. Transfer by contract usually breaks down into two forms: transfer as *beneficiary* and transfer through *trusts*. If you name someone as a beneficiary for a retirement plan or an insurance policy, that is a transfer by contract. Such transfers are subject to estate taxation but occur immediately and avoid the probate process. A trust is essentially a custom-designed transfer contract, again executed outside of probate, with any set of conditions you might choose. Trusts not only smooth the transfer but also allow you to "get things to go where you want them to go when you want them to go there," including the authority to spend your assets or further transfer them to others. Some kinds of trusts can be used to reduce the impact of taxation. We'll get to trusts in a minute.

By Will

Property transferred by will goes through probate. In fact, probate is the legal process for ascertaining the validity of a will. Even a well-planned estate will have a will. Why? Because wills cover a lot more than just the transfer of assets; they also transfer authority, appoint the executor, and cover other administrative details regarding your wishes for transferring the estate. Importantly, wills cover *survivorship*—that is, who's in line for what in case a named beneficiary has deceased since the will was created or if the will maker and a beneficiary die at the same time. Wills also cover assets not specified or in excess of amounts covered by contract or ownership transfers. All estates will go through probate; however, if an estate has been planned well, only a tiny fraction of the assets—and hopefully not the business—will transfer this way.

TRANSFER OF AUTHORITY

Aside from trusts, the will acts as the ultimate authority transfer mechanism *at* death. But as you know from watching the movies, the will isn't read and does not become legally binding until death. Yet, in many situations, especially where a business is involved, it makes sense for a person to name a trusted individual to act in his or her place to take care of property, financial, or health decisions should it become necessary. A *power of attorney* is the legal document used to transfer any such authority before death.

A *general* power of attorney typically grants the *agent or attorney-in-fact* the authority to do anything the *principal* could have done—make financial decisions, spend money, make gifts, run a business, change business agreements, etc. The power of attorney may specify conditions. A *limited* power of attorney grants the attorney-in-fact authority to do only certain things as specified—for instance, just run the business or just handle personal finances. A *medical* power of attorney gives someone the right to make medical or treatment decisions. The principal can revoke a power of attorney at any time. Most powers of attorney are made *durable*, that is, to stay in effect at and through the incapacity or disability of the principal.

NOW—ESTATE TAXATION

Estate taxes are almost as feared as death itself—especially for the heirs. From their standpoint, the good news is they will inherit a nice chunk and a piece of the family legacy; the bad news is the government is poised to take away a big chunk, nearly half in a worst-case scenario. This is scary, but the government doesn't just automatically take half of everything. There are ways, with effective planning, to reduce the bite. And for estates under $2 million ($4 million if owned by a married couple) there's likely to be no federal tax bite at all.

Estate taxes have a bad rap—largely justified—for taking huge sums from families and especially for killing family legacies such as family farms and businesses. Yes, it's true: it happens. Estate taxes can indeed have an enormous impact on the financial well-being of your heirs or family—or no impact at all. Estate taxes are among the highest and most complex forms of taxation in the free world, with effective marginal rates running as high as 45 percent.

The good news comes in the form of a generous and steadily growing exclusion and a sketch of a promise that estate taxes will go away altogether. (We don't think that will happen, but they may be modified to reduce their impact.) The federal exclusion, known as the *unified credit*, negates estate taxes in 2006–2008 for estates up to $2 million per individual. (This figure was $675,000 as recently as 2001.) In 2010, for *one year*, estate taxes go away altogether. Whether that provision continues, gets changed, or "sunsets" in 2010 is a subject of extensive congressional debate at the time of this writing and we think it will be modified to reduce impact but not eliminated.

The upshot: *even as a business owner, you likely won't have to worry about estate taxes*. But if your estate grows beyond these thresholds or if your financial planning includes possible inheritances that might be subject to the estate tax, you should understand how estate taxes work and how they are changing and you should build a precise estate plan to keep them at a minimum. Particularly when estate taxes are involved, it makes sense to get professional help with your estate plan.

The Uniform Gift and Estate Tax System

Before getting into the estate tax tables, it is necessary to understand estate taxes as part of something bigger, set up by the government as the *uniform gift and estate tax* system. As is the case for most rules and regulations set up by Congress for the IRS to enforce, this concept started simple and got a lot more complicated.

As mentioned earlier, assets can be transferred at, before, or after death. It's natural to think that, if you transfer your assets before death by giving them away, they won't be subject to estate taxes. Wrong. The federal government figured that one out long ago and imposes gift taxes on such transfers. In fact, for many years, gift taxes and estate taxes were applied to the same "whole" under the unified taxation system; that is, your taxable gifts and taxable estate at death were added up and a uniform tax was applied to both.

The 2001 law that prescribed the 2010 elimination of estate taxes and the rapid rise in the exclusion amount also, unfortunately, decoupled the estate and gift taxes. While estate tax exclusions steadily rose from 2001 forward, the gift tax exclusion stopped rising in 2004. In that year, the estate exclusion rose to $1.5 million per individual, but the gift tax exclusion stayed at $1 million, and in fact it stays the same even through the sunset of the estate tax altogether in 2010. If there is any good news, it's that the gift tax rate tops out at 35 percent after 2009, instead of 45 percent as in the unified system now. There's more good news, but only if you're an estate planning attorney—more complex planning is the obvious and inevitable result. We expect, however, that the estate and gift taxes will become unified once again (maybe it's a hope, not an expectation) when the members of Congress finally figure out what they want to do with estate and gift taxation in 2011 and beyond.

Annual Gift Exclusion

For large estates, the annual gift exclusion is one of the simplest and most powerful tools at your disposal. As of 2006, any person can give $12,000 to any other person in one year with no tax consequences. These gifts obviously reduce the taxable value of the estate. The amount—$12K—may not seem like much, but the power comes in with the "per donor, per recipient" part.

If you're a husband-wife household with three kids, you can give away $72,000 each year tax-free. How so? Because both of you can each give $12,000 to each kid. This is called *gift-splitting*. If there are more recipients, say, for instance, grandchildren, you can reduce the value of your estate even faster. You can see how effective gift planning can help drive down estate value pretty quickly. Of course, you can give more to charities, etc.—we'll get to that. And one unusual provision of section 529 college savings plans, covered in the last chapter, allows you to accelerate such gifting five years, an equivalent of $60,000 per donor, per recipient in the first year. If you're putting three kids through college, you could drain $360,000 from your estate this year. The best part: since 529 assets are held in an educational trust but still technically yours, you don't really have to give away control of the money.

Qualified Transfers

The uniform gift and estate taxation system allows payments for qualified medical or education expenses to be excluded above and beyond the annual $12,000 gift exclusion. The catch: these amounts must be paid directly to the medical or educational institution involved, not to the person benefiting from your gift. This exclusion applies whether the recipient is a member of the immediate family or not. This is a way favored by grandparents for moving funds out of an estate to benefit their grandchildren. A recent letter ruling held that this mechanism can be used for prepaid tuition plans as well as current tuition.

Estate Tax Rates

The following two tables highlight the changes in estate taxation over the years brought on mainly by the 2001 Economic Growth and Tax Relief Reconciliation Act (EGTRRA). First, the maximum federal estate tax rate (Figure 11.1).

Year	Top Marginal Rates	
2002 and before	55%	
2003	49%	
2004	48%	
2005	47%	
2006	46%	
2007-2009	45%	
2010 and beyond	35%	gift only

Source: IRS

FIGURE 11.1. Marginal Estate Tax Rates

Next, the exclusion amounts (Figure 11.2). Note the decoupling of the estate tax and the gift tax and, starting in 2003, the growing difference between the rising estate exclusion and the static gift exclusion.

THE TAXABLE ESTATE

All taxes, of course, are determined by applying a rate to a basis. We've touched on rates; now, just like calculating taxable income for income taxes, we must calculate *estate* taxable income for estate taxes. Your estate will, by law, include some items and

Year	Estate Exclusion Amount	Gift Exclusion Amount
1987-1997	$600,000	$600,000
1998	$625,000	$625,000
1999	$650,000	$650,000
2000-2001	$675,000	$675,000
2002-2003	$1,000,000	$1,000,000
2004-2005	$1,500,000	$1,000,000
2006-2008	$2,000,000	$1,000,000
2009	$3,500,000	$1,000,000

Source: IRS

FIGURE 11.2. Effective Estate and Gift Tax Exclusions

exclude others. For proper estate planning, you need to understand these items.

What's Included

Estate assets include items owned in your own name, like investment accounts, real estate in your name, retirement accounts, and life insurance. Business assets or shares in a business held in your name are routinely included in an estate. Your estate includes half of anything owned JTWROS with your spouse and a proportionate share of properties held in other joint ownership arrangements, so long as other owners paid their fair share. If other owners did not pay for their share of a jointly held asset, their share is considered a gift from you and handled as part of the unified estate. All other gifts in excess of your annual

▼ **WHAT ABOUT LIFE INSURANCE?**

Insurance salespeople are quick to tout the tax-free status of any benefit paid on a life insurance policy. If you're the beneficiary of a $500,000 policy, you won't pay a dime of federal *income* tax. But the proceeds might be subject to *estate* tax if the estate is large enough. There are some exceptions, such as when the policy is set up in an *irrevocable life insurance trust*, which we'll cover shortly.

exclusion are considered as part of your taxable estate and brought into the sum.

Valuation

Asset valuation plays a key consideration in estate planning, especially where a business is involved. Obviously, the lower the value, the less exposure to estate taxes. How does the business or your share of it get valued for estate tax purposes? It's complex.

Typically businesses are valued as an investor might value them, driven by the value of hard assets and future cash flows. But after that, it is common, and perfectly legal as guided by tax laws, to discount the value. Why? Basically, because tax authorities have some common sense and realize that a small business probably has less value without your presence. Business values are commonly discounted up to 25 percent for *marketability:* the assumption is that the business is small and not a household name and it might not sell for its true worth. Minority ownership can add another 25 percent discount, because an ownership share that is limited in its scope of control over critical aspects of the business is less attractive to an outside investor. This is often referred to as a *control* discount. Valuations may be thus 50 percent off the "book value" of a business. Such discounting can be especially effective when transferring a family business.

Exemptions and Exclusions

Exemptions start with any debts, taxes owed (other than estate taxes), administrative costs, or funeral costs associated with death. Further, they include the personal exclusion, which is really defined in terms of a credit, but effectively excludes $2 million of estate value from taxation in the years 2006–2008.

Marital Deduction

Since the early 1980s, all property transferred to a spouse is exempt from taxation. Cynics observe that

Congress was just trying to let estates grow bigger to exact a larger tax bite eventually, but the change probably was intended to keep the assets of a household together without undue stress or maneuvering to ensure preservation.

Now, if you simply transfer all assets to your spouse upon death, will you be able to take advantage of your $2 million deduction? Not really, since the assets would have transferred tax-free anyway. Suppose you and your spouse together have a taxable estate worth $4 million. If you die without using your exclusion, your spouse has the $4 million and, when he or she dies, only $2 million of that estate will be exempted—the rest will be subject to tax. This isn't good. So what happens in most good estate plans is that $2 million is set aside in a marital trust, usually with the spouse as beneficiary, to capture the $2 million exclusion. So for estates exceeding $2 million, there is more planning for a married couple to do beyond simply relying on the marital deduction.

Charitable Deduction

Congress likes to encourage people to donate to qualified charities, in order to help achieve desired social goals. Consequently, amounts donated to such charities at death are exempt from estate taxes.

STEP-UP IN BASIS

So your kids will have the great fortune, hopefully a long way into the future, to inherit your business and all of your other stuff. You did really well, so even with the best estate and gift planning, there were still some estate tax liabilities. Fine. You've taken care of that: you took out a life insurance policy to pay the taxes. Now, if your heirs decide to sell the business, will they suddenly create a big capital gains tax liability for themselves, because they own a business worth $6 million that you started for $100,000?

The answer—at least for now—is *no*. Reason: a very handy estate transfer feature known as *step-up in basis*. Step-up in basis means that any property transfers to the heirs at the value assigned to it when the estate transfers. Obviously this is a great way to preserve family wealth whether or not the estates are big enough to create estate tax liabilities.

When Congress passed EGTRRA in 2001, it first looked like the step-up in basis rules were going to go away in 2010, effectively replacing estate taxes with capital gains taxes for a great many estates—in fact, for all estates, regardless of whether or not they were large enough to be subject to estate taxes. Not only would this change probably have brought in more revenue than the estate tax would have raised, but the revenue would have been collected from a far greater number of people. Furthermore, the accounting challenge of figuring out each heir's basis in everything going back years and even decades would have been enormous.

Fortunately, Congress came to its senses at least a little and is allowing step-up in basis to continue for the first $1,300,000 in assets transferred and the first $3,000,000 transferred to a spouse. Still, it is far from simple—especially considering that the entire estate taxation scheme—for now, anyway—is scheduled to revert to pre-2001 status on January 1, 2011 unless Congress extends or amends the 2001 EGTRRA provisions. These provisions are giving financial and estate planners fits, because nobody knows what laws will apply at that point.

STATE INHERITANCE TAXES

And if these headaches weren't enough, most states have some form of death or inheritance tax in addition to federal taxes. For years, the issue was largely irrelevant, as state tax laws matched the federal tax code and the federal code allowed a credit for any amount of state tax paid so long as the laws matched. But many states haven't followed the federal changes since 2001, particularly the rise in exclusion amounts—Connecticut, District of Columbia, Illinois, Maine, Maryland, Massachusetts, Minnesota, Nebraska, New Jersey, New York, North Carolina, Ohio, Oklahoma, Oregon, Pennsylvania, Rhode Island, Vermont, Virginia, Washington, and Wisconsin. Four states—Kansas, New York, Oregon, and Virginia—didn't match even prior to 2001. If you're in one of these states, you and your advisor will need to take a close look at state law when planning your estate.

THE TRUTH ABOUT TRUSTS

The first word most people think of when they hear the words "estate planning" is *taxes*. The second word is probably "trust." The word "trust" sounds sophisticated and seems to go well with the words "money" and "wealth." We've all heard about rich folks using trusts to manage their millions, hand them out to their spoiled offspring, fund charitable causes, and do all sorts of other things. An investment company that manages *fiduciary trusts* simply must be in the know, right?

For estate planning purposes, trusts are legal entities set up and created to own assets in lieu of specific individuals to achieve any of numerous planning objectives, including the following:

- **Facilitate asset transfer.** Trusts transfer assets contractually, therefore avoiding probate and saving time, money, and publicity.
- **Manage finances** for beneficiaries unable or unwilling to do so. A widower or widow may not want to or be able to manage investments after his or her spouse's death. Or the widower or widow may be inclined to spend everything! Setting up a managed trust enables a spouse to keep control "from the grave," as people in estate planning circles put it.
- **Shelter money from estate and gift taxes.** Certain types of trusts may help shelter assets from taxes by taking advantage of the gift exclusion or by "playing games" with asset valuation.

- **Split assets and income from those assets** among beneficiaries. If you're remarried and you have children from the first marriage, you may want to provide income for your second spouse but leave your assets to your kids. Trusts can accomplish this split.
- **Control the direction of assets** after your death. Again, in complex divorce-remarriage situations, you can control where your assets—including a business—end up. If you want your assets to revert to your kids if your spouse remarries, a trust can make that happen.
- **Achieve charitable objectives.** Charitable trusts can be set up to provide assets or interest income to charities upon death.

Trust Terminology

It's helpful to understand the major players and some of the terminology of the trust world before looking at specific trust types.

Donor or *trust maker*—the person who creates and funds the trust, names the beneficiaries, and chooses the trustee.

- **Trustee**—the person or entity *managing* the trust, including investments and payouts. That could be you or a family member or it could be a fee-based professional organization, such as a bank trust department.
- **Beneficiary**—any person or organization receiving assets, income, or both from the trust.
- **Corpus**—a technical term for the assets owned by the trust.
- **Trust documents**—paperwork that you (and normally an attorney) create to define the trust and its terms and conditions. You can specify almost anything (that's legal) in a trust. If you want your kids to receive payments only when they get good grades in school or graduate from college, you can set it up that way. The "control from the grave" possibilities are endless.

TYPES OF TRUSTS

There are dozens of types of trusts. Here we will cover the more popular or frequently used varieties.

Living Trusts

Living, *revocable,* or *inter vivos* trusts are set up while the donor is living and are a part of the donor's estate. The living trust defines asset and income distribution to named beneficiaries. The main purposes are to bypass probate and, if the trust is set up to continue after death, maintain asset management and distribution at that time. Contrary to popular myth, these trusts *do not* avoid estate taxes. As they are living trusts, you retain ownership, which is why they are part of your estate. As they are revocable, you may change them at any time.

Irrevocable Trusts. Irrevocable trusts, as the name states, cannot be changed; they effect a complete transfer of ownership. The trust is still administered according to your terms, but you can't change it and you can no longer benefit directly from the assets. When you fund an irrevocable trust, you are in effect making a *gift* to its beneficiaries. If kept within the annual gift exclusion or if used to buy a life insurance policy owned by the trust, irrevocable trusts can reduce estate taxes.

Testamentary Trusts. This fancy-named trust actually comes into existence when you die—as part of the probate process. Testamentary trusts are usually created by a will and are usually used to manage assets and control asset direction after death.

QTIP Trusts

The Qualified Terminable Interest Property (QTIP) trust is designed to control asset direction primarily when there are spouses beyond a first marriage. A QTIP trust is usually used where the donor wants to provide income security for a subsequent spouse in trust, but have the assets revert to children (or elsewhere) upon the spouse's death. Typically that spouse receives income from the trust but can't touch the assets. The interest terminates when that spouse dies or often if he or she remarries.

Bypass or Marital Trusts

Touched on earlier and often called *A/B trusts,* these trusts are set up to pass assets outside the marital couple to take advantage of the unified credit available to each spouse. The trust simply separates an asset amount, usually the exclusion amount for that year, from the family estate. Typically these trusts are set up to pay income to the surviving spouse and distribute to downstream heirs upon the death of that spouse. The surviving spouse may serve as trustee. These trusts also avoid estate taxes on the increase in trust value between the death of the first spouse and the death of the second spouse, for the assets will not technically be part of the latter's estate.

Charitable Trusts

Charitable remainder and *charitable lead* trusts are designed to transfer a portion of an estate to a charity or charities before death or upon death. A chari-

---

▼ THE OLD TRUST MILL

Watch out for "trust mills"—the B-grade law firms appearing on daytime TV or matchbook covers hawking their versions of living trusts. They make living trusts sound indispensable. While revocable trusts have value for complex estates and to avoid probate, they often don't live up to the hype. Trust mills may charge only $500-$1,000, but you'll get only a very simple trust that may not suit your needs. These trusts fall far short of a true estate plan, especially if you must cover the nuances of business ownership or avoid estate taxation.

table *remainder* trust pays an annual sum back to the beneficiary (the trust maker or another party) and then transfers any remaining assets to the charity upon death. The donor gets a charitable income tax deduction upfront and, since the remaining corpus goes to charity, it avoids estate tax. The charitable *lead* trust pays an annual sum to the charity and then reverts the remainder principal to the beneficiary. Either way, these trusts are powerful tools for achieving charitable objectives and reducing taxes.

Life Insurance Trusts

The fancy-sounding *irrevocable life insurance trusts* (ILITs) are irrevocable trusts designed to own a life insurance policy. The policy usually is set up to pay heirs as beneficiaries. As they are irrevocable and uncontrollable by the insured, they pass outside the estate and avoid estate taxes. Funds used to pay *premiums* can be subject to gift taxes or may fall within the gift exclusion. ILITs can be powerful tools to pass on a large, tax-free sum at relatively low cost to the donor.

▼ IN THE BIG BAG OF TRUST TRICKS

Do you want to take advantage of a popular estate planning strategy used by the wealthy? Set up a *charitable remainder trust* to preserve income for as long as you live for yourself, pass the remainder to charity tax free, and take an upfront income tax deduction. That sounds good, but isn't something missing? What will your heirs get? Nothing.

So to fix that, set up and fund an ILIT with an insurance policy naming them as beneficiaries. Upon your death it will replace the wealth they're not inheriting. No estate taxes and little to no gift taxes if any on premiums paid. Or, keep your kids cut out of the estate altogether. It's your choice.

Grantor-Retained Interest Trusts

The fancy-sounding *grantor-retained interest trusts* (GRITs) are fancy indeed and are often used where a business or other rapidly appreciating asset is involved. The grantor (owner) places an asset in the trust at its current value. The grantor retains an interest, usually defined as an annuity payment from the asset, but gives up the value, or corpus, of the asset. If the grantor survives the annuity term, the asset passes on to the beneficiary at the fixed value—not the value to which it may have appreciated, thus potentially avoiding a big estate tax hit. If the grantor does not survive the trust term, the asset transfers at the market value at time of death. GRITs are especially effective for transferring a growing business, especially when the owner is otherwise financially secure. The value is frozen in time.

One special form of grantor trust allows much the same transaction for a personal residence. With a *qualified personal residence trust* (QPRT), you can freeze the value of your family home, which will transfer at the end of the trust period. If you think real estate values will grow substantially on a residence you plan to keep in the family and could be subject to estate taxes some day, a QPRT can help.

Family Limited Partnerships

Technically and legally, a *family limited partnership* (FLP) is not really a trust at all but a true legal limited partnership. In use and function, however, it resembles the GRIT or the QPRT. A business asset, which can include a rental property, can be put into the partnership. Each descendant family member gets a limited partnership percentage, which can grow in time through gifting, using the annual exclusion if possible to make it free of estate and gift taxes. The parent retains an interest as a general partner, which can drop as low as 1 percent, and continues to operate the business. The parent continues to make day-to-day operating decisions. But for estate planning purposes, the valuation for limited partners is subject to marketability and *minority interest* or *control* discounts discussed above. The parents can also shift business income to their descendants, who may be able to pay income taxes at lower rates. (The "kiddie tax" reduces this benefit somewhat for dependent children earning more than $5,000 per year. Consult a tax advisor.) Families should take care to make sure the FLP really is a legitimate business and is operated that way—the IRS has recently cracked down on using such devices for family vacation homes and similar assets.

Needless to say, family limited partnerships and grantor trusts are complex and should be designed and implemented by professionals—as is true for most all trusts.

ESTATE PLANNING CONSIDERATIONS FOR BUSINESSES

Business ownership, especially when the value of the business is high enough or growing fast enough to put an estate into the taxable range, can make estate planning complex—and entirely necessary. As mentioned at the outset, the exercise is twofold: planning for transfer or disposition of assets and planning for succession of ownership and management.

There are many challenges. First among them is to avoid a major estate tax hit that would wipe out family assets—and possibly the business. Second, a transition plan must be sensitive to the needs and sense of fairness of family members and the needs and comfort zones of employees. Transfer by death is a very emotional situation; the more it can happen according to plan, the better.

Business Estate Planning Strategies

When there is a substantial business involved, estate planning usually involves a combination of complex and simple estate planning tools. Here is a brief list, of which some have already been covered and some have not:

1. **Gifting and preemptive gifting.** Eventual owners are brought in gradually with higher ownership percentages or ownership of specific assets. Certain assets like buildings or real estate may be pulled out and sold or gifted to others. *Employee stock ownership plans* (ESOPs) work like retirement accounts to build stock gradually in the accounts of future owners in a manner that minimizes income and estate taxes, but ESOPs get complicated as they must include all employees.

2. **Valuation strategies and tactics,** like marketability and control discounts, are commonly used. Also, strategies to *freeze* asset values, like grantor trusts, work well, especially when asset values are growing or expected to grow rapidly.

3. **Business continuation agreements** should be in place to define management and responsibilities beyond ownership when an owner passes. There may be life insurance plans, including *buy-sell* policies to make sure designated parties have sufficient funds to purchase shares left by a deceased owner.

4. **Estate tax financing strategies.** The Tax Code allows families to spread out estate taxes over a period of 14 years, with payments for the first five years interest-only at favorable rates, if the business exceeds 35 percent of the entire value of the estate. Life insurance policies can be purchased to pay off estimated estate taxes at the time of death and, of course, provide a nice sum to beneficiaries if it is not needed for estate taxes.

Some of the tools for these strategies and tactics have already been outlined—grantor trusts, life trusts, and valuation discounts, to name three. There are many more. A good estate planner who specializes in small businesses can help you navigate your way through the maze. As mentioned several times in this book, many entrepreneurs are prone to forsake their own finances as they focus on their business. Don't do this with estate planning: don't forsake your personal estate plan just to "take care of business" with your business.

SUCCESSION PLANNING

As mentioned at the outset, the transition of businesses from the original owner to second-, third-, and fourth-generation heirs is fraught with hazards and pitfalls. The success rate is relatively low. Issues beyond the "pure" financial and tax considerations of estate planning include the following:

- **Control.** Who gets what percentage of ownership and who runs the business? Furthermore, when does the business really transition to the owners? Will the "retired" parent stay out of its affairs or stay in the face of the new owners? Can the parent let go? Can he or she acknowledge mortality and accept the fact that a plan must be constructed? These issues, often highly emotionally charged, must be dealt with at the outset. Leadership is key; it often helps to bring in an outside party, particularly a succession planning specialist, to help facilitate the discussion and resolve potential conflicts with rationale, experience, and handholding.

- **Credibility of heirs.** Do the heirs have the experience, expertise, desire, and, most of all, maturity to run the business? If not, there will be perpetual conflicts with siblings and other descendants and owners—and with employees. Such conflicts are explosive and can wreck a business or set it back years. Strategies include (again) leadership, training, and education. It is almost always best to have descendants start out in entry-level positions and work their way up to "pay their dues" and learn the ropes. When relatives are assigned status just because of the family name, it breeds resentment, contempt, and long-lasting discord.

- **Family harmony.** Business owners are smart and have dynamic personalities. Such personalities aren't always "functional" when it comes to getting along with others—particularly other family members. Good business succession involves at least a degree of family harmony, which if nothing else requires basic elements of communication, empathy, and dedication to task. Old rivalries need to be brought out into the open and discussed, including their potential impacts on the successful transition. Here, the planner often becomes counselor, but it's often better if someone from the family can play that role.

SETTING UP YOUR ESTATE AND SUCCESSION PLAN

Planners recommend varied approaches to getting started and carrying out an estate planning and succession planning exercise. Here's what we recommend:

Step 1: *Acknowledge mortality.* You won't live forever. Nobody has. You and your business partners need to recognize that there will be a "someday."

Step 2: *Identify a leader.* Choose someone from within or outside the family with the capability, interest, time, and willingness to learn

Step 3: *Form a team.* Include owners, potential heirs, and key managers in the business as appropriate.

Step 4: *Set objectives.* Define the desired outcomes clearly—e.g., transfer assets, transfer income, avoid taxes, fill management roles and positions, sell all or part of business.

Step 5: *Commit and meet regularly.* This is important business.

Step 6: *Identify alternatives.* Bring in professional advice. The leader may work alone with professionals to sketch a framework. Explain alternatives clearly to whole team.

Step 7: *Choose one or more alternatives.* Clearly the identify ramifications, upsides, downsides, and financial consequences of each. Explain the choice(s). Make sure everyone is on board.

Step 8: *Develop and document an action plan.* It should indicate action items and provide timelines for those items, including financial transfers and transfers of authority.

Step 9: *Meet periodically to check progress.* Review the plan for changes in the situation, changes in tax law, etc.

It's important to be clear, deliberate, transparent, and—most of all—*patient* during this touchy but crucial process.

Federal and State Corporate Income Tax Tables

REGARDLESS OF WHERE YOU INCORPORATE your business, you will be subject to federal corporate income tax rates. These tax rates, presented earlier in chapter 3, differ widely from personal income tax rates but are fairly simple and straightforward. They are shown again here for convenience.

But as with personal income taxes, the story isn't finished at the federal level. Each state; with the notable exception of South Dakota, levies a corporate income tax of its own. And like personal income taxes, state corporate income taxes vary widely. The following table gives a summary of state corporate income tax rates. We say "summary," because in most states there is considerable detail lying underneath, with alternative minimum taxes, various property and franchise taxes, and separate or alternate taxes on corporate capitalization, sales, or even payroll. It is important, naturally, to get the details, a task usually best accomplished by contacting a tax professional in the state in question.

2006		
Over	**But Not Over**	**Tax Rate**
$0	$50,000	15%
50,000	75,000	25%
75,000	100,000	34%
100,000	335,000	39%
335,000	10,000,000	34%
10,000,000	15,000,000	35%
15,000,000	18,333,333	38%
18,333,333		35%

Source: IRS

FIGURE A-1. U.S. Corporate Income Tax Rates

State	Rate	Brackets	Notes
Alabama	6.5%		
Alaska	1.0%–9.4%	$10,000-$90,000	
Arizona	6.97%		Minimum tax $50
Arkansas	1.0%–6.5%	$3,000-$100,000	
California	8.84%		Minimum tax $800, 1.5% tax on S corps
Colorado	4.63%		
Connecticut	7.5%		
Delaware	8.7%		
Florida	5.5%		Exemption $5,000, 3.3% AMT
Georgia	6.0%		
Hawaii	4.4%-6.4%	$25,000-$100,000	Capital gains tax is 4%
Idaho	7.6%		Minimum tax $30
Illinois	7.3%		
Indiana	8.5%		
Iowa	6.0%		
Kansas	4.0%		Surtax 3.35% on income > $50,000
Kentucky	4.0%		Minimum tax $175
Louisiana	4.0%		
Maine	3.5%		
Maryland	7.0%		
Massachusetts	9.5%		Minimum tax $456, additional property tax
Minnesota	9.8%		
Mississippi	3.0%		
Missouri	6.25%		
Montana	6.75%		Minimum tax $50
Nebraska	5.58%		
New Hampshire	8.5%		Plus 0.5% enterprise base tax
New Jersey	9.0%		Minimum tax $500
New Mexico	4.8%		
New York	7.5%		
North Carolina	6.9%		
North Dakota	2.6%–7.0%	$3,000 - $30,000	
Ohio	5.1%–8.5%	above $50,000	
Oklahoma	6.0%		
Oregon	6.6%		Minimum tax $10
Pennsylvania	9.99%		
Rhode Island	9.0%		Minimum tax $250
South Carolina	5.0%		
South Dakota	–		
Tennessee	6.5%		
Utah	5.0%		Minimum tax $100
Vermont	7.0%–8.9%	$10,000-$250,000	Minimum tax $250, rate decrease after 2006
Virginia	6.0%		
West	9.0%		
Wisconsin	7.9%		
Dist. of Columbia	9.98%		Minimum tax $100

Source: Federation of Tax Administrators, January 2006

FIGURE A.2. 2006 State Corporate Income Tax Rates

Special Situation Tips and Tricks

The following lists are intended to help you think through special business situations and the personal financial planning that might accompany them.

FAMILY BUSINESSES

In general, family businesses provide special tax planning opportunities (and challenges) in the structure, the employment of family members, and the eventual transition or distribution of the business. Here are some tips:

Employ family members. Employing family members, especially dependents, allows income splitting, that is, shifting income to individuals in lower tax brackets or who pay no tax at all.

Set up IRAs for family members. Contributions to individual IRAs for family members can be written off on the family tax return. There is no minimum age for IRAs. Even if the funds are eventually withdrawn before age 59½, the tax-free growth and savings make them worthwhile. With an IRA, a dependent can earn $9,000 ($5,000 exempt plus $4,000 deductible for the IRA) before paying taxes; the family can write off the amount of the contribution.

Deduct travel expenses for both spouses if they are co-owners.

Have one spouse "volunteer." This will save on employment taxes—but make sure that spouse otherwise is eligible for Social Security.

Prepare both an estate plan and a succession plan. The estate plan handles transfer of assets and personal authority, while the succession plan prepares successors and transfers business authority.

Transfer business assets to dependent children to reduce income taxes. But take care that the income from those assets doesn't trigger the "kiddie tax." Use the annual $12,000 exclusion and gift splitting to reduce eventual estate taxes.

HOME-BASED BUSINESS

If you use your home as a primary place of business, you not only save on rent, lease, or the purchase of business premises but you can also realize significant write-offs and income tax savings.

Direct expenses related to your home business can be deducted. Office fixtures, lighting, clocks, wall art, etc. used in the designated place of business are all business expenses.

Indirect expenses can be deducted in proportion to the total area of the home used exclusively for business. Utility bills, home maintenance, repairs, cleaning, homeowner's dues, etc. all qualify.

Net operating losses can offset other income so long as the business is legitimate (i.e., not a hobby), run for profit, and generally profitable in three of five business years.

The capital gains exclusion ($250,000 single or $500,000 married filing jointly) still applies even if the home is used for business. However, any depreciation taken on the home may be recaptured and taxed at a rate higher than personal capital gains rates.

The mileage deduction for the use of personal vehicles has grown to 44 cents in 2006, a nice deduction especially if you have an older, mostly depreciated vehicle.

Liability risk is expanded for home-based businesses, for many homeowner's policies don't cover business use or events related to that use. Insurance should be expanded to cover business uses, even if the home is only a delivery location with no customer interaction.

BUSINESSES WITH EMPLOYEES

Hiring employees opens up new challenges for the business that may also spill over into personal finances.

Employers must get an Employer Identification Number (EIN) immediately.

Payroll tax and accounting rules and regulations are very rigid. Failure to properly meet payroll tax obligations can spell disaster. The IRS can "pierce the corporate veil" to come after owners despite corporate protection against liability.

Employers can offer many deductible benefits to employees—including life insurance, health insur-

ance, and tuition reimbursement. Some, like the Health Savings Account, can be set up in lieu of expensive health coverage or even pay.

There are many retirement plan choices for employer-employee retirement plans. The rules are complex. Many require employer contributions for employees. Employers do best to seek plans that depend mostly on employee contributions, like the 401(k) plan.

Many retirement plans otherwise requiring employer contributions for employees don't apply to short-time, part-time, or under-21 employees.

It is tempting to avoid employee issues and costs by hiring contractors. This works for many businesses, but take care to make sure workers really qualify as contractors. Control and authority, place of work, time of work, and number of clients or jobs besides yours are all factors.

BUYING A BUSINESS

Bottom line: a business is really no more than an investment—a rather large one for most individuals and families. Special care must be taken to correctly evaluate the business from business, financial, marketplace, and tax standpoints.

A business is no more than a set of assets, some tangible, some intangible.

Return on those assets, now and in the future, is the yardstick by which to judge the value and price of the business.

Good business records indicate a well-run business with few surprises for the new owners.

Review past, present, and future cash flow projection, income statements, and balance sheets. Look for businesses that produce rather than consume capital. Look not just at the dollar figures but also at the quality and value of the assets reported. Remember that liabilities are real, while asset values may not always be.

Review employment and tax history carefully. Make sure there are no lurking payroll or income tax bombs. Look also for unrealized depreciation to help reduce future taxes and other opportunities in the form of credits.

Understand asset basis. How are assets valued? What is the future capital gain exposure?

Is the organization form right? If it needs to change, e.g., be incorporated, better to do it at the time of acquisition.

Evaluate the intangibles. How is the business perceived in the marketplace? By customers? By suppliers? Banks? Creditors? What reputation does it have?

Set up an escrow account for contingencies. It is impossible to know everything about a business when you buy it; purchase terms should include a fund to handle the unexpected.

A small business advisor or a CPA specializing in small business acquisitions can help evaluate the business and identify the right questions to ask.

BIGGEST TAX LEVERS

It may seem that you're taxed to death—and even more so if you own a business. But Congress has provided some relief. Here are some of the bigger sources of relief for an entrepreneur.

Retirement savings plans can help an entrepreneur not only save for retirement but also pull a lot of pretax money out of the business for eventual personal use. Different plans adapt to different situations. Individual or very closely held businesses can shelter a lot of income with SEP-IRAs (up to $42,000 annually) or defined-benefit pension plans (up to $170,000 annually). Combinations of plans can work well for businesses with larger payrolls. The choices are complex and many are expensive, but well worth it.

Section 179 expensing allows smaller businesses to expense up to $105,000 in acquired equipment or other assets (besides real estate) without capitalizing and depreciating those assets.

Income splitting can help family businesses shift income to other family members, often tax free or at far lower tax rates. (See earlier Family Businesses section.)

Income splitting can also be used among owners to achieve tax-effective balance of wage and investment income. For instance, S corporations can distribute income free of self-employment taxes so long as they pay reasonable wages for services performed.

Putting an office in your home can turn a situation in which money would have been paid for rent into a situation in which ordinary home expenses can be deducted.

Health insurance and health savings account (HSA) contributions can be fully deducted.

Direct health care expenses can be deducted by C corporations.

Individuals can purchase and lease assets, like buildings, to corporations, receiving better capital gains treatment and sheltering those assets from creditors.

General business credits are far reaching.

Estate and succession planning are very important to ensure business continuity and successful transition to new owners. Planning tools include:

- *Annual gifting and gift splitting,* which can move up to $12,000 per donor per recipient from an estate without incurring gift taxes
- *Selling or sale/leaseback of key assets*
- *Valuation discounts,* including marketability and control discounts, to moderate the appraised estate value of the business
- *Grantor trusts,* to maintain an income stream for the owner, while transferring an appreciating asset and fixing its value at the current level
- *Family limited partnerships* with planned gift-

ing, to transfer assets to family members at favorable values, usually through valuation discounts

- *Charitable trusts,* which can be used to preserve income as long as necessary, contribute to charities upon death or transition, and get a healthy current income tax deduction

CHOOSING A FINANCIAL ADVISOR

Professional financial help comes in many forms. More so than tax advisors, financial advisors focus on the personal financial space – personal cash flow, investing, insurance, retirement, college and estate planning needs. Naturally, advisors are aware of the linkages to business ownership and finances, but most do not specialize in the specific financial needs of the business owner, Most professional financial advisors, particularly the more generalized Certified Financial Planner (registered trademark), are like the "MBAs" of personal finance, understanding how the products and practice of each area like insurance, investments, and trusts work together. Once a financial plan is assembled, advisors can then serve as a "general contractor," working with specialists in the many fields to get things done. But many financial advisors cut their teeth selling some form of financial product—insurance, investments, even worse, mortgages—so may have a bias to talking about their area of expertise with little general financial common sense and even less for the business owner's situation. . Beware. Just as with professionals you hire to help with your business, make sure you know where your financial advisor "comes from" in the sense of experience and expertise.

The best way to find a good advisor is through referrals from other satisfied clients, so we would recommend talking to friends and acquaintances in the small business space. That will considerably narrow the field. And just as you'd interview a construction or engineering contactor to build a facility for your business, make sure you practice the same dili-

gence with a financial advisor. Selecting a financial advisor is a bit more subjective and nuanced than selecting a tax professional, for all tax professionals operate off the same tax code. Tax work is more science that art, whereas financial planning is more art than science.

Here are some characteristics to look for..

- **Accreditation.** There are literally dozens of three- and four-letter accreditations which have hit the pavement over the years. Many are specialized, such as CLU (chartered life underwriter) for life insurance or QPA (Qualified Pension Adminstrator) for business retirement and benefit plans. Some are more generalized. Investment advisors must register with the Securities and Exchange Commission and become RIAs (Registered Investment Advisors). The Certified Financial Planner (CFP™) and ChFC (Chartered Financial Consultant) often work with more sophisticated clients and have one of the highest sets of standards, but even here you must go further than the pedigree to assure the value of an advisor.
- **Compensation.** How is the advisor compensated? By commission on sales of investment and insurance products? Fee-based where they charge you a fee for service but also can get commissions for products they sell? Or fee only, where a set fee is charged to manage assets and perform services without regard to what financial products are implemented. Watch for inherent conflicts of interest in any advisor being paid to sell a product; the fee-only structure is probably best but there are good advisors in the other categories. Fee structures vary and can be based on assets, hours of work performed or on specific deliverables, a complete financial plan, for example.
- **Small business knowledge and experience.** It's not that hard to find a financial advisor, but it is less common to find one with a special expertise in small business and entrepreneur-

ial issues. Most have had some training in the area, but an advisor with special experience or expertise in small business and entrepreneurial issues brings a lot of value; Word of mouth is probably the best way to find this specialty – talk to other entpreneurs individually, in trade meetings, etc. Ask prospective advisors about their small business expertise and client base,

- **Expert network.** A good advisor covers all fields and topics in personal finance and usually will not be the expert or purveyor of product in any one area. Advisors, for example, don't write buy-sell agreements or write trusts. They find experts who do. A good advisor will have a good Rolodex, or may have specialists in his/her office or nearby in a financial "mall" arrangement. Ask who their experts are.

- **Goal and style congruence.** When you work with a financial advisor, will build a relationship if all goes well. As with any other personal or professional relationship, you want someone who respects you, thinks like you at least to a degree, and who you can get along with. If you like to take risks and your advisor tells you to stuff cash into a mattress, that may be a problem. Bad or awkward communication is also a problem—if you like high level concepts and all you get from him or her is unintelligible jargon, buzzwords, and detail, watch out. If they waste your time, watch out. If you wouldn't hire the individual to work in your business, you probably don't want him or her as your advisor.

- **Reputation and references.** This is largely self explanatory—an advisor already well known to your entrepreneurial colleagues is a plus. Talk to a prospective advisor about who their clients are, and get a name or two to chat informally with yourself. A good advisor

should support your request, but keep in mind that client confidentiality is a high priority and advisors will only give references if they've been given permission beforehand.

CHOOSING A TAX ADVISOR

Many of the same tenets that apply to choosing a financial advisor also apply to choosing a tax advisor. Familiarity with small business and entrepreneurial issues (and of course, relevant tax law) is naturally important. The choice may depend on how much you rely on your tax advisor for advice beyond the preparation, filing and possible defense of tax returns. Do you seek their services as a tax preparer, or something beyond? Some tax advisors, especially CPAs and attorneys, are trained and qualified to offer more complete business and personal financial advice; some are not. A CPA/CFP combination in this space is especially powerful.

Just as with financial advisors, tax advisors come with different credentials. Many tax preparers or bookkeepers have minimal formal credentials but lots of experience and can give savvy real-world advice and find quick solutions to problems. Enrolled agents are a step up the ladder, being certified by the IRS (many are former IRS agents) to give tax advice and prepare tax returns. But for those with more complex tax issues or decisions to make about incorporating or any other major business move, you should seek a Certified Public Accountant (CPA) or tax attorney, and especially one with a small business specialty. Only attorneys, CPAs and enrolled agents can represent taxpayers before the IRS in all matters including audits, collection actions and appeals. As with much else in life, you get what you pay for, and the depth and breadth of advice, will determine the cost.

IRS Publications for Entrepreneurs

THE FOLLOWING IS A HANDY LIST OF IRS PUB-lications covering topics of most interest to entrepreneurs and their families. These generally readable documents can be downloaded as PDF files from the IRS Web site (www.irs.gov) or more directly from the Forms and Publications page (*www.irs.gov/formspubs/index.html*).

Publication 1, Your Rights as a Taxpayer

Publication 15A, Employer's Supplemental Tax Guide

Publication 15B, Employer's Tax Guide to Fringe Benefits

Publication 334, Tax Guide for Small Business

Publication 463, Travel, Entertainment, Gift, and Car Expenses

Publication 505, Tax Withholding and Estimated Tax

Publication 525, Taxable and Nontaxable Income

Publication 535, Business Expenses

Publication 536, Net Operating Losses (NOLs) for Individuals, Estates, and Trusts

Publication 538, Accounting Periods and Methods

Publication 541, Partnerships

Publication 542, Corporations

Publication 544, Sales and Other Dispositions of Assets

Publication 550, Investment Income and Expenses

Publication 551, Basis of Assets

Publication 560, Retirement Plans for Small Business (SEP, SIMPLE, and Qualified Plans)

Publication 583, Starting a Business and Keeping Records

Publication 587, Business Use of Your Home

Publication 590, Individual Retirement Arrangements

Publication 925, Passive Activity and At-Risk Rules

Publication 946, How to Depreciate Property

Publication 954, Tax Incentives for Distressed Communities

Publication 970, Tax Benefits for Education

Publication 3402, Tax Issues for Limited Liability Companies

CD-ROM: Small Business Resource Guide

Handy Forms and Tables

FOR YOUR CONVENIENCE, ON THE FOLLOWING pages we've provided full-size versions of some of the forms and tables you'll find most useful.

Bob's Bagels Start-up Budget		
Revision 1.0	Date: 10/01/06	
Category	**Item**	**Amount**
BUSINESS PURCHASE	Business or Franchise Cost Professional Fees	$ $
LEGAL	Partnership Agreement Incorporation Business Name Search Zoning Compliance Business License and Registration	$ $ $ $ $
ACCOUNTING	Business Structure Advice Business and Tax Process Setup	$ $
INSURANCE	Property Liability Health Disability Life	$ $ $ $ $
BUILDING/OFFICE	Initial Lease or Rent Deposit Remodeling Costs Fixtures Rent for Storage Space or Other Deposits for Utility Connections, etc.	$ $ $ $ $
MATERIALS AND EQUIPMENT (M&E)	Production Equipment Computers and Software Communications Equipment Deposits for Phone, etc. Furniture Tools Vehicles	$ $ $ $ $ $ $
INVENTORY	Initial Stock Purchase	$
SUPPLIES	Production Supplies Office Supplies	$ $
MARKETING	Brochures, Cards, etc. Yellow Pages Ad Initial Advertising Campaign Web Site Design and Build	$ $ $ $
Assumptions 1. 2. 3.		

FIGURE D-1. Sample Start-up Budget Form

Bob's Bagels
Operating Budget

Revision 1.0	Date: 10/01/06	Cash Flow												
Category	**Item**	**Jan**	**Feb**	**Mar**	**Apr**	**May**	**Jun**	**Jul**	**Aug**	**Sep**	**Oct**	**Nov**	**Dec**	**Total**
INCOME	GROSS SALES	$												
	Returns and allowances (% or $)	$												
	Cost of goods sold (% or $)	$												
	GROSS PROFIT	$												
	Other Income	$												
	NET INCOME	$												
EXPENSES	Advertising	$												
	Car and truck	$												
	Commissions and fees	$												
	Contract labor	$												
	Depreciation (not for cash flow)	$												
	Employee benefits	$												
	Insurance	$												
	Interest	$												
	Legal and professional	$												
	Office expense	$												
	Pension and profit sharing	$												
	Rent or lease	$												
	Repairs and maintenance	$												
	Supplies	$												
	Taxes and licenses	$												
	Travel, meals, and entertainment	$												
	Utilities	$												
	Wages	$												
	Owner compensation	$												
	Other expenses	$												
	TOTAL EXPENSES	$												
	Net Profit or Cash Flow from Operations	$												
	Investments to Capital Exp.	$												
	Commitments to Reserves	$												
	Net Cash Provided or Required	$												
	Cash Paid to Owner(s)	$												

ASSUMPTIONS
1.
2.
3.

FIGURE D-2. Sample Operating Budget

Bob and Mary Bagelmeister Family
Family Budget

Revision 1.0 — Date: 10/01/06

Category	Item	Jan	Feb	Mar	Apr	May	Jun	Jul	Aug	Sep	Oct	Nov	Dec	Total
INCOME	Wages, Mary	$												
	Bonus and Commissions, Mary													
	Business Income, Bob													
	Interest and Dividends													
DEDUCTIONS	Mary, FICA, other taxes, misc.	$												
SAVINGS RESERVE	401(k), Mary	$												
	SEP-IRA, Bob													
	Rainy Day Fund													
	Big Purchase Fund													
	TAKE HOME	$												
OBLIGATIONS	Mortage/rent	$												
	Property/renters' insurance													
	Property taxes													
	Property dues or fees													
	Day care													
	Private school tuition													
	AVAILABLE	$												
NECESSITIES	Groceries	$												
	Utilities: gas and electric													
	Utilities: water, sewer, trash, other													
	Phone/communications													
	Gas													
	Cable													
	Medical expenses													
	School lunches, expenses													
	Home maintenance, cleaning													
	dry cleaning, laundry													
	Pest control													
	Other maintenance, cleaning													
	SPENDABLE	$												
DISCRE-TIONARY	POCKET MONEY ("Taschengeld")	$												
	PERSONAL ALLOWANCE	$												
	FAMILY ALLOWANCE	$												
	NET BALANCE	**$**												

ASSUMPTIONS
1.
2.
3.

FIGURE D-3. The Personal Budget

FUTURE VALUE FACTORS

Calculates future value of $1 deposited once, upfront, for a given number of years and rate of return. Multiply this factor by the amount deposited to calculate its future value.

	Future Value of $1 Present Sum							
Number of years	**1**	**2**	**5**	**10**	**15**	**20**	**30**	**40**
4.0%	$1.04	$1.08	$1.22	$1.48	$1.80	$2.19	$3.24	$4.80
5.0%	1.05	1.10	1.28	1.63	2.08	2.65	4.32	7.04
6.0%	1.06	1.12	1.34	1.79	2.40	3.21	5.74	10.29
7.0%	1.07	1.14	1.40	1.97	2.76	3.87	7.61	14.97
8.0%	1.08	1.17	1.47	2.16	3.17	4.66	10.06	21.72
9.0%	1.09	1.19	1.54	2.37	3.64	5.60	13.27	31.41
10.0%	1.10	1.21	1.61	2.59	4.18	6.73	17.45	45.26
12.0%	1.12	1.25	1.76	3.11	5.47	9.66	29.96	93.05
15.0%	1.15	1.32	2.01	4.05	8.14	16.37	66.21	267.86
20.0%	1.20	1.44	2.49	6.19	15.41	38.34	237.38	1,469.77
25.0%	1.25	1.56	3.05	9.31	28.42	86.74	807.79	7,523.16

Rate of Return (%)

TABLE D-4. Future Value Factor Table

PRESENT VALUE FACTORS

Calculates today's approximate worth of $1 received a given number of years in the future. Multiply this factor by the future sum, the amount to be received.

	Present Value of $1 Future Sum							
Number of years	**1**	**2**	**5**	**10**	**15**	**20**	**30**	**40**
4.0%	$0.96	$0.92	$0.82	$0.68	$0.56	$0.46	$0.31	$0.21
5.0%	0.95	0.91	0.78	0.61	0.48	0.38	0.23	0.14
6.0%	0.94	0.89	0.75	0.56	0.42	0.31	0.17	0.10
7.0%	0.93	0.87	0.71	0.51	0.36	0.26	0.13	0.07
8.0%	0.93	0.86	0.68	0.46	0.32	0.21	0.10	0.05
9.0%	0.92	0.84	0.65	0.42	0.27	0.18	0.08	0.03
10.0%	0.91	0.83	0.62	0.39	0.24	0.15	0.06	0.02
12.0%	0.89	0.80	0.57	0.32	0.18	0.10	0.03	0.01
15.0%	0.87	0.76	0.50	0.25	0.12	0.08	0.02	0.00
20.0%	0.83	0.69	0.40	0.16	0.06	0.03	0.00	0.00
25.0%	0.80	0.64	0.33	0.11	0.04	0.01	0.00	0.00

Rate of Return (%)

TABLE D-5. Present Value Factor Table

ACCUMULATION ANNUITY FACTORS

The accumulation annuity calculates the future value of an equal sum saved each year for a number of years at a given rate of return. Alternatively, you can work backwards to figure out the equal annual sum you will need to save to reach a specified financial goal. Take that goal (your "number) and divide it by the appropriate factor for the number of years and the appropriate rate of return on your investments to estimate the annual savings required.

	Sum accumulated with $1 deposited end of each year for n years							
Number of years	1	2	5	10	15	20	30	40
4.0%	$1.00	$2.04	$5.42	$12.01	$20.02	$29.78	$56.08	$95.03
5.0%	1.00	2.05	5.53	12.58	21.58	33.07	66.44	120.80
6.0%	1.00	2.06	5.64	13.18	23.28	36.79	79.06	154.76
7.0%	1.00	2.07	5.75	13.82	25.13	41.00	94.46	199.64
8.0%	1.00	2.08	5.87	14.49	27.15	45.76	113.28	259.06
10.0%	1.00	2.10	6.11	15.94	31.77	57.27	164.49	442.59
12.0%	1.00	2.12	6.35	17.55	37.28	72.05	241.33	767.09
15.0%	1.00	2.15	6.74	20.30	47.58	102.44	434.75	1,177.09
20.0%	1.00	2.20	7.44	25.96	72.04	186.69	1,181.88	7,343.86

(Rate of Return (%) is the label for the leftmost column of percentages)

TABLE D-6. Accumulation Annuity Factor Table

DISTRIBUTION ANNUITY FACTORS

The distribution annuity calculates the annual fixed payment available for a specified number of years given a fixed sum deposited at the beginning of the term. To calculate the monthly payment you can get for a fixed sum, divide the fixed sum by the appropriate factor. That will give you the annual payment available; divide by 12 for the monthly payment. (The actual monthly payment will be slightly different due to continuous or monthly compounding; this table assumes the sum to be paid at the end of the year.)

	Sum required to receive $1 paid out each year for n years							
Number of years	1	2	5	10	15	20	30	40
4.0%	$0.96	$1.89	$4.45	$8.11	$11.12	$13.59	$17.29	$19.79
5.0%	0.95	1.86	4.33	7.72	10.36	12.46	15.37	17.16
6.0%	0.94	1.83	4.21	7.36	9.71	11.47	13.76	15.05
7.0%	0.93	1.81	4.10	7.02	9.11	10.59	12.41	13.33
8.0%	0.93	1.78	3.99	6.71	8.56	9.82	11.26	11.92
10.0%	0.91	1.74	3.79	6.14	7.61	8.51	9.43	9.78
12.0%	0.89	1.69	3.60	5.65	6.81	7.47	8.06	8.24
15.0%	0.87	1.63	3.35	5.02	5.85	6.26	6.57	6.64
20.0%	0.83	1.53	2.99	4.19	4.68	4.87	4.98	5.00

(Rate of Return (%) is the label for the leftmost column of percentages)

TABLE D-7. Distribution Annuity Factor Table

Index